DI0929361

WITHDRAWN

Shakespeare's
London

Shakespeare's London

Everyday Life in London 1580-1616

STEPHEN PORTER

AMBERLEY

First published 2009

Amberley Publishing plc
Cirencester Road, Chalford,
Stroud, Gloucestershire, GL6 8PE

www.amberley-books.com

Copyright © Stephen Porter 2009

The right of Stephen Porter to be identified as
the Author of this work has been asserted in
accordance with the Copyrights, Designs and
Patents Act 1988.

ISBN 978 1 84868 333 4

All rights reserved. No part of this book
may be reprinted or reproduced or utilised
in any form or by any electronic, mechanical
or other means, now known or hereafter
invented, including photocopying and
recording, or in any information storage or
retrieval system, without the permission in
writing from the Publishers.

British Library Cataloguing in Publication
Data. A catalogue record for this book is
available from the British Library.

Typeset in 11 pt on 15 pt Sabon.
Typesetting and Origination by Diagraf.
Printed in the UK.

Contents

Acknowledgements

One day Jonathan Reeve of Amberley Publishing phoned and asked if I was interested in writing a book on Shakespeare's London, as observed by contemporaries. This was an invitation that I could not refuse. I am very grateful to him for giving me the opportunity and to the staff at Amberley for making such a good job of producing the book. It is a study of London in Shakespeare's time, not of Shakespeare in London. However, the plays provide a rich source for contemporary life, from which I have drawn a number of examples. I have been fortunate over the years to see many fine productions and, in particular, the Royal Shakespeare Company's 2009 production of *The Winter's Tale* was both stimulating and timely. Gillian Tindall and Peter Day kindly read the text and made a number of helpful suggestions. The staffs of Warwickshire Libraries and the Library and Archive of the Shakespeare Birthplace Trust were very efficient in dealing with my requests.

My wife Carolyn's excellent knowledge of Shakespeare's works has been a great help. Despite my insistence that she was far better qualified to write a book on Shakespeare's world than I was, she protested that was not the case, and preferred to supply much helpful advice, for which I am truly grateful.

1

A Little World in Itself

'Come to London, to plaguy London, a place full of danger and vanity and vice.' John Donne's damning description of his native city was perhaps a little harsh, but he was writing in August 1607, when fear of plague had sharpened his revulsion.[1] Most visitors were favourably impressed, rather than dismayed or repelled. Such contrasting responses reflect the difference between someone who knew London intimately and those who were visiting, perhaps for the first time.

Visitors inevitably gained a snapshot impression, seeing the metropolis over a relatively short period. The problems and tensions that are part of the life of any great city were not so obvious to them as they were to Londoners themselves, and to their rulers. Those who lived there were also more aware of its diversity, its many facets and the varied districts and neighbourhoods. They were conscious, too, of the changes which the city was experiencing, which were not always welcome, to them or to the government.

During the four decades in which Shakespeare knew London, from the 1580s until the 1610s, it was a bustling, teeming metropolis that was by far the largest and richest city in the British Isles and one of the biggest in Europe. The descriptions of visitors, comments by its citizens, official orders and administrative records together provide insights into the life of the metropolis, seemingly stable and yet growing and changing. Its streets and buildings showed the pressures, with the infilling of open spaces, change of use of buildings and the growth of the suburbs, not only within living memory but apparently taking place before the citizens' eyes. Yet there was social and political stability, both in the neighbourhoods and in the city as a whole.

Growth was fuelled by immigration. The city was drawing in migrants, from Britain and the continent. Its inexorable expansion created concerns for its rulers, with anxieties about overcrowding, congestion, public health and disorder. The stranger communities attracted attention and the numbers of immigrants were counted, yet it was domestic migration that was providing the largest numbers of incomers. The government followed a policy of containment, attempting to prevent new buildings and the subdivision of existing ones. One spur to controlling growth was the fear of plague, the worst outbreaks of which killed up to one-fifth of the inhabitants. Polluted air and a foul environment were thought to be among the causes of disease and they were worsened by the overcrowding in such a large city. Yet people continued to be drawn to London, some because it was the national capital and the place where the court was resident for most of the year, providing opportunities, for influence, income and patronage. And the proximity of the monarch and government gave Londoners a feeling of being close to the centre of affairs. They reacted to both foreign and domestic issues and often expressed their opinions somewhat stridently.

The growing population generated greater demand for food, water and fuel, which altered the way in which goods were sold. It produced, too, problems of distribution, with traffic congestion another issue that prompted intervention and regulation. The incomers were drawn by London's expanding economy and growing prosperity, which produced a market for luxury goods among the wealthy citizens and the courtiers. This was supplied by London's burgeoning overseas trade. But the city had a broad and developing economy; it was an economic powerhouse, a great commercial city. Some of her merchants grew to be very rich. They were at the top of a pyramid of wealth in a city which contained a range of manufacturing and service trades, members of the professions, and a body of skilled and semi-skilled workers, some of whom periodically slipped into poverty.

London's rulers feared social instability and unrest, produced by an increase in the number of paupers and those seemingly without a stake in the urban community. Indeed, an important concern was to provide enough charitable help for the poor, to replace that previously channelled through the religious houses, and charitable giving did keep pace with their needs. But life could be insecure and short. Accidents, violence, theft, impoverishment and fraud could mar the citizens' lives. Yet Londoners also enjoyed a rich cultural life, with civic ceremonial and a variety of entertainments, including those at the new theatres, which grew and developed during the forty years that spanned the sixteenth and seventeenth centuries.

With such a complex city, the varied reactions are understandable. Donne was not alone in his gloomy comment, for one of his contemporaries wrote from London to William Trumbull, English ambassador in Brussels, that 'Heere I am in a great, vast, durtie, stinking cittie, o that I had but a little of your Brabant ayre, howe greedily would I suck it in.'[2] Visitors agreed with the description of its sheer size, but did not focus on the pollution which it caused and generally gained more positive impressions. Jacob Rathgeb, from Würtemberg, described it as 'a large, excellent, and mighty city of business and the most important in the whole kingdom'. And its economy was tersely summarized by Lupold von Wedel, from Pomerania, in 1585 as consisting of 'great trade and many handicrafts'. London was just so difficult to summarize briefly, a problem succinctly expressed by Thomas Adams in 1612 with the comment: 'Looking one way you see a beautiful virgin; another way, some deformed monster.'[3]

The task was all the harder because the metropolis consisted of three distinct parts: London itself, on the north side of the Thames, Westminster and Southwark. London was the commercial city, while Westminster was the focus of the political nation, containing the principal royal palace, the court and the meeting place of parliament, with all the functions of government, the courts of law, and the nobility's mansions. On the south side of the Thames, across London Bridge, Southwark was larger than some provincial cities. Together they held an unrivalled position in the country's economic, social, legal and cultural life. Thomas Platter, from Switzerland, visited England in

1599 and in his account of his travels commented that, 'London is not said to be in England, but rather England to be in London'.⁴

Seen from Southwark, the length of the river frontage was impressive. It ran from the riverside suburb of Wapping, past the prominent fortress of the Tower to the bridge, and beyond that along to the Temple and then the aristocratic mansions between the Strand and the river, as far as Whitehall Palace and the abbey at Westminster. Behind the congested riverside wharves lay the city, its skyline punctuated by the towers and spires of more than 120 churches and the great cathedral of St Paul. That panorama gave an indication of the city's size. In 1588 the playwright William Smith estimated it to be three miles long, including Westminster which 'lyeth at the West end of London, lyke the suburbs', and two miles from north to south, 'reckoning Southwark and its bridge'.⁵

Von Wedel contented himself with the remark that, 'The City of London is large.' Others were more ambitious and attempted to estimate the size of its population. In 1590 Giovanni Botero, an Italian diplomat, placed it in a group of cities with populations of around 160,000, and in 1607 the Venetian ambassador Niccolò Molin wrote that London was 'rightly considered one of the chief cities of Europe for its size, its site, and its population, which in common opinion surpasses three hundred thousand souls'.⁶

That was a considerable over-estimate, but Botero's figure, on the other hand, was too low, for the whole metropolis contained approximately 200,000 inhabitants at the end of the sixteenth century, when the population of England was around four million. London's population had risen from 160,000 over the previous forty years and continued to expand, reaching 260,000 by 1625. The national total was also growing, but at a slower rate, and so the proportion of the population living in London steadily increased.

Other European cities grew significantly over the same period and by 1600 at least eight of them had populations in excess of 100,000. London was smaller than Constantinople, Paris and Naples, but had outstripped Venice, Seville and Lisbon. A significant change had occurred in the Low Countries, where Antwerp had gone into a sharp decline, a victim of Spain's attempt to re-conquer its rebellious provinces. The city was north-west Europe's largest port and the most important destination for exports from London, but was sacked by Spanish troops in 1572, and captured by them in 1585. The Dutch kept control of the mouth of the Scheldt and charged high customs dues on ships trading with Antwerp, devastating its overseas trade. It declined from 90,000 inhabitants in 1550 to only a little over a half that number by 1600. Antwerp's misfortune was Amsterdam's gain and it began a rapid rise as a major port, becoming London's chief trading rival, and more than doubling its population in the second half of the sixteenth century, although it was still much smaller than London. In 1596 Francesco Gradenigo, a Venetian gentleman, attributed London's growing prosperity to the wars in the Low Countries and the Wars of Religion in France, which erupted intermittently between 1562 and 1598. He wrote that those conflicts, 'have so increased its riches that London may fairly be called a little world in itself'.[7]

The sheer number of people produced congestion. According to Rathgeb: 'It is a very populous city, so that one can scarcely pass along the streets, on account of the throng.' Platter made a similar comment, that 'one simply cannot walk along the streets for the crowd'.[8] In 1606 the playwright Thomas Dekker wrote facetiously that: 'at every corner, men, women and children meet in such shoals, that posts are set up of purpose to strengthen the houses, lest with jostling one another they should shoulder them down.'[9]

The narrowness of the streets was a part of the problem. Baron Waldstein, who arrived in London from Moravia in 1600, commented that most of them were 'rather dark and narrow'.[10] Tall buildings contributed to their gloominess. A common house type was two rooms deep and three or four storeys high. The Wallington family in St Leonard's Eastcheap, near London Bridge, were wood turners and a typical artisan family. Their house was four storeys high, with a shop and workroom on the ground floor, parlour and kitchen on the first floor, bedchambers on the second, with a garret and store-room above them.[11] The experienced traveller Fynes Moryson described London's houses as, 'very narrow in the front towards the street, but are built five or six roofs high, commonly of timber and clay with plaster'. He thought that the street frontages were not attractive because the best houses were hidden from view. They were built facing a courtyard, which was flanked by stables, warehouse and counting house, while the street front was lined with a row of shops or houses. Those buildings, perhaps only one room deep, formed a screen between the grand house and the street. In Moryson's words:

> the aldermen's and chief citizens' houses, howsoever they are stately for building, yet being built all inward, that the whole room towards the street may be reserved for shops of tradesmen, make no shew outwardly, so as in truth all the magnificence of London building is hidden from the view of strangers at the first sight.[12]

Only after long familiarity with the city would they come to appreciate its buildings.

Few people can have had such an intimate knowledge of the topography of late sixteenth-century London as the historian John Stow. Born in the parish of St Michael, Cornhill in 1525, Stow spent his life in the city and was familiar with its streets, alleys, courts and buildings. He published his *Survey of London* in 1598, with a second edition in 1603, two years before his death. By the time that his work was nearing completion age and infirmity were catching up with him: 'being (by the good pleasure of God) visited with sickness, such as my feet (which have borne me many a mile) have of late years refused, once in four or five months, to convey me from my bed to my study'.[13]

The *Survey* is a history and description of London, its citizens and buildings, spiced with personal memories. Having described the history of the convent of the Poor Clares at the Minories, he adds that a farm had stood on its south side, at the which farm I myself in my youth have fetched many a halfpenny worth of milk, and never had less than three ale pints for a halfpenny in the summer, nor less than one ale quart for a halfpenny in the winter, always hot from the kine, as the same was milked and strained.[14]

He had a less pleasant memory from when he was living in Leadenhall Street in 1549 and the Bailiff of Romford was executed 'upon the pavement of my door where I then kept house'. Stow was close enough to the gibbet to hear the unfortunate man's last words, that he was executed for an innocuous comment he had made just the previous evening to the curate of St Katherine Cree, concerning the uprisings in East Anglia.[15]

Stow also provides a glimpse into the process of compiling his great work. When researching the histories of the livery companies he went to the Vintners' hall, showed them what he already had on the company's history and asked that, 'if they knew any more which might sound to their worship or commendation, at their leisure to send it me, and I would joyne it to my former collection'. But he was rebuffed, was told that it was an inferior company, not one of the principal ones, and was asked to leave, which he did. He heard no more from the company, which, as he noted, 'hath somewhat discouraged me any farther to travail amongst the companies to learne ought at their handes'.[16] Those who sent him away empty handed perhaps saved themselves the mild inconvenience of making available records for his research, but also earned for their company an indignant comment in his timeless history of the city.

His work conveys the economic and social characteristics of a street or district and the predominant trades. On both sides of Bread Street Hill stood 'divers fair houses, inhabited by fishmongers, cheesemongers, and merchants of divers trades'; Watling Street was inhabited by 'wealthy drapers, retailers of woollen cloth, both broad and narrow, of all sorts, more than in any one street of this city'; and St Dunstan-in-the-East was 'a great parish of many rich merchants, and other occupiers of divers trades, namely salters and ironmongers'.

He explained the derivation of names. Three Cranes Lane was named from three cranes 'on the Vintry wharf by Thames side, to crane up wines there'. The northern section of Bow Lane was Hosier Street until the sixteenth century, but that name had lapsed. Stow wrote that this was because the hosiers, who had replaced the cordwainers, had themselves been supplanted by members of other trades. He recorded the loss of a trade, not just to London but to the country. The stainers produced images on woven cloth. They merged in 1500 with the painters, and the joint company was incorporated in 1581, but before the end of the century 'that workmanship of staining is departed out of England'.[17]

Among the streets with good buildings were Aldermanbury, which contained 'divers fair houses on both sides, meet for merchants or men of worship' and Addle Street, which was 'replenished with fair buildings on both sides'. Milk Street consisted of 'many fair houses for wealthy merchants and other'; the shops in Poultry and Bucklesbury were occupied by grocers, haberdashers and upholsterers; St Mary-at-Hill was 'furnished with many fair houses for merchants'; Bartholomew Lane had 'divers fair houses on both sides'.[18] But Stow did not shrink from mentioning the city's dark corners and its imperfections. A lane which had connected Fenchurch Street with Lime Street, 'was stopped up for suspicion of thieves that lurked there by night'.[19]

Londoners lived where they worked; shopkeepers behind and above their shops, merchants and artisans on the same premises as their warehouses and workshops. The best, and so most expensive, sites were those along the principal streets in the city centre. Houses in the alleys and courts were smaller and their occupants poorer, and so were those in the suburbs, beyond the corporation's jurisdiction. The corporation governed London's historic core, between Temple Bar in the west and the precincts of the Tower of London in the east. Conveniently described as 'the City', it covered a slightly larger area than that enclosed within the medieval walls, which were still largely intact. As the built-up area expanded, a growing proportion of Londoners lived outside its boundaries. And expansion produced problems within the city, with the infilling of spaces and subdivision of sometimes grand houses into tenements.

Stow was aware of the changes affecting his city. He described their impact and indeed his critical remarks at times verge on disgust. Outside Aldgate there had been just a few scattered tenements, 'but now that street is not only fully replenished with buildings outward, and also pestered with divers alleys, on either side to the bars, but to White Chappell and beyond.'[20] The development then continued, with 'filthy cottages' and rubbish dumps, for half a mile beyond St Mary's church, so that the district, in his opinion, provided 'no small blemish to so famous a city to have so unsavoury and unseemly an entrance or passage thereunto'. Another main road into the city passed through the extra-mural suburb beyond Bishopsgate, where 'many houses have been built with alleys backward, of late time too much pestered with people (a great cause of infection)'. The street continued up to Shoreditch with, 'a continual building of small and base tenements, for the most part lately erected'.[21]

Gold Lane off Holborn had been 'a filthy passage into the fields, now on both sides built with small tenements' and Leather Lane was 'lately replenished with houses built'. In recent years the Earl of Shrewsbury had acquired Poultney's Inn, off Upper Thames Street, where he erected 'a great number of small tenements, now letten out for great rents to people of all sorts'. Over the previous fifty years houses had been built even in the churchyard of St Michael, Cornhill, 'whereby the church is darkened and other ways annoyed', and in Billiter Lane 'three fair houses' were built in 1590, on land that had been a garden. At Pie Corner, on the edge of Smithfield, there had been 'a fair inn for receipt of travellers, but now divided into tenements' and the large open space of Smithfield itself had been greatly reduced in size by new 'enroachments and enclosure'. Even Tower Hill had not escaped the inexorable increase of buildings. It had been 'a large plot of ground, now greatly straitened by incroachments (unlawfully made and suffered) for gardens and houses'.[22]

Stow also regretted the damage to churches and former monastic properties, following the Reformation. The church of the secular college of St Martin le Grand was demolished in 1548. According to Stow, a 'large wine tavern' was built on part of the site and on the remainder 'many other houses were built and highly prized, letten to strangers born and other such'. In 1574 the Privy Council had commented on the 'strangers, inmates and many lewd persons' there, and by 1583 the precinct contained about 100 immigrant families. They were attracted by the privileges granted to the college that continued after its dissolution, creating what was said to be the largest sanctuary from the law in England. Stow disapproved, as those privileges were not intended to benefit 'artificers, buyers and sellers'.[23]

All Hallows the Great, close to London Bridge, was 'a fair church, with a large cloister on the south side thereof... but foully defaced and ruinated. The church also hath had many fair monuments, but now defaced.' St Mary Somerset was 'a proper church, but the monuments are all defaced'. That was not unusual. Stow commented that a vicar of St Leonard's, Shoreditch had taken memorial brasses from gravestones and sold them for coining, despite a proclamation of Elizabeth I forbidding the practice.[24] Stow thoroughly disapproved of the destruction of memorials and John Manningham, a lawyer, recorded that during a conversation:

> He gave me this good reason why in his Survey he omittes manie newe monumentes: because those men have bin the defacers of the monumentes of others, and soe thinkes them worthy to be deprived of that memory whereof they have injuriously robbed others.[25]

The nave of the former priory of the Austin Friars was granted to the Dutch community in 1550 as their church. The remainder was used as storehouses until it was demolished in 1600; the tombs having been sold for £100, to be broken up for their stone. Stow greatly admired the steeple of the Dutch church, describing it as 'a most fine spired steeple, small, high, and straight, I have not seen the like'. But it became unsafe because of neglect and was dismantled in 1613. Other churches were in bad repair. Collections by the parishioners of Holy Trinity near Queenhithe to repair their church had been inadequate, and Stow described the building as 'very old, and in danger of down falling... it leaneth upon props or stilts'.[26]

St Paul's Cathedral was also in disrepair and its presence was sadly diminished after the steeple had been destroyed by fire, started by a lightning strike, in 1561. The blaze destroyed part of the roof as well as the steeple. The roof was repaired over the next ten years, but the steeple was not replaced, despite the queen's insistence that it should be rebuilt. The cost of that and other necessary work was estimated in 1584 at almost £11,500 and was not carried out. The fabric was neglected and in 1600 a horse was killed by a piece of masonry that fell from the south battlements. In 1616 Henry Farley, a scrivener, began a campaign for the repair and renovation of the building, which he described as 'cracked, defaced, rent, and almost undone'.[27]

The imperfections were not so obvious to visitors, who found it an impressive structure; Rathgeb described it as 'large and remarkable'.[28] Its size certainly was striking, with a length of 596 feet and a height to the crown of the roof of 93 feet. Many visitors climbed the 285-foot-high tower and carved their initials on the lead there. They also descended into the crypt, part of which was occupied by St Faith's church. This was the church of the stationers and booksellers whose businesses were located around the edge of the churchyard and in Paternoster Row on its north side. The churchyard also contained a pulpit on the site of Paul's Cross, from which weekly sermons were delivered to a numerous and varied outdoor congregation, whose distinguished members were provided with shelter from the weather in a gallery. Above that was the royal box. Baron Waldstein described this area as, 'an open space where they hold open air services which the Mayor of the City himself attends. The services last for nearly 3 hours.'[29]

The cathedral was a place of business as well as worship, a meeting place, a promenade, a haunt of pickpockets and thieves, somewhere to pick up a prostitute, and a refuge for the poor. Its long central aisle was commonly known as Paul's Walk, where servants were hired, lawyers met their clients and business deals were struck. Debts were settled at the font. Dekker described it as being, 'like a common Mart where all Commodities (both the good and the bad) are to be bought and solde'.[30] Gossip was exchanged among acquaintances. John Chamberlain sadly reported the death of his friend Tom Powell, 'whose companie I shall much want for my walke in Powles'. There he gathered news, both domestic and international, including 'whatsoever is stirring in Fraunce'.[31] In many respects the aisle functioned like a high street, but the City's true high street lay eastwards from the cathedral, in Cheapside. From Cheapside tradesmen passed through St Paul's, taking the shortest route to Ludgate Hill, carrying their loads and treating the building as a thoroughfare. The profanation of the cathedral was condemned occasionally, and attempts were made to prevent it. In November 1602 Chamberlain wrote to Sir Dudley Carleton excusing his lack of gossip, blaming this upon 'a new devised order to shut the upper doores in Powles in service time, whereby the old entercourse is cleane chaunged, and the trafficke of newes much decayed'.[32] But its many and varied secular functions were too well-established to be so easily suppressed.

Those who came out of the cathedral and set off down Ludgate Hill went through the gate, rebuilt in 1586, and then passed the Belle Sauvage, or Bel Savage, inn. First recorded in the mid-fifteenth century, it was used as a theatre from c.1579 until c.1588; the Queen's Men, formed in 1583, acted there. From Ludgate the route from St Paul's continued along Fleet Street – a centre of printing since Wynkyn de Worde, who had worked with William Caxton, took premises there in 1500–01 – to Temple Bar, then along the Strand, lined with the mansions of the nobility, to Charing Cross, Whitehall Palace and Westminster. The palace did not impress visitors; Justus Zinzerling c.1610 thought it 'not very magnificent'. Westminster Abbey, on the other hand, made a favourable impression. Rathgeb described it as 'the beautiful and large royal church... situated at the end, outside the city'.[33] It was a popular destination for visitors, who admired the tombs; the antiquary William Camden published a list and description of the monuments in 1600, which went through two more editions within the next six years. The French ambassador, André Hurault, Sieur de Maisse, in 1597, was most impressed by Henry VII's chapel and its tombs:

> a very fair sight and of marvellous workmanship, and one cannot see nor speak of anything fairer, be it for the work within and without this chapel, or because of these tombs; nor do I think that anywhere in the world can the like be seen, nor one so fairly adorned.[34]

To the north of Westminster and Charing Cross the city's limit was St Giles-in-the-Fields. The route from Newgate along Holborn had been built up, according to Stow, with 'many fair houses built, and lodgings for gentlemen, inns for travellers, and such like up almost (for it lacketh but little) to St Giles-in-the-fields'.[35]

Eastwards from Newgate ran Newgate Street, which led to Cheapside, the most admired street in the city; according to Paul Hentzner, visiting from Brandeburg in 1598, 'it surpasses all the rest'. Visitors referred to it as the goldsmiths' street because of the number of their shops, with eye-catching window displays of gold and silver wares. Thomas Platter wrote: 'In one very long street called Cheapside dwell almost only goldsmiths and money changers on either hand, so that inexpressibly great treasures and vast amounts of money may be seen here.' The account of the Duke of Saxe-Weimar's visit to London in 1613 describes it as 'the finest and richest' street in the city.[36]

It had developed from late Saxon times as the City's principal market, sometimes known as West Cheap, to distinguish it from Eastcheap. The names of the adjacent streets indicate the specialities of their medieval markets, such as Honey Lane, Bread Street, Milk Street and Wood Street, and Cheapside continued eastwards as Poultry. Cheapside provided a fine setting for civic processions, especially the annual Lord Mayor's show. Because of its prominence, it was also used for less pleasant purposes; shoddy goods which contravened the regulations of the livery companies were burned there, miscreants stood in the pillory, apprentices skirmished among themselves, and criminals and traitors were executed.

Its inhabitants' wealth was reflected in the fine buildings, some four or five storeys high, with elaborately carved façades. Goldsmiths' Row, on the south side, attracted particular attention. Built by Thomas Wood in 1491, the row contained ten houses and fourteen shops and was four storeys high 'uniformly built', with decoration on the street front that included the Goldsmiths' arms and lead figures of woodmen 'riding on monstrous beasts'.

But during the early seventeenth century the street began to lose some of its gloss, as the goldsmiths gradually moved away and their shops were taken by other tradesmen. According to John Chamberlain they included booksellers, stocking men, haberdashers, lace-makers and 'other mean trades, crept into the Goldsmith's Row, that was wont to be the beauty and glory of Cheapside'. Nor was it only the shops that were lowering the street's reputation. The title of Thomas Middleton's *A Chaste Maid in Cheapside* (c.1613) is clearly ironic, with illicit sex one of the themes running through the play. A few years later Thomas Dekker, in *The Owles Almanacke*, contrasted its outward respectability with prostitution, commenting that, 'A fair wench is to be seen every morning in some shop in Cheapside: And in summer afternoones the self-same Faire opens her Booth at one of the Garden-houses about Bun-hill.'[37]

To the north of Cheapside stood Guildhall, rarely mentioned in the accounts of visitors from abroad, although it is a fine example of a north-European civic hall. Begun in 1411 during the mayoralty of Thomas Knolles, a merchant active in the cloth trade, it took almost twenty years to complete. Its great hall is a grand space, 151 feet by 48 feet, and the undercroft is also impressive, with three aisles and central piers of Purbeck marble, with clustered columns and moulded capitals and bases. Guildhall was the centre of the City's administration, where its elections and meetings were held and where its courts sat. The City was divided into twenty-five wards until 1550, when Southwark was acquired from Edward VI and became the twenty-sixth. Each sent one alderman to sit in the council of aldermen, and the wards also elected the members of the less powerful Common Council of more than 200 members. The Lord Mayor was chosen from among the aldermen and served for one year. Niccolò Molin described the extent of the aldermen's authority with the comment that they 'govern the City absolutely, almost as though it were an independent Republic'.[38]

The choice of Lord Mayors indicates that no one trade dominated the City's political life, nor was the office held by members of a few families. No surname is repeated in the list of those who held the office between 1580 and 1616. From 1580 until the end of Elizabeth's reign in 1603, the office was held by twenty-seven men, some serving for the balance of the mayoral year when the incumbent had died. They were members of eleven livery companies, the City's guilds which oversaw membership and the practice of a trade. Six of them were from the haberdashers' company and five from the clothworkers' company; no other company supplied more than three Lord Mayors and only two were goldsmiths, perhaps surprisingly given the comments about their wealth.

The goldsmiths were in the process of shifting their base. From Cheapside, some of them moved eastwards, beyond Poultry to the area around Cornhill, Threadneedle Street and Lombard Street, which was developing as the centre of trade and finance. This was greatly enhanced by the building of the Royal Exchange, completed in 1568 on the north side of Cornhill. Its founder was Sir Thomas Gresham, who had been a very successful merchant trading with Antwerp and acting as the government's representative in that city. Its design was based on the first purpose-built bourse, opened in Antwerp in 1531. In January 1571 the queen visited Sir Thomas at his house before going on to the Exchange, where, according to John Stow, 'she caused the same burse by an herald and trumpet to be proclaimed the Royal Exchange, and so to be called from thenceforth, and not otherwise'.[39] It had an open courtyard flanked by ranges of three-storey buildings, with arcades. The merchants met in the courtyard, in groups according to the region or city with which they were trading. Its presence, as the hub of London's trade, confirmed the area as the centre of business and finance, and also as a rival to Paul's Walk for the exchange of news and information.

Banking was already well established in and around Lombard Street, which had been known as Longebrod, taking its new name from the Italian merchants, from Lombardy and elsewhere, who had settled there. The word Lombard came to be applied to places where money transactions took place, which developed into banks, or pawnshops.

Lombard Street, Threadneedle Street and Cornhill ran eastwards to meet the main north-south route through the City, from Southwark across London Bridge to Bishopsgate. The corporation had built its granary in 1455 where this intersected with the principal east-west route along Cornhill and Fenchurch Street. Known as Leadenhall, this stone building consisted of four ranges with corner towers around an open courtyard, with an arcaded ground floor providing stalls for sellers of foodstuffs, and the upper floors contained granaries. The building was reserved for traders who were citizens and so 'country butchers' had to hold their market in the street outside. It also served as the City's arsenal for weapons and as the place where alms were distributed to the poor.

Leadenhall Street and Fenchurch Street led to Aldgate, and Eastcheap to Tower Street and beyond that to Tower Hill. Virtually all visitors went to the Tower. Von Wedel's impression was of a 'great castle surrounded by a moat and walls'. He looked around the armoury and visited the Mint, 'where on either side many persons were sitting and working continuously'. Virtually all of the coins in circulation had been minted there. The artillery and the bows, arrows and cross-bows attracted the especial attention of those who were shown around the buildings. They also commented on the beautiful, rich furnishings: 'gilt bedsteads, curtains, tapestries, tablecovers, cushions... all royally wrought in gold and silver'.[40] The menagerie provided another source of interest, with its lions and lionesses, a lynx, a wolf (who was 'excessively old'), an eagle and a large porcupine. The animals were kept 'in a remote place, fitted up for the purpose with wooden lattices'.[41]

Space inside the walls was limited because of overcrowding. Waldstein described it as 'defended with several moats, encircled by triple walls, and inside it is so full of houses that it gives visitors the impression of a town'. Overcrowding caused problems. A survey was taken in 1597 and the report included the observation that: 'By means of the newe erected Tenements within the liberties of the Tower, the inhabitants are so encreased, as ther is not within the Tower anie place sufficient for their buriall s.'

Waldstein also alluded to a potential function of the Tower as the means to intimidate the citizens, should they become restive. On the White Tower he saw sixteen cannon 'which are trained upon the City'. The buildings were not in good repair. Waldstein was shown 'an ancient dining-hall, almost falling to pieces with age'. On the plan accompanying the survey of 1597 the hall is noted as 'decayed', and the surveyors' report contains the comment that, 'your Majesties lodgings and manie other buildings within the Tower are in decaye'.[42]

De Maisse evidently thought that it had little military value and could not serve as a modern fortress. He noted that the city ditch was full of water, but 'There are no earthworks and no fortress.' Niccolò Molin echoed that view, describing the Tower as:

> a right noble pile for age, but not for strength, as it has neither bulwarks nor bastions nor other fortifications. The royal treasure... is kept there. There is also an arsenal of arms; but its chief use is as a ward for prisoners of State.[43]

Masonry walls were easily breached by siege artillery and needed additional earthwork defences to give them protection. Most cities had constructed such defences some distance from the built-up area, but that was not undertaken at London until 1642–3, during the

Civil War. Although the walls and ditches were obsolete militarily, the gates had been maintained. Those on London Bridge had provided an effective defence for London as recently as 1554, when they had been closed against Sir Thomas Wyatt's rebel force, compelling it to cross the Thames at Kingston. But Drawbridge Gate was demolished in 1577 and the drawbridge replaced by a fixed roadway, leaving only the fifteenth-century Great Stone Gate close to the bridge's southern end.

Built between 1176 and 1209, the bridge consisted of twenty piers on broad platforms, known as starlings, with narrow gaps between them through which the water flowed at considerable speed. This made passage through the bridge hazardous, except at slack water between the tides. Some passengers preferred to alight before the bridge and re-embark after it, rather than experience the discomfort of a rocking boat and the risk of it being overturned by the turbulent current, or crashing into one of the starlings.

The roadway was lined on both sides with tall buildings, so that, in Stow's phrase, 'it seemeth rather a continual street than a bridge'.[44] Most visitors thought it to be one of London's most imposing features. Von Wedel wrote that the bridge was 'built over with fine houses, which are daily full of commodities and are right splendid to behold'. Rathgeb was equally laudatory, describing it as 'a beautiful long bridge, with quite splendid, handsome, and well-built houses, which are occupied by merchants of consequence'. But Molin thought that the shops on the bridge, 'make it very narrow and spoil its beauty, and if two carriages meet there they can hardly pass one another'.[45] Despite the congestion, there was no question of widening the way by clearing buildings from such valuable and prestigious sites. Some houses were rebuilt under new leases granted in 1579 and Drawbridge Gate was replaced by a large and impressive timber-framed building known as Nonesuch House.

The thoroughfare northwards from the bridge to Bishopsgate ran through St Helen's parish, where William Shakespeare lived during the mid-1590s. He was born in Stratford-upon-Avon in 1564 and married Anne Hathaway in 1582, when he was eighteen years old. Their three children were baptized at Holy Trinity church in Stratford, Susannah in May 1583 and the twins Hamnet and Judith in February 1585. By 1588 Shakespeare was in London, dealing with a property dispute through his lawyer at the Middle Temple, and within four years he was well-established in the capital, as an actor and playwright.

In October 1596 Shakespeare was assessed in St Helen's to pay 5s for the second collection of a parliamentary tax imposed in 1593. In November 1597 he was recorded as a defaulter. He was again assessed in that parish in October 1598, but once more was noted as a defaulter, having failed to pay the 13s 4d due and listed with others who had not paid the tax, with the note 'Surrey', indicating that he had moved south of the river. The 13s 4d had still not been paid when another list was compiled in October 1600, which has the marginal note 'Episcopo Wintonensi', for it had become the responsibility of the Bishop of Winchester, who had jurisdiction of the Clink Liberty in Bankside, Southwark.

St Helen's was a relatively small parish, with seventy-three households in the 1590s. Stow described the approach to the church as being along 'a winding lane' and the church itself as 'a fair parish church, but wanteth such a steeple as Sir Thomas Gresham promised to have built, in recompense of ground in their church filled up with his monument'.[46] Gresham was one of the parish's wealthiest inhabitants in the mid-sixteenth century. He built a large mansion between Bishopsgate Street and Old Broad Street, where Gresham College was established by his bequest.

Sir John Spencer was also a parishioner of St Helen's and is commemorated by a grand tomb in the parish church. An extremely wealthy merchant, 'Rich Spencer' served as Lord Mayor in 1594–5. In 1594 he bought Crosby Hall, built in 1466 on the east side of Bishopsgate by Sir John Crosby, a rich wool merchant and a member of the Grocers' Company. Stow described the house as 'very large and beautiful, and the highest at that time in London'. Shakespeare referred to it in *Richard III* (as both Crosby Place and Crosby Hall), as the London base of Richard, Duke of Gloucester.

As one of the chief streets into the city, Bishopsgate had, according to Stow, 'divers fair innes, large for receipt of travellers', with courtyards and stabling.[47] Some of them were used for performances and the area developed as one of the theatrical districts of Elizabethan London. The Black Bull – where plays were being performed by 1578 – had a permanent stage and was licensed in 1583 as a venue for the Queen's Company of players. Further along, in Gracechurch (or Gracious) Street, the Bell and the Cross Keys, close to each other on the west side, were used as playhouses, the Bell from at least 1576 and the Cross Keys by 1579. The Queen's Company used the Bell as one of its winter theatres. Shakespeare may have played at the Cross Keys with Lord Strange's men in 1589, and in 1594 as a member of the Lord Chamberlain's Company, which played 'this winter time within the city at the Cross Keys in Gracious Street'. In Great Eastcheap, close to the junction with Gracechurch Street, stood the Boar's Head, perhaps the tavern kept by Shakespeare's character Mistress Quickly in *Henry IV*. When Prince Hal enquires after Falstaff by asking, 'Doth the old boar feed in the old frank?' he is told, 'At the old place, my lord, in Eastcheap.'[48]

Shakespeare lived near that part of Bishopsgate Street where, according to Stow, 'amongst other tenements, are divers fair and large built houses for merchants, and such like'. He was conveniently placed for the inn theatres. But they had somewhat tainted the district's respectability. When Anthony Bacon settled in Bishopsgate Street in 1594 a friend wrote to his mother complaining that performances at the Bull had 'infected the inhabitants there with corrupt & lewd dispositions' and the area had become 'a place haunted with such pernicious & obscene plays & theatre'.[49] For Shakespeare, however, it had the further advantage of being within easy reach of two playhouses to the north, in Shoreditch. These were the Theatre, erected in 1576, and the Curtain, built close by in the following year, both of which were under the management of the actor and impresario James Burbage. Shakespeare was a member of his company and in 1594, with Burbage's son Richard and other members of the company, formed the Lord Chamberlain's Men, based at the Theatre.

The implication of the tax returns is that before the end of the decade Shakespeare had left St Helen's and was living in Southwark, in the Paris Garden area of Bankside. Southwark was expanding along the riverfront on both sides of the bridge, where by the end of the sixteenth century it extended, according to Stow's rather vague phrase, for 'more than a large mile in length'. Running southwards from the bridge was Southwark Street, 'built on both sides with divers lanes and alleys'. St Saviour's church and the Bishop of Winchester's palace were the finest buildings. The Earl of Suffolk's 'large and sumptuous house' known as Southwark Place had been pulled down in the late 1550s and replaced by 'many small cottages of great rents, to the increasing of beggars in that borough'. St Olave's church, close to the Thames, was 'a fair and meet large church, but a far larger parish especially of aliens or strangers, and poor people'.[50]

Many of Southwark's inhabitants were watermen, who provided the carrying service on the river, and those working in the inns and hostelries that catered for travellers arriving in London from the south. The district also contained five prisons, alehouses, brothels, St Thomas's Hospital, and, by 1600, three playhouses on Bankside and two arenas for animal baiting. John Stow described them as:

> two bear gardens, the old and new places, wherein be kept bears, bulls, and other beasts, to be baited; as also mastiffs in several kennels, nourished to bait them. These bears and other beasts are there baited in plots of ground, scaffolded about for the beholders to stand safe.[51]

Attempts to close down the brothels, or stew-houses, had all failed. Because of those in the Bishop of Winchester's Clink liberty the prostitutes were known as 'Winchester Geese'. An alternative name was 'Flemish Frows', as many of the women were from the Low Countries. The brothels and playhouses gave Bankside a rather disreputable character.

By 1602 Shakespeare had returned to the City and was lodging in Silver Street, near Cripplegate, where he lived for at least two years.

The move from Bankside to Silver Street took Shakespeare away from the playhouses, but to a district where other members of the acting fraternity lived. His friends and fellow-actors, John Hemming (or Heminges) and Henry Condell, were long-time residents of the nearby parish of St Mary Aldermanbury. Condell was a churchwarden and Hemming a sidesman, eight of Condell's nine children and thirteen of Hemming's fourteen children were baptized in the church, and both men and their wives were buried there. In his will Shakespeare bequeathed them and Richard Burbage £1 6s 8d each, to buy rings.

John Stow assumed that the name Silver Street derived from silversmiths living there. He noted that it contained 'divers fair houses'. On its south side stood St Olave's church, which he dismissed as 'a small thing, and without any noteworthy monuments'.[52] By the late sixteenth century those who made wigs and decorative attire lived in the street. Monkwell Street ran northwards from Silver Street almost to the city wall; the large gabled house at the north-east corner of the junction of the two streets was occupied by Christopher and Mary Mountjoy, French Huguenot refugees, who specialized in making ornamental and expensive head-dresses, decorated with precious stones, gold and silver. In 1604 Shakespeare, their lodger, acted as the go-between when Christopher's former apprentice Stephen Belott was courting Mary, the Mountjoys' only child. The couple were married at St Olave's in 1604, but after Christopher's wife Mary died in 1606 family arguments followed, so much so that in 1612 the Belotts sued Christopher for £60 unpaid dowry and, afraid that Mary would be disinherited, for a legacy of £200 to be included in Christopher's will. Shakespeare gave evidence concerning the arrangements made when the marriage was being negotiated. The case was referred to the elders of the French church, in Threadneedle Street, who made a small award in the Belotts' favour. But they disapproved of both Christopher and his son-in-law, describing them as 'debauched' and expelled Christopher, citing his 'irregular and outlandish life; and... his lewd acts and adulteries'.[53]

It is not known where Shakespeare lived after he left the house in Silver Street. In 1613 he bought the gatehouse buildings on the eastern edge of the Blackfriars precinct, built over 'a great gate', which opened into St Andrew's Hill. Shakespeare paid the owner Henry Walker, a minstrel, £140 for the property, perhaps acquired as an investment rather than a residence. One of his three trustees for the purchase was William Johnson, proprietor of the Mermaid in Bread Street, a convivial meeting place in the early seventeenth century for members of London's literati, including Francis Beaumont and Ben Jonson. The contemporary traveller and letter-writer Thomas Coryate wrote that 'the company of right worshipful Sirenaicall Gentlemen' met there on the first Friday of every month.[54] Johnson could have known Shakespeare for business reasons, or perhaps because the playwright frequented the Mermaid. By the time that Shakespeare bought the gatehouse property he may have been spending much of his time at Stratford, where he died on 23 April 1616.

The gatehouse was only a few yards from the Blackfriars theatre, formed by James Burbage in 1596 from the great hall, or Parliament Hall, of the Dominican priory, dissolved in 1538. Objections from local residents delayed its opening, but it was used as a playhouse from 1600 and the King's Men, Shakespeare's company, acted there from 1608, during the winter months.

Until 1608 Blackfriars was beyond the Lord Mayor's jurisdiction, one of the liberties and precincts inside the City's boundaries with rights inherited from the monastic houses. It also lay outside the authority of the diocese. Following the dissolution of the priory a new parish of St Anne, Blackfriars, had been formed. Part of the priory church was adapted as the parish church, until Sir Thomas Cawarden, the king's Keeper of the Tents and Master of the Revels, came into the possession of the former monastic buildings, in 1550. He developed the area and built himself a house there. Sir Henry Carey, Lord Hunsdon, Privy Councillor under Elizabeth I and a patron of the theatre, also lived in the district.

Cawarden used the church as a store. According to Stow, he later demolished the building, allocating as a replacement, 'a lodging chamber above a stair, which... in the year 1597, fell down, and was again by collection therefore made, new built and enlarged in the same year'.[55] After the new church was built, the religious life of the precinct came to be dominated by the Calvinist preacher William Gouge, whose sermons attracted large congregations. Appointed minister in 1608, Gouge was the best-known Puritan clergyman in London during the early decades of the seventeenth century. Yet during Elizabeth's reign some of the buildings were used to conceal fugitive Roman Catholic priests. An inhabitant described one building as having 'sundry back-dores and bye-wayes, and many secret vaults and corners'.[56]

Blackfriars was a compact precinct, but despite its size it contained affluent residents and fine houses, brothels and flimsy buildings, Puritans and Roman Catholics, and the Huguenot artist Isaac Oliver, who died there in 1617. Like the other varied neighbourhoods where Shakespeare lodged and where the playhouses stood, it was one of the complex patchwork of communities which made up London. And his connections among the theatrical fraternity exemplify the city's networks, centred on occupation and social relations. The legal cases in which he was involved were typical of a litigious age, while the Mountjoy family in Silver Street, supplying members of the court with luxury goods, illustrates the presence in the metropolis of specialist craftsmen who were immigrants from the continent, attracted to the crowded and bustling city as it continued to grow.

2

A Great Multitude of People

The expanding city drew many people from abroad, some for a short stay, others to settle there. As a port city, it attracted merchants and their agents for business reasons; as the national capital it hosted diplomatic representatives and their retinues. Its communities of strangers included those who came to benefit from the economic opportunities which it offered and others hoping for a refuge from religious or political persecution. They attracted some hostility, yet were gradually assimilated into the metropolitan economy. And they were, in any case, far outnumbered by internal migrants, arriving from within Britain in such numbers that the government felt compelled to try to stem the flow.

Control was attempted through prohibiting new buildings and demolishing those erected in defiance of the ban. The wording of the orders which set out the policy reveals the anxiety concerning the social composition of those who lived in the new housing, especially the small, often shoddy, houses in the suburbs. By extension, they were thought to be people whose living conditions were such that they would create an environment in which disease would flourish, especially plague. The policy to restrict London's growth was, therefore, related to the plague regulations introduced during the sixteenth century.

The building and environmental regulations were not implicitly directed at the stranger communities. In any case, some visitors were in London for only brief periods and had little interaction with the citizens, while those engaged in commerce or diplomacy, or who came as part of a European tour, were relatively few in number.

From 1282 until 1598 the merchants of the Hanseatic League were based at the Steelyard, or Stahlhof, a trading yard on the Thames alongside Dowgate. By the sixteenth century it covered three acres, but housed only twenty or so merchants, who led quite separate lives from the Londoners and followed their own rules. The Steelyard was the only such privileged enclave for foreign traders; the others made their arrangements independently. Travellers and diplomatic representatives were more likely to record their impressions than were merchants, although their comments probably reflected commonly-held impressions.

Most foreigners in London during the late sixteenth and early seventeenth centuries came from northern and western Europe, especially the Low Countries, Germany and France. But others were from further afield, from Spain, Portugal and Italy, and from beyond Europe. The Moorish ambassador to Elizabeth I arrived in August 1600 with his retinue, for 'a half year's abode in London'.[1] In 1593 three 'blackamores' were noted as servants of Alderman Paul Blanning in Farringdon and parish records from across London include the baptisms, marriages and interments of persons described as 'negro' and 'blackamore'. The churchwardens of St Martin-in-the-Fields recorded the burial in September 1570 of 'Margarete a blakeamore', in August 1593 the burial of 'Thomas Morino A Moore', and in November 1596 that of 'John of Carata an Indian from Sr Walter Rayleighes'.[2] A proclamation of 1601 declared that the queen was 'discontented at the great number of negars and blackamoores' that had settled in England since the outbreak of the war with Spain sixteen years earlier, 'to the annoyance of her own people', and it ordered that they should be deported. A merchant of Lubeck was given the task of supervising their expulsion.[3]

Visitors were generally critical of the way in which they were treated and of how Londoners seemed to regard foreigners. In 1557 the Venetian ambassador Giovanni Michiel wrote of 'the insolence with which foreigners are treated by the English', and in the following year the French traveller Etienne Perlin complained that, 'These villains hate all sorts of foreigners.'[4] Jacob Rathgeb, in 1592, was more specific when describing the attitude of Londoners, who he found to be:

> extremely proud and overbearing; and because the greater part, especially the trades people, seldom go into other countries, but always remain in their houses in the city attending to their business, they care little for foreigners, but scoff and laugh at them.[5]

Even someone who lived in the city for a long time, rather than paying a short visit, came to a similar conclusion. Emanuel van Meteren, a merchant from Antwerp, was in London for almost the whole of Elizabeth I's reign (1558–1603) and his summary of Londoners was that they were 'not vindictive, but very inconstant, rash, vainglorious, light, and deceiving, and very suspicious, especially of foreigners, whom they despise.'[6]

The Florentine writer Petruccio Ubaldini, a Protestant and long-standing resident of the city, commented sardonically in 1588 that it was easier 'to find flocks of white crows than one Englishman (and let him believe what he will about religion) who loves a foreigner'.[7] Things had not changed by 1617, when the Venetian chaplain Orazio Busino explained that:

> Foreigners are ill regarded not to say detested in London, so sensible people dress in the English fashion, or in that of France, which is adopted by nearly the whole court, and thus mishaps are avoided or passed over in silence. The Spaniards alone maintain the prerogative of wearing their own costume, so they are easily recognised and most mortally hated.[8]

Londoners could be intimidating, even violent. Isaac Casaubon was a distinguished Protestant scholar who had found the rigid Calvinism of Geneva oppressive and so moved to Paris, where he came under strong pressure from members of the court to convert to the Roman Catholic church. He felt increasingly uncomfortable after the assassination of Henri IV in May 1610 and later that year accepted an invitation from Archbishop Bancroft to visit London, where he stayed until his death in 1614. Casaubon was welcomed at court, where he had conversations with James I, and he made friends with a number of senior churchmen. But he never learned English and his years in London were made difficult by the citizens' behaviour. He claimed that he was insulted more than he had been in Paris, stones were thrown at his windows, he was attacked and injured one day as he was going to court, his children were abused in the streets, he and his family were pelted with stones, and their house was burgled.[9]

Members of diplomatic missions were also liable to experience harassment, especially those from countries regarded as hostile to England. Perlin wrote that 'the people of this nation have a mortal hatred for the French as their ancient enemies'.[10] During the late sixteenth century the Spanish came close to supplanting the French as the main objects of popular resentment and derision. This was fuelled by the violent attempts to quell the revolts in the Low Countries, the war with England from 1585, and especially the Great Armada and threatened invasion in 1588. That hostility continued, even after James I had made peace with Spain in the Treaty of London of 1604.

After the peace of 1604, Bridgewater House in the Barbican was used as the Spanish embassy. In 1613 the Count de Gondomar arrived in England as ambassador and he ingratiated himself with James I, not only promoting Spanish interests but making the house a centre for Roman Catholic services in London. This was unpopular with the citizens, both because of the presence of such a centre of Catholicism and the king's reversal of Elizabeth's foreign policy. In 1623 John Chamberlain complained that, 'priests and Jesuites swarme here extraordinarilie'.[11]

Busino related an incident in which a Spaniard, thought to be a member of the embassy, was belaboured by a crowd incited by a woman wielding 'a cabbage stalk and calling him a Spanish rogue, and although in very brave array his garments were foully smeared with a sort of soft and very stinking mud, which abounds here at all seasons, so that the place better deserves to be called Lorda (filth) than Londra (London). Had not the don saved himself in a shop they would assuredly have torn his eyes out.'[12]

Another episode, in 1618, attracted more attention. A horse ridden by one of Gondomar's men knocked over a boy in the street. The man rode on and, mistakenly thinking that the boy had been killed, a growing crowd pursued the rider to the embassy. He arrived safely ahead of them and they had to content themselves with throwing stones at the windows. The king was outraged and insisted that the rioters be brought to trial; seven were found guilty and were fined and given prison sentences. Gondomar pleaded for their pardon, because, as the Venetian ambassador explained, he was aware that, 'the populace, which already detests their nation, would resent the punishment of the rioters who attacked the house'. The king's pardon was a grudging one, describing the incident as 'that outrageous & seditious assault' and noting that the punishments had been too lenient. It demonstrated the government's concern that major public disturbances could develop from such minor events: 'and the scumme of the Suburbes may joyne to the youth and Prentises of the Citie, and proceede from fury to pillage, and fill all things with mischiefe and combustion'.

The pardon also revealed its anxiety that the justices were sympathetic to the rioters, declaring that if offenders were not dealt with speedily or adequately by the civil authorities, the crown would 'command the offenders to be executed by Martiall Law without delay, or other formality of proceeding'. Such a disproportionate response to a minor accident was hardly likely to lessen Londoners' resentment of the Spanish entourage, but it did reflect the government's fear of social disorder.[13]

Fynes Moryson felt the need to answer 'the Imputation of strangers that the English are inhospitable towardes them, and to this day apt to use insolent wronges towards them'. This he attributed partly to their first impressions, gained from the people of Gravesend, where travellers disembarked, to travel to London overland and so avoid sailing on the long loop of the Thames around the Isle of Dogs. Many who lived in the town had travelled abroad and retained a smouldering resentment at the way in which they had been treated, settling their scores by taking financial advantage of visitors. They then directed them to landlords in London who had a similar attitude, 'where they may be ill used for expences, and there perhaps are sometyme arronged by the insolency of the baser sorte of Prentisces, serving men, Dray men, and like people'.

This behaviour Moryson excused with the comment that those groups treated English gentlemen and ladies in the same way. To be received courteously and hospitably a traveller needed 'an honest guide' and should 'converse with the better sorte'.[14] But even sightseeing could produce suspicion of discrimination through over-charging. When Valentin Arithmaeus, Professor of Poetry at Frankfort-on-Oder, visited Westminster Abbey in 1617, a verger offered him a copy of Camden's guide-book to the monuments, 'but after the manner of his nation, eaten up with avarice, he demanded a great price'. And at St Paul's, where many visitors climbed the tower, his comment was that, 'No German is admitted to it, unless he pays his money beforehand, so intense is the avarice of the English'.[15] Despite such reactions, Moryson insisted that the English did respect strangers, especially military men and scholars, and indeed were liable to have more regard for foreign physicians and others than for their own countrymen.

Yet Moryson also admitted that, 'the Cittizens of London and of lesse Cittyes, have had and may have a spleane against strangers for growing rich among them by traffique used to theire prejudice'.[16] For the merchants, travellers and diplomats were far outnumbered by the tens of thousands of incomers from Europe, who braved the resentment of Londoners to settle in the city and practise their trades. That resentment could erupt into violence at times of heightened tension, when prices were high or work was short. In 1580 the Lord Mayor summarized the nature of the fears concerning the strangers:

> Great complaint was made by Her Majesty's subjects, that they were
> eaten out by stranger artificers, to the suffering of this country, whereas
> none of Her Majesty's subjects were suffered in their country to live by
> their work.[17]

Memories still lingered of the violent disturbances on May Day
1517, which were directed at strangers and began, according to the
chronicler Edward Hall, after an Italian stole a pair of pigeons and
another abducted a goldsmith's wife, purloining some of his silver as
well. In the xenophobic atmosphere of the time those incidents were
enough to provoke a riot. Italians were resented, for living in comfort
in fine houses, gaining control of the import trade in luxuries, and
exporting too much English wool, which could have been made into
cloth in London, providing employment and selling for a higher price
than raw wool. But the violence was directed mainly at immigrant
Flemish workers, as about a thousand young men rampaged through
the area around Cheapside.

Those Evil May Day riots were recalled when the economy faltered.
In 1587 the City's Recorder, William Fleetwood, was afraid that grain
shortages in London would lead to rioting by apprentices 'as like unto
ill May Day as could be devised'.[18] Neither the corporation nor the
government had the means to respond rapidly to large-scale disorder,
and feared that an outbreak may gather momentum, beginning with
attacks on the strangers and then spreading to the plunder of the
wealthy citizens and nobility. The Evil May Day riots in 1517 had
been suppressed not by the City justices, but by the Duke of Norfolk,
who led a force of his own retainers into the city; 278 people were
arrested and 15 of them were executed.

The issue of public disorder was confronted in the play *Sir Thomas
More*. Written by Anthony Munday and Henry Chettle, probably
in 1592–4, it drew the disapproval of Sir Edmund Tilney, Master of
the Revels and official censor. He asked for changes, specifically the
removal of the section on the Evil May Day riots, a sensitive subject
however it was handled. The text was revised by Chettle, Shakespeare,

Thomas Dekker and Thomas Heywood, with Shakespeare writing the passages based on the riots. His text presents More as a humane conciliator. When More asks the crowd what their objectives are, a spokesman replies, 'the removing of the strangers, which cannot choose but much advantage the poor handicrafts of the city'. More points out that, if they achieve their purpose, with 'Authority quite silenced by your brawl', they will have shown how insolence and violence could prevail and create the conditions in which they, too, would be vulnerable to prejudice. Other ruffians could do the same, and they 'Would shark on you, and men like ravenous fishes would feed one on the other.' Would they really benefit if the social order broke down, through their example? And what if the king did not pardon them and expelled them for their crime, would they find a refuge?

> What country, by the nature of your error, Should give you harbour?...
> Why, you must needs be strangers. Would you be pleased
> To find a nation of such barbarous temper
> That breaking out in hideous violence
> Would not afford you an abode on earth... ?

Shakespeare used the example of the riots, more than seventy years earlier, to probe a contemporary issue.[19]

The view expressed by Shakespeare echoed that of Henry Finch, MP for Canterbury, in a debate in the House of Commons in March 1593. A Bill before the House would have prevented strangers from acting as retailers of imports. Finch, who often put the Puritans' point of view, was concerned that it would lead to a campaign for their expulsion, and pointed out that English Protestant refugees had been given asylum abroad during Mary I's reign (1553–8),

> when our case was as theirs now, those contryes did allow us those liberties which now we seeke to deny them. They are strangers now. We may be strangers hereafter, therefore let us doe as we would be done to.

Others spoke in favour of a tolerant policy. Sir John Wolley was afraid that if the Bill passed into law, it would damage London, 'for the Riches and Renown of the City cometh by entertaining of Strangers, and giving liberty unto them'.[20]

Some who favoured the Bill alleged that strangers had a commercial advantage over English traders in exporting, because of their network of contacts abroad. Other economic arguments were put forward, including fear that strangers trading overseas paid in English coin, reducing the amount in circulation in England. The debate provided the opportunity for other complaints to be aired, not directly concerned with the question of retailing. Sir Walter Raleigh claimed that the Dutch would not settle under any government for long and that 'here they live disliking our Church'. Nicholas Fuller, one of London's MPs, objected that strangers did not integrate: 'they will not commerce with us. They mar[r]y not into our nation. They will not buy any thinge of our contry men', while another speaker 'imputed the beggery of this City to strangers, and sayd, that in some one parish there were 1100 that lyved by begging'. The immigrant communities were convenient targets for such allegations and fears, and the Bill passed the Commons, only to be rejected by the Lords.[21]

Londoners were indeed concerned about unfair competition, which breached the structures of the city's economy and society. The City's social and economic system, which strangers were accused of evading, was centred on its freemen, who held the right to trade. They were members of the livery companies, which controlled entry to a trade and maintained the quality of the product. Stow listed sixty companies. Freemen's sons were entitled to claim the freedom of the City, others could obtain it by payment of a fee, or by serving an apprenticeship with a master. The lawyer John Manningham explained that, 'almost any man for some 40£. may buy his freedome, and these are called freed by redemption'.[22] Yet more than eighty per cent of admissions to the livery companies were through apprenticeship. Apprentices commonly served seven or more years and were in their early twenties when they completed their term, were proficient in their trade and could become freemen. Orazio Busino explained that citizens, 'served bare-headed for seven years in their youth in some workshop for the sake of obtaining the mere title of apprentice. This enables them to open a shop.'[23] Of course, many others, semi-skilled and unskilled, were employed in the metropolitan economy and they were not members of the companies. But the basic unit, and the safeguard of social order, was seen to be the household, consisting of a family, apprentices, employees and domestic servants, under the direction and discipline of its head, who was a citizen.

The corporation was concerned that strangers did not merge into this pattern, yet it complied with requests from the Privy Council to grant the freedom to individual strangers. The livery companies were also suspected of granting the freedom to strangers, circumventing the usual process. In 1583 a pamphlet was scattered around the streets, directed 'against strangers, especially handicraftsmen, and [who] were of no church'. It suggested that the livery companies were taking money to allow 'sundry Flemings to set up what trade they liked'. That was an economic objection; the allegation that strangers were 'of no church' was a social and religious one, that they did not attend parish churches.[24] Many attended their own churches, formed in 1550; the French church in St Anthony's chapel on the north side of Threadneedle Street and the Dutch church in the nave of the church of the former Augustine friary, where the Dutch community had worshipped before the Reformation. In 1593, 2,720 attended those two churches, in roughly equal numbers, and 29 the Italian church, and only 549, or one in six, attended parish churches.[25] This had an impact on the parishes where they lived, for if they did not attend church and pay their parish rates, its revenues were reduced. By the 1590s Billingsgate Ward contained roughly 150 households of strangers, 30 of them in St Botolph's parish, where collections for the poor had fallen from £27 per year to £11, 'for the stranger will not contribute to such charges as other citizens do'. But thirty years earlier there had been no more than 'three Netherlanders' in the whole ward.[26]

In fact, strangers were subject to rules that did not apply to citizens. By a regulation of 1550 they had to work with their shops' shutters closed, not keep 'open shop', so that passers-by would not be tempted by their wares. The citizens complained that such measures against strangers were not enforced, while the strangers grumbled about being harassed. In 1611 the Dutch and French communities objected to being molested by the City's officers for practising their trades, as they had been doing peaceably hitherto. The Lord Mayor and Aldermen responded by writing to the Privy Council, pointing out the strength of feeling among the freemen against strangers: 'The manual artificers found their work taken from them by the sufferance of so many stranger artisans, and the merchant and retailer complained of the stranger's manner of trading.' Their letter could have been written at any time over the previous fifty years or more. And they did respond to complaints and attempt to enforce the orders. After repeated protests that Nicholas Loe, of St Andrew's, Holborn, a crossbow-maker, 'used his trade by keeping an open shop within the freedom with as much privileges as any freeman', the Chamberlain was instructed to shut up his shop windows. This he did, but 'for doing whereof he received very ill treatment from the servants of Loe', whose employment was threatened by his action. Loe argued that he and his father had worked there for thirty years and, undaunted, continued to trade as before, and so was imprisoned.[27]

Government policy distinguished between Protestant refugees fleeing from persecution, who could stay, and others, who were expelled. In 1574 it believed that London contained 1,500 strangers who were not Protestant, and they were ordered to leave. The strategy was renewed in 1586, with a Privy Council order for the expulsion of strangers in London, Maidstone, Dover and Sandwich, 'not being of any church or congregation'. Even so, tensions were high in the 1590s, because the number of strangers in London seemed to be increasing, especially in districts such as Southwark and St Katherine-by-the-Tower. A return of 1571 recorded 698 foreigners in Southwark, and another, in the following year, found 425 in St Katherine's, 328 of them Dutch; the district was known as 'Petty Flanders'.[28] The increased numbers in the 1590s were attributable to the wars on the near continent during the previous decade. The situation prompted some apprentices to issue a pamphlet in April 1593, demanding that all French and Flemish should leave, setting 9 July as the deadline. If they did not do so, 'all the apprentices and journeymen will down with the Flemish and strangers'.[29]

Against this background, the government ordered an enumeration of strangers. The returns showed that London contained 7,113 strangers, with twice as many having arrived from the Low Countries as from France, and fewer still from Germany. They did not include Westminster, and the true figure may have been around 10,000, but still no more than five or six per cent of the total population. A comparable return twenty years earlier had put the figure at 7,143, and so the proportion of strangers had fallen, from about ten per cent, as the population of the metropolis had increased. Not all were refugees, for roughly a third of those recorded in 1573 were economic migrants, who admitted 'that their coming hither was onlie to seeke woorke for their livinge'. This need not produce resentment, either from the state which they had left, or in London. When the Duke of Würtemberg was being shown around the Tower in 1592, 'one of his Highness's subjects... presented himself to his Highness. He was by trade a gunsmith, and had married and settled in London.'[30]

The return for 1593 must have been a relief to the government, for it demonstrated that the number of strangers was not increasing, and that they formed a stable group. It also showed considerable integration. A third of those recorded, and three-quarters of the children, had been born in England. And it contradicted the common complaint that the strangers deprived Londoners of work, for over a half of their householders employed indigenous workers or servants. This probably was the result of government pressure that they should do so.[31] Indeed, the investigation seemed to have vindicated government policy, which Sir Robert Cecil summarized by saying that:

It is a great charity to releeve strangers, specially being such as doe not greive our eyes. This hath brought great honour to our kingdome for it is therefore counted the refuge for all distressed nations. But yet our charity to them must not iniury our selves.

The balance was difficult to achieve. While Thomas Platter, in 1599, had the impression that the thousands of religious refugees 'have been very kindly received', complaints against strangers continued.[32] These were largely based on the fear that they were putting Londoners out of work, using cheap, unskilled labour and cutting costs further by living in poor and overcrowded accommodation. Those who lost their livelihoods as a result of such practices increased the number and expense of the poor.

London's stranger population probably peaked in the mid-1590s. Thereafter the inward flow of refugees from France was reduced by the issuing of the Edict of Nantes in 1598, which allowed French Protestants freedom of worship, and from the Low Countries by the effective recognition by Spain of the United Provinces, with the agreement of a truce in 1609. The changed political circumstances from the late 1590s also encouraged outward migration, from London to the United Provinces. And, for diplomatic reasons, in 1598 Elizabeth withdrew the privileges of the Hanseatic merchants and expelled them from the Steelyard, in retaliation for the Emperor Rudolf II's expulsion of the Merchant Adventurers from the port of Stade, on the River Elbe. Even though James I allowed them to return eight years later, they did not recover their earlier privileges and the League itself was in decline.

The numbers of strangers in the returns showed that immigration was not a significant cause of London's inexorable population growth. That was largely produced by internal migration, by those drawn to London for economic reasons, many of whom took up a trade through apprenticeship. In the mid-sixteenth century, London contained approximately 7,000 young men serving apprenticeships; by the end of the century that figure had risen to 15,000, with another 12,000 working as journeymen, wage-earners not serving an apprenticeship. By the first decade of the seventeenth century the number of apprentices enrolled to masters in thirteen of the livery companies was two-thirds higher than it had been forty years before. This was one cause of London's increasing population, for most apprentices, perhaps as many as four-fifths, came from outside the capital. Roughly a half arrived from south-east England, East Anglia and the Midlands. In the 1610s, only one-twelfth of apprentices enrolled with the wood turners' company were Londoners.[33] Domestic servants formed another category of incomers, and they, too, were drawn mainly from within England.

As at least four-fifths of freemen gained that status by apprenticeship, not as freemen's sons, and as four-fifths of apprentices were new to London, then a high proportion of males practising trades in the City were incomers. James Dalton in *An Apology of the City of London* of *c.*1580 described Londoners as 'by birth for the most part a mixture' from all the regions of the country.[34] High mortality within the metropolis also influenced the character of the population. Deaths exceeded births, even in non-plague years, and during an epidemic they greatly outnumbered them. There were few plague deaths in 1612–19, yet burials were seven per cent higher than baptisms. Thus the city required incomers just to replenish its population and a considerable inflow for it to grow at the rate at which it did expand.

London therefore contained a high proportion of newcomers, anxious to establish themselves within its economy and society. The high level of immigration produced a young and dynamic society. Dalton described Londoners as 'by profession busy bees, and travailers for their living in the hive of this commonwealth', and almost forty years later Orazio Busino commented, 'From this busy commonwealth all idlers are banished.'[35] But it could also have created some anxious insecurity and tensions between those who were born in London and incomers, if so many citizens were no more firmly established in the city than were the strangers. It was during this period that native Londoners came to be described as Cockneys, acknowledging their sense of identity. In 1600 John Rowlands referred to 'a Bow-bell Cockney', in his satire *The Letting of Humours Blood in the Head-Vaine*. The lexicographer John Minsheu defined the term in 1617 as, 'applied only to one borne within the sound of Bow-bell, that is, within the City of London', and in the same year Fynes Moryson wrote that, 'Londiners, and all within the sound of Bow-bell, are in reproch called Cocknies, and eaters of buttered tostes'.[36]

Those entering the city's economy through the formal channels were also suspicious and resentful of their own countrymen who lived and worked outside the system, on the fringes of society. Attention and concern were focused on those masterless men, inmates (or lodgers), and others, who provided casual labour. They operated outside the structure of the livery companies and were thought to be criminal and disorderly elements, a potential threat to the community, and to the corporation's orderly control of the city. Such groups were seen as a major cause of London's growth, which was so striking that it could not be ignored.

That growth became a cause of concern to Elizabeth's government, alarmed that London was attracting so many people from the rest of the country that agriculture and manufacturing would be adversely affected. The increasing size of the metropolitan market was thought to be altering the balance between the numbers of consumers and producers of food. In other words, so many were leaving the countryside that there would not be enough remaining to till the land and raise the livestock needed to supply the city's increasing demands. Agricultural output would fall as metropolitan demand was rising, producing shortages and high food prices, which, in turn, could provoke discontent and disorder among the poor. Moreover, the growing city was using great amounts of fuel, including timber that should have been used for shipbuilding. And the maintenance of justice was also a worry, with the awareness that, because of the greater numbers of people, it could not be upheld without 'more new jurisdictions and officers for that purpose'.[37] A further concern was that overcrowding created the nasty conditions and contaminated air in which diseases could thrive. While public health was acknowledged to be better than at any time within living memory, there was no room for complacency.

High prices, disorder, epidemics; those concerns were expressed in the preamble to a royal proclamation issued in 1580, which initiated a policy to restrict the growth of London. Unable to prevent or control the arrival of people, the strategy followed was aimed at limiting the amount of accommodation, by keeping the number of dwellings at the existing level. That approach was continued by successive governments, intermittently and ineffectively, until the mid-seventeenth century.

The proclamation made it clear that the policy had the support of the corporation, with the statement that it was issued with the agreement of the Lord Mayor, Aldermen and 'other grave wise men in or about the Citie'. It ordered everyone:

> To desist and forbeare from any new buildings of any house or tenement, within three miles from any of the gates of the sayd Citie of London, to serve for habitation or lodging for any person, where no former house hath bene knowen to have bene, in the memorie of such as are now living, and also to forbeare from letting or setting, or suffering any more families than one onely to be placed or inhabit from henceforth in any house that heretofore hathe bene inhabited.

The penalties were harsh. If those found to have begun new buildings continued with the work after they had been warned, then they were to be imprisoned, without bail. They would be released only when sureties were found who entered into bonds that they would not attempt to continue with those buildings. The proclamation also instructed the City to take action against those who, within the previous seven years, had allowed an increase in the number of 'indwellers, inmates or undersitters', terms which were used to describe lodgers.[38]

Such a policy was difficult to enforce, given the size of the city, its expanding economy, the financial investment in property and the profits to be made from rents. Wages were higher in London than in provincial cities, reflecting the level of demand for labour. In the late sixteenth century they were generally one-quarter to one-third higher in London than in southern England, and by the early seventeenth century the differential was closer to fifty per cent.[39] That created a powerful economic force that was difficult to resist through legislation aimed at restricting living space.

The Privy Council complained to the Lord Mayor and Aldermen in 1583 that they had been given the authority to enforce the terms of the proclamation, but that had been 'so ineffectually carried out, that buildings had greatly increased within the City and liberties, to the danger of pestilence and riot'. They responded by claiming that when they were required to provide the numbers of houses that contravened the order, they had been instructed, 'not to include any erected in the late dissolved monasteries and such other places, pretending exemption from the City's liberties of Middlesex, as parcel of that county'. They pointed out that the Lord Mayor, those Aldermen who had served in that office and the Recorder were, by its charter, Justices of the Peace for the City, and that:

> it had been the custom to make return of all places as well within the liberties as without, without the intervention of foreign Justices; that these places being in the heart of the City, and being daily filled with a great multitude of people of the meaner sort, it would greatly prejudice the citizens, if they should be delivered from their authority.

This was a clear case of conflicting jurisdictions hindering the implementation of policy. The Lord Mayor's writ did not run in the liberties or the suburbs beyond the City's boundaries on both sides of the Thames, which were the responsibility of the county justices.[40]

An Act of Parliament of 1592 set out the government's intentions once again, stating that because of the erection of new buildings and the subdivision of existing ones:

Great Infection of Sickness and dearth of Victuals and Fuel hath growen and ensued and many idle vagrant and wicked persons have harboured themselves there and divers remote places of the Realme have been disappointed of Workmen and dispeopled.

The ban on new building and conversion of houses into 'severall Habitacions or Dwellings' was repeated, although with the qualification that it could be allowed if a dwelling created by subdivision was occupied by someone wealthy enough to be assessed for parliamentary taxes at £5 for goods or £3 for land. The regulation against taking in lodgers was renewed, with the order that no householder should 'receyve or take into his or their House or Houses any Inmate or Undersitter'. William Shakespeare maintained a household in Stratford, but in London was a lodger, and so, by the letter of the law, could have been construed as living in the city illegally.[41]

The growth of the suburbs was especially alarming to the authorities. Stow remarked that they had been 'mightily increased with buildings'. For instance, the extra-mural part of Cripplegate contained more than 1,800 householders and 'above four thousand communicants'. Infilling and subdivision were less conspicuous, but attracted the attention of the Weavers' Company, which made a connection between the stranger population and overcrowded premises. It alleged that, 'The most part of strangers and foreigners dwellings are in chambers and odd corners, being divers families in one house.'[42]

The Act of 1592 lapsed after ten years, but the policy was continued under James I, who came to the throne in March 1603. The size of his new capital city dismayed the king and he complained that because of its rapid expansion, 'soon London will be all England'. His government did not develop a new approach and continued existing policies. A proclamation issued just five months after he came to the throne, during the plague epidemic, was directed against, 'Inmates and multitudes of dwellers in strait Roomes and places in and about the Citie of London: And for the rasing and pulling downe of certaine new erected buildings'. Those living in 'small and strait roomes and habitations' were condemned as 'idle, indigent, dissolute and dangerous persons', in other words, unruly and lawless people likely to be a threat to social stability. Without a family or economic attachment to the household with which they were lodging, they were regarded as lacking connections or allegiance to the city. That concern was made explicit in another proclamation against new building in London and the suburbs, issued in 1607, which also mentioned:

> the filling & pestering of houses with Inmates and severall dwellers (and those of the worse sort) almost in every roome, whereby both the people increasing to so great numbers, are not well to be governed by the wonted Officers and ordinarie Jurisdiction of the same.

The proclamation contained the unambiguous order 'that no person doe hereafter receive into any House any Inmates or Undersitters, or any more families than one'. The corporation still supported the policy and had asked that the proclamation be issued, having failed to get a Bill into Parliament. In 1611 the Common Council ordered that each dwelling in converted buildings should contain at least three rooms, each 14 feet square, with penalty fines for non-compliance and for housing an inmate who was not included in the taxation lists.[43]

The authorities attempted to enforce the measures; some cases were brought before the Court of Star Chamber, whose functions included the enforcement of royal proclamations. In 1614, for example, charitable trustees of property in Holborn and Bloomsbury brought an action in the court against:

> greedy & covitously minded persons pursuing only theire owne corupte gaine without respect of the good of the Common Wealthe... [building] divers houses and cotages in sundry places where noe house houses cotage or cotages have formerly been erected.[44]

Most such buildings were small and slight, and erected quickly. The prefabricated nature of timber-frame buildings created a difficulty with enforcement, as the Privy Council acknowledged in 1598, because 'those that doe make new buildinges doe cause the frames to be made in other places, and suddainly sett up the same'. And so buildings were erected before action could be taken to prevent it, especially when the courts were not sitting. At the same time the Council expressed dissatisfaction with the efforts of the Lord Mayor, Aldermen and justices, warning them that, 'your slack and negligent oversight therein doth deserve some sharp and severe reprehension'.[45]

In 1602 the Council authorized determined and practical action against infilling caused by 'building over stables, in gardens, and other od corners'. Its solution was demolition, as John Chamberlain explained:

> they have taken order to have them puld downe, and this weeke they have begun almost in every parish to light on the unluckiest, here and there one, which God knowes is far from removing the mischeife.[46]

Demolition was tried again in 1618, when Sir Francis Bacon told the judges in the Star Chamber court that illegal houses should be destroyed, 'and those of the rich first'. The Privy Council duly ordered that some new buildings should be pulled down as an example, and at least forty-seven were demolished accordingly.[47]

This could deal with just a small proportion of the offending structures and have only a temporary impact, for the profit from letting them would encourage landlords to rebuild. In one case in Star Chamber, the Attorney General brought an action against two men who had built in Drury Lane and the Strand, taking the opportunity to build on a space that was vacant because a building had been demolished on the Privy Council's orders.[48] And if there was a probability that a new building would be pulled down, then owners had no incentive to build a substantial one, and would erect a flimsy structure, minimising their loss if they should be one of the unlucky ones whose property was demolished.

Pulling down was not an option for the larger and better-built houses of influential owners, and compromises had to be made. But they were not always successful. For example, a servant of the Countess

Dowager of Derby was reprimanded for dividing a house into no less than twenty-one tenements, and was instructed to reduce the number to four, not to restore the house to a single dwelling. Nevertheless, he refused to do so. In 1606 the Lord Mayor reported to the Privy Council a case in Southwark, where 'an ancient brewhouse' was being converted into 'several small tenements'. The owner had ignored orders to stop the work, and the Lord Mayor now recommended that he should be allowed to convert the property into no more than three tenements. And so its conversion would be permitted, even though this was an example of just the kind of alteration, from non-residential to residential use, that the policy was designed to prevent.[49]

Other landlords and their tenants were harshly dealt with. In 1610 a householder in Petty France who had 'receiv'd William Dicker and his wife Robert Down and his wife Inmates into his Tenemt contrary to his Maities Laws and to the hurt of this Citty' was ordered to expel them within four days, 'and to receive no more' tenants or be committed to the Gatehouse prison. Four years later a carpenter who had built a small tenement in the same street was condemned to sit in the stocks for six hours and then be gaoled, until he could find sureties for his good behaviour. The justices alleged that just one room of that tenement housed, 'six masterless persons, both men and women... being newly come out of the Country', who were to be sent back to the place of their last known residence. In 1614 a woman living alone was brought before the sessions in Westminster, 'for living suspiciously and out of service att her own hand... [she] shall either forthwith get her into some honest service, or else avoid out of the said Thomas Westmills house... upon pain of whipping'.

Also in that year, a builder erecting a new tenement in St Martin's Lane had to submit a bond 'to save the Parish harmless of such Tennant or Tennants as he shall hereafter receive into that Tenement or are now inhabiting therein'.[50] Such actions against lodgers and newcomers not only enforced the law curbing the growth of the city, but also reflected the concern that people living as lodgers who were without work might claim poor relief from the parish.

The regulations effectively imposed a measure of social control, attempting to restrict the influx of too many poor people without the certainty of employment, or beyond the control of household or trade. But the continued growth of the metropolis showed that policies to control its expansion were futile. That was just as well. Had they been assiduously and successfully enforced, they would have threatened the city's prosperity, and the welfare of its inhabitants. If new housing had been prevented, while London continued to draw in newcomers, then the overcrowding that resulted would have produced the environmental conditions which the government acknowledged endangered public health.

Foul and tainted air was believed to provide the ideal environment for the venomous sticky atoms that were thought to carry plague. Decaying rubbish and nasty and malodorous living conditions could corrupt clean and wholesome air. In 1582 the corporation complained of those living in overcrowded conditions because, 'filthie keeping of their houses and of noisome and yll savors in the streets is one of the greatest occasions of the infection of the plague'.[51] Simon Kellwaye included an example in his *A Defensative against the plague* (1593), which summarized the measures that should be taken to prevent the plague. He recommended that innkeepers should clean out their stables daily and remove the contents from the city, because:

> by suffering it in their houses, as some used to do, a whole week or fortnight, it doth so putrifie that when it is removed, there is such a stinking savour and unwholesome smell, as is able to infect the whole street where it is.[52]

Devastating plague epidemics had hit the city periodically since the Black Death in 1348–9. Plague was distinguishable from fevers and other diseases by the swelling of the lymph nodes, especially in the groin and armpits and on the neck, forming buboes, and excruciatingly painful blotches or carbuncles up to an inch across, caused by haemorrhaging beneath the skin. Contemporaries described the blotches as tokens, and plague as 'spotted death'. They knew that when, 'the tokens, tumors, or carbuncle do appeare, there is no cause of suspition or doubt of the disease'.[53] Those who contracted the disease suffered in agony and died within days, while those who had been in contact with them experienced terrible anxiety, in case they, too, fell victim to plague, which was virtually a death sentence, for few survived. In *Antony and Cleopatra* Shakespeare mentions, 'the token'd pestilence, Where death is sure'.[54]

Preventive measures evolved during the sixteenth century were based upon cleanliness, including the removal of dung and rubbish from the streets, quarantining the sick in their houses, the killing of stray dogs and cats because they were thought to transmit the disease, and bans on people meeting in groups. When an outbreak threatened, statistics were collected that distinguished plague deaths from the others, to allow measures to be put in place. The first such London Bill of Mortality was compiled in 1519 and in 1555 the parish clerks were instructed to make a return of 'the numbers of all the persons who die and whereof they die'.[55]

Such measures were implemented in 1563, as a plague epidemic began. The corporation instructed that houses where someone was suffering from the plague should be marked, and its occupants confined to the house for a month. Houses and streets were to be washed and fires were lit in the streets to circulate the air and prevent it stagnating. These were ineffective and the policy of household quarantine in particular was much resented, and was difficult to enforce when so many houses contained plague victims. Despite the steps taken, the outbreak grew into one of the most destructive of the century, with the number of deaths across the city almost eight times higher than in recent years. The total number of deaths was 23,660, of which 20,136 were attributed to plague.

The corporation continued to issue regulations, especially when plague threatened, and in May 1583 produced a codification of its plague orders, under twenty-one headings. The marking of infected houses, household quarantine, cleaning of the streets, identification of the cause of death by 'sober anciente women', the killing of stray dogs, rules governing burials, punishment of plague victims who walked the streets, prohibition of plays and interludes, and the washing or destruction of bedding from infected houses were all included.[56] These were sound and sensible measures, based upon continental practices, appropriate for the control of a contagious disease transmitted directly from person to person. But they could not prevent the spread of plague, for they were produced by a society which was wholly ignorant of the nature of the disease and struggled to deal with its effects. Not until the end of the nineteenth century was the plague bacillus, *Yersinia pestis*, isolated and its transmission by the bite of a rat's flea, *Xenopsylla cheopis*, understood.

In any case, the implementation of the regulations could not always be efficient, especially during the traumatic period of a plague epidemic, when many better-off citizens left the city, as the only way to escape the disease. But Londoners were not negligent and attempted to maintain cleanliness. Some householders kept their premises clean and smelling sweetly. During an outbreak in 1593, Edward Alleyn wrote from Bristol to his wife at their house in Bankside, hoping that the disease would miss their house. He recommended that she should, 'kepe your house fayr and clean which I knowe you will and every evening throwe water before your dore and in your bakcsid and have in your windowes good store of rwe and herbe of grace.'[57]

That epidemic, which began in 1592 and continued into the early months of 1594, was the most serious since 1563, with 25,886 deaths, 15,003 of them from plague. Overall, burials were over four times higher than in a normal year, but at St Vedast, Foster Lane and All Hallows, London Wall they were five times higher, and in St Botolph, Bishopsgate they were seven times higher than normal. Roughly thirteen per cent of London's population died in the outbreak. The Privy Council took a close interest in the progress of the epidemic, complaining that the regulations were not being implemented. It summarized contemporaries' reaction to disease with the comment that:

althoughe we do acknowledge these plagues and sicknes to proceede
from the handes of God as a due punyshement of our synnes, nevertheles
we oughte to use all possible meanes by all good waies to prevente the
increase of the same.[58]

But such a view was challenged during the next, and far more
destructive, outbreak, in 1603. The question then posed was that if
God did indeed send the plague, as a punishment, then surely he alone
could end it, and any measures which government or city might devise
must be futile? The clergyman Henoch Clapham both published and
preached such sceptical observations, and eventually was imprisoned,
in an attempt to reduce his influence.

The usual steps were taken once the plague began to claim victims
during the spring. But the outbreak grew remorselessly throughout
the summer and continued until the early winter. During the year,
43,154 deaths were recorded, eighty-one per cent of them attributed
to plague. The outer areas were the worst affected; Southwark, St
Giles, St Sepulchre's, Cripplegate and Bishopsgate. Roughly twenty
per cent of Londoners died during the epidemic. Taken as a proportion
of those who remained in the city, the figure would have been rather
higher, for the population fell when some citizens left to escape the
unfolding disaster. Contemporaries recognized that going away was
the safest course, but the morality of leaving at such a time was hotly
debated, especially as the wealthier were those who were able to leave
and the poor had no choice but to stay and take their chances. The
disease erupted among the poorer people in the suburbs. Thomas
Dekker wrote that:

Death... hath pitcht his tents... in the sinfully-polluted suburbs... which
they within the gates perceiving, it was no boot to bid them take their
heeles, for away they trudge thicke & threefolde, some riding, some on
foote, some without bootes, some in their slippers, by water, by land...
so that within a short time, there was not a good horse in Smithfield,
nor a Coach to be set eye on.[59]

He was also critical of the physicians, because the treatments and medicines which they prescribed were quite useless; 'they hid their Synodicall heads aswell as the prowdest'. The citizens had recourse to their own cures, such as 'a pot of Pinders Ale and a Nutmeg', and they hoped that sweet smells would protect them, so that 'the price of flowers, hearbes and garlands, rose wonderfully'. Dekker grieved for his native city: 'In this pittifull (or rather pittilesse) perplexitie stood London, forsaken Like a Lover, forlorne like a widow, and disarmde of all comfort.' [60]

But recovery came quickly. Niccolò Molin arrived in London in mid-December 1603, as the epidemic was dying away, and commented that, 'No one ever mentions the plague, no more than if it had never been.'[61] Winter always brought a respite from plague and so the citizens knew that the worst was over, which helps to explain the response which Molin witnessed. That proved to be the case, but the disease lingered on through the remainder of the decade, claiming hundreds of victims in every year until 1611.

Plague epidemics periodically caused a frighteningly high death-toll, but did not deter people from moving to London, and the loss of life created openings for others to fill. The city's population recovered to its pre-plague level within two years of the epidemic of 1603. Partly this came from children born to those who remarried after losing their spouse to the disease, but migrants must have made the major contribution, for the losses to have been replaced within such a short time.

Nor did the reactions of Londoners to incomers or the building regulations reduce the inflow of people. In practice, the laws against new buildings became a source of income through the fines that were levied, rather than an effective deterrent to growth. Not all who came to the city were vagrants and potential burdens on the system of poor relief, and not all stayed. Indeed, many incomers were in London quite legitimately and temporarily, on business, to attend to legal matters, or to get the attention of a courtier, in the hope of a favour or a reward. Like many foreign visitors, they came because London was the capital city.

3

The Greatest City of the Christian World

London's position as the capital city of England made it the unrivalled centre of power and patronage. Here were royal palaces, the meeting place of Parliament, the law courts and offices of state. The functions of government were centred on the monarch and so the court acted as a magnet, drawing in members of the aristocracy and gentry. The accession of James I in 1603 united the crowns of England and Scotland and the focus of Scottish political life inevitably moved south with the king, enhancing London's role. In his view, it had effectively become the capital of the British Isles and he took a keen interest in improvements, to services and buildings. London inevitably attracted those who hoped to make a living at court, which in turn prompted action to stem the flow, a policy which was in tune with the wider attempts to prevent London's growth. The gentry were discouraged from coming to the city, no less than the poor.

The citizens had sometimes strained relations with the young gentlemen who lodged to the west of the City, in the growing legal quarter around Chancery Lane, along the Strand and in Westminster. But they also had a keen interest in the goings on at court, in national politics and foreign affairs. When state matters threatened to impinge on their city, they could react quite vociferously. A generation that had grown up since Elizabeth I had settled England's religion as Protestant viewed with anxious concern attempts to place a Catholic monarch on the throne, by plot or invasion. Court and city shared common interests.

The court and government were centred on Whitehall Palace. This had been the London palace of the Archbishops of York, rebuilt by Archbishop George Neville in the 1460s and 1470s, and again by Thomas Wolsey, archbishop from 1514 and created a cardinal in 1516. On his fall from power York Place, as it was known, was appropriated by Henry VIII. The living apartments of the royal palace of Westminster had been destroyed by fire in 1512, leaving the king without a palace in Westminster. York Place fulfilled that function. Henry added new apartments and extended the site, partly by acquisitions and partly by reclaiming marshy land along the river, for a frontage of over 500 feet. After his death in 1547, the buildings remained much as he had left them, for neither his son nor his daughters made significant alterations.

Whitehall Palace's exterior did not impress visitors, despite its size and position alongside the Thames. When arriving by boat, in 1597, the French ambassador, de Maisse, found the entrance from the riverside to be 'small and inconvenient' and the palace itself 'very low and has no great appearance for a royal house... the place is passing melancholy'. He moderated this opinion a few days later, when he 'entered by the land gate, which is far more magnificent and royal than the water gate, and well becomes the Court of a great Prince'.[1]

The interior created a much better impression, certainly on Lupold von Wedel, in 1584: 'On the whole the inside of this house is regally and very beautifully furnished, though one would not judge so from the exterior.'[2] Baron Waldstein, in 1600, was even more delighted, commenting that the palace was 'a place which fills one with wonder, not so much because of its great size as because of the magnificence of its bed chambers and living rooms which are furnished with the most gorgeous splendour'. South of the Holbein Gate was the great hall, described by Waldstein as a 'vast hall', where members of the household dined. De Maisse noted that 'the ladies-in-waiting eat in the Hall where the guards sit'.[3] Close by was the Chapel Royal, and then the ceremonial rooms, known collectively as the Chamber. That part of the palace was accessible to all members of the aristocracy and to anyone who looked presentable enough to enter, in the opinion of the Gentlemen Ushers, who controlled entry. It included the Presence

Chamber, where ambassadors and their retinues were received. Von Wedel described it as 'a large, lofty room with a gilded ceiling'.[4]

Beyond the Presence Chamber lay the monarch's Privy Lodgings, to which access was much more restricted, and where the Privy Council met. De Maisse was received in that inner part of the palace. He described crossing 'a chamber of moderate size wherein were the guards of the Queen, and thence into the Presence Chamber'. From there he was taken by the Lord Chamberlain:

> who has charge of the Queen's household... to arrange audiences and to escort those who demand them and especially ambassadors... along a passage somewhat dark, into a chamber which they call the Privy Chamber, at the head of which was the Queen seated in a low chair, by herself.[5]

Waldstein was there as a visitor, not a diplomat, yet was shown the royal bed-chamber, which had 'rich tapestries all around' and an adjoining room, 'reserved for the Queen's bath: the water pours from oyster shells and different kinds of rock'. Next was her library, which led to 'a long majestic gallery where various knights have their shields displayed, painted with their devices', and he was also shown 'a large and lofty banqueting hall which the Queen suddenly arranged to be put up within 20 days when she was expecting the visit of a prince of France'.[6] This was the Duc d'Alençon, a prospective suitor, in 1581.

The hall was intended to be a temporary structure, but was retained until 1606, when James I replaced it with a more substantial building. Orazio Busino admired that structure:

> with its two orders of columns, one above the other, their distance from the wall equalling the breadth of the passage, that of the second row being upheld by Doric pillars, while above these rise Ionic columns supporting the roof. The whole is of wood, including even the shafts, which are carved and gilt with much skill. From the roof of these hang festoons and angels in relief with two rows of lights.[7]

That banqueting house was destroyed by fire in 1619 and the Banqueting House designed by Inigo Jones was built on its site. It was also used as a presence chamber. Jones's building is the only part of the palace to have survived a fire that swept through the buildings in 1698.

When Waldstein finished his tour of Whitehall Palace he noticed that, 'beyond the grounds of this royal residence there is another palace'. He was referring to St James's Palace, built by Henry VIII on the site of the former leper hospital of St James, dissolved in 1532. John Norden described it in 1592 as being 'of quadrite forme, erected of brick, the exterior shape whereof although it appeare without anie sumptuous or superfluous devises; yet is the plott verie princely, and the same with arte continued, within and without'.[8]

The whole court based in the two palaces had over 1,000 members, some three-quarters of whom were servants, and the remainder members of the aristocracy and gentlemen, who held a range of posts. De Maisse noted that the queen 'bears the charges of all her officers and those of her Council from term to term without any lack, so that her expense is very great'.[9] It offered an opportunity for those who needed an income or position which would enhance their influence within their own communities. The court was away from London during the hot summer months, but for the remainder of the year drew those hopeful of advancement.

South of Whitehall Palace stood the buildings that had escaped the fire of 1512: the magnificent hall built by William II, St Stephen's Chapel at its east end, the Painted Chamber, and the Court of Requests. Westminster was the location for the courts of common law and equity from the late twelfth century and for King's Bench from the early fifteenth century. By the late Middle Ages three courts met in Westminster Hall: Chancery and King's Bench on either side of the south end, and Common Pleas along the west wall. The three equity courts of Chancery, Exchequer and Requests had grown up alongside the common law courts and, according to Sir Thomas Smith, in his *De Republica Anglorum* of 1583, heard cases where those without 'remedie in the common law' could seek redress 'according to equity and reason'. All of them attracted much business from a wide social range. Requests and Exchequer had developed in the sixteenth century, Requests as a court accessible to 'poor men'. The Court of Star Chamber was created under Henry VIII and took its name from the Star, or Starred, Chamber, built by Edward II as part of Westminster Palace. Its functions were the enforcement of royal proclamations and investigation of cases of riot, broadly interpreted to include conspiracy, fraud, perjury, forgery, threats and acts of violence, and duelling.

Westminster was the meeting place for Parliament. Von Wedel coincided with a sitting: 'The House of Parliament is as large as a fair-sized castle. I saw the Lord Chancellor sitting in council with the other gentlemen, and it was an impressive sight.'[10] Parliament sat intermittently. Elizabeth called six Parliaments between the outbreak of the war with Spain in 1585 and her death eighteen years later; James I called his first Parliament in 1604 and it sat until 1611. He summoned others in 1614 (the 'Addled Parliament'), 1621 and 1624. According to John Norden, in 1592, both the sittings of the courts during the legal terms and the more irregular meetings of Parliament drew large numbers to London. He wrote that 'greate multitudes of people usually flocke and resort' to the courts and that Parliament:

> causeth a great assembly both of the nobilitie and inferiour persons
> to give attendaunce within this Cytie, which is noe small releefe unto
> the same which also wee reed, hath bene helde at dyvers other places
> within this realme. And maye be at her Majesties pleasure also removed
> hence.[11]

The fear that removal of the courts and Parliament out of London could be used as an economic threat by the crown to cow the citizens was addressed in an anecdote recorded by James Dalton in *An Apology of the City of London*, *c*.1580. When an alderman was told by a courtier:

that Queen Mary, in her displeasure against London, had appointed to remove the parliament and term to Oxford, this plain man demanded whether she meant also to divert the river of Thames from London, or no? and when the gentleman had answered 'No,' 'Then,' quoth the alderman 'by God's grace, we shall do well enough at London, whatsoever became of the term and parliament'.[12]

This made the point that London was a commercial city and by no means solely dependent on its role as the seat of government. But such a threat was deployed by the Privy Council, in 1593, when it told the corporation that if it neglected to implement the regulations against overcrowding, the queen would call Parliament elsewhere. That would 'greatly prejudice the state of the cittie and people in generall', and it hinted that London's rulers would be have to endure, 'the clamour and complaintes of the people and the inconvenience that maie follow therof in case they shall finde their ruyne to have proceeded from you'.[13]

Dalton explained the drift to London of country landowners in terms of the presence of the court, which:

is now-a-days much greater and more gallant than in former times, and which was wont to be contented to remain with a small company... is now for the most part either abiding at London, or else so near unto it, that the provision of things most fit for it may easily be fetched from thence.[14]

It attracted younger sons, widows, those down on their luck or with falling incomes, as well as the wealthy and successful who could indulge themselves by maintaining an expensive household and wearing fine clothes.

The City authorities were not greatly impressed with the budding young courtiers. In 1583 William Fleetwood, the Recorder of London, told Lord Burghley that, 'Here are sunderie yonge gentlmen that use the Court that most commonly terme themselffs *gyntylmen*.'[15]

1. The engraved portrait of William Shakespeare on the title-page of the First Folio of 1623, by Martin Droeshout. Martin was born in Brussels, the second son of John and Mary Droeshout; the family moved to London as refugees c.1569. Probably a member of the Painter-Stainers' Company, he was an established artist when he was chosen by the editors John Hemming and Henry Condell to execute the portrait for the volume of Shakespeare's plays.

3. The figure of Elizabeth I above the entrance to the vestry porch of the church of St Dunstan-in-the-West came from Ludgate, rebuilt in 1586 and demolished in 1760.

2. John Norden's view of London Bridge shows the substantial houses which lined the roadway. In 1599 Thomas Platter wrote that it contained 'many tall handsome merchant dwellings and expensive shops, where all manner of wares are for sale, resembling a long street'.

4. Claes Visscher's view of 1616 shows the Tower of London closely hemmed in by buildings, and the many buildings within the walls of the fortress itself.

Above: 5. Whitehall Palace from Anthonis van den Wyngaerde's pen-and-ink drawing of *c.*1544. Henry VIII made this the principal royal palace in London during the 1530s and it remained so until it was destroyed by fire in 1698.

Left: 6. The Jewel Tower was built in the mid-fourteenth century as part of the royal Palace of Westminster. It survived the fire in 1512 that gutted much of the palace, and the blaze in 1834 that destroyed most of the remainder.

Opposite: 7. Women shopping at a market, from *Tittle Tattle or the Several Branches of Gossiping* (1603). London's markets came under increasing pressure during the late sixteenth and early seventeenth centuries, as the city's population grew. As the picture illustrates, they also had a social function as meeting places.

8. A bird's eye view from the Agas plan-view of London, mid-sixteenth century. Gracechurch Street runs from north to south and the principal streets running west-east are Lombard Street, already developing as a centre of finance, and Fenchurch Street. The large building shown on the east side of Gracechurch Street, near the top of the view, is Leadenhall, the city's grain store and arsenal.

9. Devastating outbreaks of plague struck London from time to time. The worst epidemics in London during the early seventeenth century came in 1603 and 1625. In this woodcut death stands triumphantly on the coffins of Londoners, the victims of the disease lie about and citizens attempting to flee are repelled by the hostile inhabitants of places near the capital, trying to keep their communities free from the disease.

10. A section of city wall at Tower Hill; the lower sections are Roman. The open area here was steadily being reduced in size by the end of the sixteenth century by the building of small houses and tenements, right up to the wall.

11. This stone bastion at the corner of the city wall, west of the site of Cripplegate, stands on the corner of the Roman fort built in the second century. It is close to the northern end of the former Monkwell Street; Shakespeare lodged in a house at the southern end of that street in the early seventeenth century.

Avove: 12. John Norden's plan of London of 1593, showing the city from St Katherine's-by-the-Tower to the east and the Temple to the west, with Southwark south of the Thames. Much of the city wall was still intact and stretches of it are clearly shown. The suburbs are beginning to develop along the main roads into the city and at Clerkenwell, north of Smithfield.

Left: 13. The White Tower dominated the approach to London along the Thames from the east. Baron Waldstein noted in 1600 that cannon were mounted on its roof, 'trained upon the City'.

14. Guildhall, the centre of the City's administration, was begun in 1411 and completed c.1430. It was restored after the Great Fire of 1666 and in 1788–9 a new and larger porch was built, but retaining the ground storey of the fifteenth-century original.

15. The gateway to the churchyard of St Bartholomew-the-Great, Smithfield. The stone doorway was the west entrance to the priory church and was retained when the nave was demolished c.1543; the two-storey structure above it was built in 1595.

Above: 16. The houses in Southwark, close to the south end of London Bridge, are shown on Claes Visscher's view to be substantial buildings, two or three storeys high.

Left: 17. St Helen, Bishopsgate was Shakespeare's parish church when he lived in the district during the mid-1590s. The timber bell-turret was erected in 1568–9 and John Stow's comment that the church 'wanteth a steeple' still applies. The church is known as the 'Westminster Abbey of the City' because of the number of tombs which it contains.

Above: 18. The narrow gaps between the piers, or starlings, on which London Bridge was built were a hazard for the watermen in their wherries. Some passengers preferred to alight and walk around the bridge to be picked up on the other side. Others were prepared to take the uncomfortable option of staying in the wherry as it 'shot' the bridge.

Right: 19. The tower of the church of All Hallows Staining. The fifteenth-century tower was retained when the church was pulled down in 1870 and is maintained by the Clothworkers' Company.

20. The densely packed houses and the skyline punctuated by church towers and spires just west of the Tower of London, shown by Claes Visscher.

21. Middle Temple Hall, erected in 1562–70, and although much altered the architectural historian Nikolaus Pevsner described it as 'the finest Elizabethan building in central London'. It is 101 feet long and is spanned by a magnificent double hammerbeam roof. A performance of *Twelfth Night* was staged there in February 1602.

22. The new chapel of Lincoln's Inn was built in 1619–23, with this undercroft, intended as a meeting place for lawyers and their clients, and for the students. The foundation stone was laid by John Donne, the Preacher and former student, and he also preached the sermon at the service of consecration.

23. 'This was the parish church of St Olave Silver Street destroyed by the dreadful fire in the year 1666'. This tablet marks the site of the small church, which was not rebuilt. In the early years of the seventeenth century Shakespeare lived a few yards away, at the junction of Silver Street and Monkwell Street, now covered by the roadway of London Wall.

tectum

porticus

sedilia

orchestra

ingressus

mimorum ædes

proscænium

planities siue arena

quintum sed dispari et structura, bestiarum conflictat oni destinatum, in quo multi vrsi tauri, et stupendæ magnitudinis canes, distinctis caueis & septis aluntur; qua la

Above: 25. The Custom House, rebuilt in 1559 after a fire. London dominated England's growing overseas trade and the customs dues collected here were a significant part of the crown's revenues.

Right: 26. The church of St Dunstan-in-the-East, shown in Claes Visscher's view of 1616. In 1598 John Stow described it as 'a fair and large church' standing in a large churchyard and serving 'a great parish of many rich merchants, and other occupiers of divers trades, namely salters and ironmongers'.

Opposite: 24. The Swan Theatre on Bankside, built in 1595. A Dutch visitor, Johannes de Witt, was there in 1596 and sent a sketch of the interior to Arendt de Buchel, who copied it into his commonplace book. This copy survives as the only contemporary illustration of the interior of a playhouse of the Elizabethan and Jacobean period.

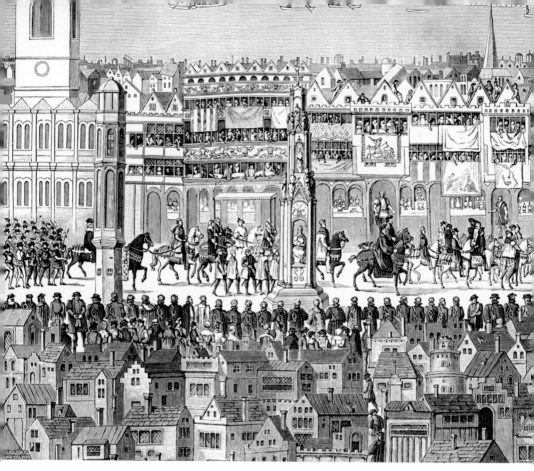

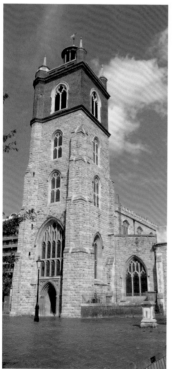

Above: 27. The coronation procession of Edward VI in 1547, passing along Cheapside on its way to Westminster Abbey, with Cheapside Cross in the foreground. The windows are crowded with onlookers and there are even spectators on the roofs. Such enthusiasm was typical of the citizens' response to the pageants and processions in Cheapside, including the annual Lord Mayor's show.

Left: 28. The church of St Giles, Cripplegate was close to Shakespeare's lodgings in Silver Street. It was rebuilt in 1390 and restored after a bad fire in 1545. The top stage of the tower was rebuilt in brick in 1682–4. Gutted by incendiary bombs in 1940, the church was re-opened in 1960 after restoration.

Opposite: 29. Elizabeth I at prayer is the frontispiece to *Christian Prayers* (1569), which reputedly was for the queen's private use. It was printed by John Day, whose print works were at Aldersgate, where he 'built much upon the wall of the city'. The most notable works printed by Day were the *Folio Bible* of 1549, John Foxes's influential *Book of Martyrs* (1567 and later editions) and his edition of the works of the reformers William Tyndale, John Frith and Robert Barnes (1572–3), Roger Ascham's *The Scholemaster* (1570) and a translation of Euclid's *Elements of Geometry* (1570). Day died in 1584.

Above: 30. Richard Quiney was a mercer in Stratford-upon-Avon and a friend of Shakespeare's. While he was in London in 1598 on the town's business he wrote to Shakespeare on 25 October from the Bell Inn in Carter Lane, near St Paul's, asking for a loan and beginning the letter 'Loveinge contreyman'. But he did not send the letter.

Left: 31. The Tower of London: Cradle Tower, from where John Gerard, a Roman Catholic priest, made an ingenious escape in 1598, swinging across the moat by rope to a waiting boat.

Above: 32. The Charterhouse: the almsmen's lodgings on the west side of the Great Court, built in 1613–14, when the buildings of the Tudor mansion on the site of the Carthusian priory were adapted as an almshouse and school. This print was by J. Sewell, 1797.

Right: 33. Temple Church, built c.1160–85 for the Knights Templar; in 1240 a rectangular chancel or choir on its east side was consecrated. In the early fourteenth century the Templars were suppressed and their property was granted to the Knights of St John, known as the Knights Hospitaller. A community of lawyers grew up near the church, which by the mid-fifteenth century had evolved into the two Inns of Court, the Inner Temple and Middle Temple. The lawyers were allowed to remain after the Knights Hospitaller were suppressed in 1539, with the church serving both societies.

Above: 34. In 1591 Common Council ordered that water-wheels for mills should be built at the southern end of London Bridge, where the poor could grind their corn. These were later used to raise water for householders in Southwark.

Left: 35. Londoners enthusiastically celebrated both civic and national events. Here a street party is gathered around a bonfire and a large flagon of drink is being carried out to the revellers.

Above: 36. The Great
Hall of the Charterhouse,
built in 1545–6,
overlooking the principal
courtyard, now Master's
Court. This splendid room
has been the almsmen's
dining-room since 1614.
By Thomas Hosmer
Shepherd, *c.*1830.

Right: 37. The former
churchyard of St Mary
Aldermanbury contains
a memorial garden
and monument to
Shakespeare's friends
and fellow-actors John
Hemming and Henry
Condell, who were
parishioners. In 1623 they
published the first edition
of his works, known
as the First Folio. The
monument was erected in
1896.

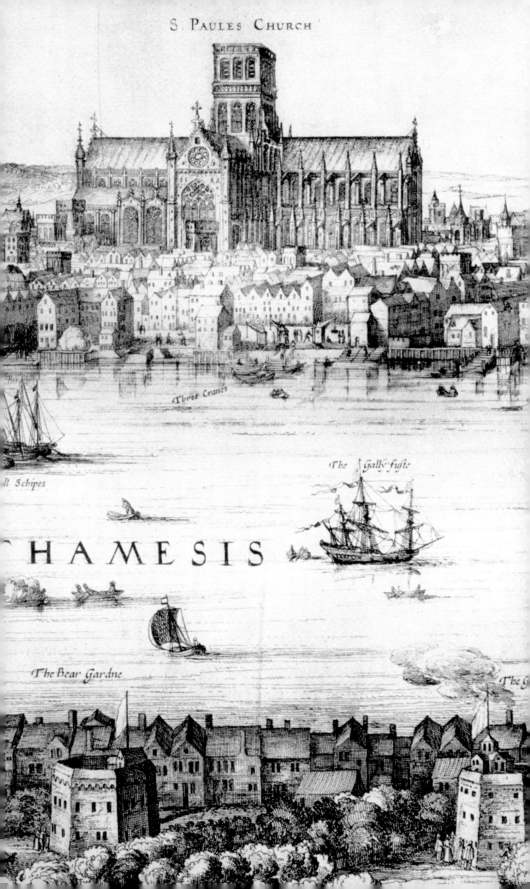

S. PAULES CHURCH

Three Cranes

The Gally fuste

lt Schipes

THAMESIS

The Bear Gardne

40. A sitting of the Court of Wards and Liveries, shown in a painting of *c*.1585. One of the courts established by Henry VIII, it was created in 1540 to collect the revenues payable by the heirs of tenants holding land directly from the crown. When the heir was a minor, the administration of the estate and the arrangement of their marriage passed to the crown, although often it was then sold. The court was abolished in 1645.

Last page spread, left: 38. Claes Visscher's Panorama of London of 1616, with St Paul's Cathedral towering above the huddle of buildings leading down to the river. It shows the dock at Queenhithe and Three Cranes Wharf. In the foreground is Bankside, with the bear garden and the second Globe theatre. On the skyline to the left is the reservoir at the New River Head near Islington, opened in 1613.

Last page spread, right: 39. The church of St Saviour, Southwark, and London Bridge, shown on Visscher's panoramic view of 1616. The heads on pikes above the Great Stone Gate of the bridge were those of traitors. Some of their descendants were said to have taken visitors to show them the skull of their ancestor, proud that a relic of a member of their family should have been so prominently displayed.

Opposite: 41. Inigo Jones's design for Candace, Queen of Ethiopia, played by Lady Anne Winter in the court masque of 1609 entitled *The Masque of Queens*.

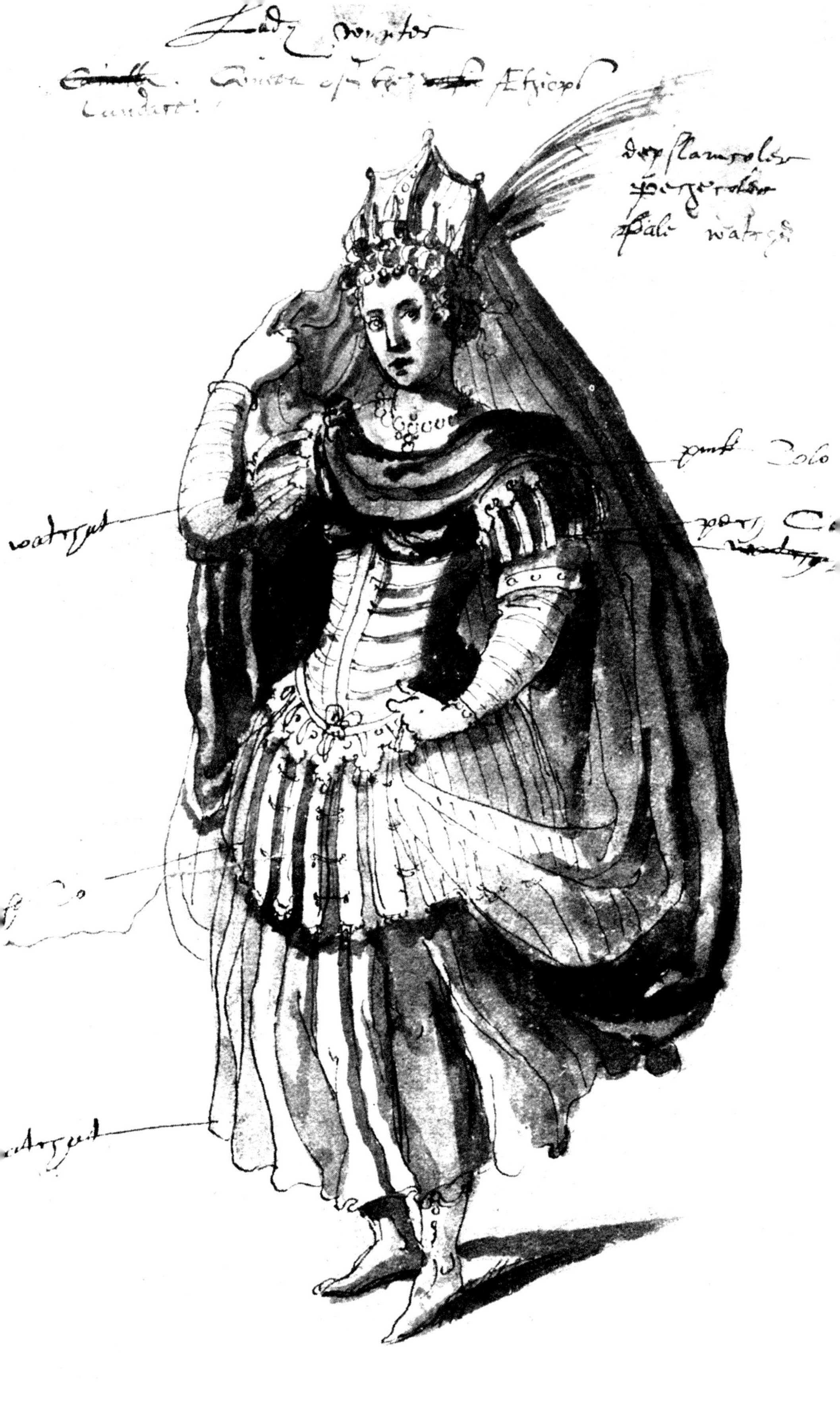

{These two pictures, liuely set out,
One bodie and soule, God send him moꝛe grace:
{This monsterous desembler, a Cranke all about,
{Vncomly coueting, of eath to imbꝛace,
{Money oꝛ wares, as he made his race,
{And sometyme a Mariner, and a seruingman:
{Oꝛ els an artificer, as he would faine that.
{Such shyftes he vsed, being well tryed,
{A bandoning labour, till he was espied:
{Conding punishment, foꝛ his dissimulation,
{He surely receaued with much exclamation.

43. An ornately carved house front in Hart Street drawn and engraved by J.T. Smith. The building was known as 'Whittington's House'.

Opposite: 42. Rogues and vagabonds were a cause for concern in London, with the fear that the city attracted them from across the country, especially 'cranks', who counterfeited sickness or necessity. This drawing, from *Groundworks of Conycatching*, depicted the same man as Nicholas Blunt, 'an upright man', and as Nicholas Jennings, as a beggar, or 'counterfeit crank'.

Opulentius mercator Londinensis in Anglia.   Nobilis puella ornatus apud Londinenses.   Vulgarium fœminarum in Anglia. vestitus gentilis.   Plebey adolescentis in Anglia ha

Above: 44. Costumes of the Elizabethan period: a merchant, a court lady, a citizen's wife, and a gallant. From Caspar Rutz, *Habitus variarum orbis gentium,* 1581.

Left: 45. The gatehouse of the Inner Temple, facing Fleet Street, photographed *c.*1905. It was erected in 1610–11 and served as an inn called the Prince's Arms, although the initials PH in the plaster ceiling of the room over the gate caused it to be dubbed 'Prince Henry's Room'.

Opposite below: 47. Engravings by the Swiss artist Jost Amman (1539–91), showing costumes worn by 'An English Lady' and 'A Lady from London'.

46. Joris Hoefnagel's illustration of English women's costumes, 1582, depicting, from the left, a young unmarried woman, two wives of merchants and three members of the nobility. In the lower illustration, country women are preparing produce, including gutting fish that are being kept fresh in a tank.

48. J.T. Smith's etching of 1791 of a house in Sweedon's Passage, Grub Street, which reputedly dated from the fifteenth century. It was demolished in 1805.

Above: 49. Card games were a popular form of recreation during the period. Here four gentlemen are playing primero, one of the commonest games, in which each player was dealt four cards. It was said to have originated in Italy and *c.*1555 was described as 'a new game'.

Right: 50. An apothecary's shop, with the apothecary preparing a prescription for two customers. The woodcut is by Jost Amman, 1574. The apothecaries were able to establish their own company in 1617, and by that date their shops were scattered about London, with one district that was 'full of apothecaries' shops'.

51. The Thames at Richmond, with the royal palace, built on the site of the Palace of Sheen, in the background. The palace was where Elizabeth spent the last weeks of her life, before her death on 24 March 1603.

52. A convivial marriage festival at Horsleydown, on the south side of the Thames, east of Southwark, with musicians and dancers, shown in a painting by Joris Hoefnagel.

Shakespeare described some of the characteristics from which a courtier could be recognized; his dress, his way of walking, his aroma and his contemptuous manner, with the air of someone declaring that, 'I am courtier cap-à-pie [from head to foot]; and one that will either push on or pluck back thy business there'. And John Donne referred to 'a briske perfum'd piert Courtier'.[16] Many young courtiers hoped for patronage, a place in the royal household, or in a nobleman's entourage. A stroke of good luck could lead to great rewards, in terms of power and wealth, creating an individual's reputation and making or repairing a family's fortunes.

Catching the monarch's eye might pay rich dividends indeed, and the examples of those who prospered in this way acted as a spur to others. Lupold von Wedel wrote in 1585 of Sir Walter Raleigh's success in attracting the queen's favour: 'but a year ago he could scarcely keep one servant, whereas now owing to her bounty he can afford to keep five hundred'.[17] The Jacobean courtier Sir Robert Naunton described how Charles Blount had achieved success. A student at the Middle Temple from 1579, about four years later, 'he came to see the fashion of the court', and was noticed by the queen. She enquired who he was, and had him brought over to her, telling him, 'Fail not to come to the court, and I will bethink myself how to doe you good.' He did not spurn his opportunity and made a successful career as a soldier as well as a courtier. Elizabeth appointed him Lord Deputy of Ireland in 1599 and he was created Earl of Devonshire by James I, in 1603. Naunton wrote that 'he lived plentifully in a fine way and garb'.[18]

Even greater success was achieved by Robert Carr. A younger son of a Scottish nobleman, he became a page to George Home, later Earl of Dunbar. After James's accession in 1603, Home went to London and probably through his influence Carr became a groom of the bedchamber. His duties brought him into frequent contact with the king, who noticed him, because of his good looks and bearing. When Carr broke a leg in a fall from his horse at a tilt in 1607 he might have lost any advantage that he had gained, for others would carry out his duties while he recuperated. But in fact it made his fortune, because the king took a personal interest in the young man's recovery and was completely smitten by him. Created Viscount Rochester in 1611 and Earl of Somerset in 1613, he acted as the king's secretary and was appointed Lord Chamberlain in 1614. His glittering career came to an abrupt and shameful end in 1615, when he was implicated in the scandal of Sir Thomas Overbury's murder in the Tower, but it showed what could be achieved by someone who had started with a junior position at court. George Villiers followed a similar path. A member of a gentry family from Leicestershire, he was created Earl of Buckingham when he was twenty-four, Marquess a year later and Duke in 1623, when he was thirty, and by far the dominant figure at court.

Unquestionably, the greasy pole could be worth climbing, but it was very slippery and considerable outlay on food and drink, fashionable clothes and jewellery was essential, without any guarantee of returning a profit. To be attached to one of the powerful factions was important, but their influence shifted and their rise or fall affected those dependent on their patronage. Discussing Elizabeth's later years, Naunton referred to, 'the feares and many jealousies of the Court and times, wherewith the Queen's age, and the malignity of her setting times were replete'.[19]

The new reign brought new hopes. In Thomas Dekker's phrase, 'now does fresh blood leape into the cheekes of the Courtier'.[20] As James and his entourage approached London, many courtiers and those on the fringes of the court went to Theobalds Palace, near Cheshunt, to see him, and perhaps be introduced. And there was a flood of people into London in anticipation of the coronation, appropriately fixed for St James's Day, 25 July. As early as 12 May Giovanni Scaramelli, the Venetian ambassador, believed that: 'The assembly at Court amounts to upwards of forty thousand persons of all conditions, and it is held for certain that by the date of the Coronation there will be more than one hundred thousand extra mouths in London.'[21] A royal proclamation issued on 6 July referred to the 'great Concourse of people to our sayd City against the time of our Coronation'. After the ceremony this became a source of complaint, expressed in another proclamation, that 'there doe continually hang upon our Court, a great number of idle and masterlesse persons, aswell Scottish as English, who can give no accompt of their abode here'. It announced measures to reduce the numbers, especially of suitors hoping to press their claims for advancement. Because of the plague epidemic a date was fixed, after which 'no Suitor shall be allowed to follow the Court, upon what pretence soever, during this Contagion'.[22]

The clamour was not without justification, for the king certainly was liberal in distributing titles and favours in the early stages of his reign. He told Parliament in 1607 that, 'My first three years were to me as a Christmas, I could not then be miserable.' His outgoings on pensions reached over £100,000 a year, nearly one-third of the crown's revenues.[23] But not everyone could benefit. Lady Anne Clifford's mother was 'all full of hopes', but like others she was disappointed: 'every Man expecting Mountains & finding Molehills, excepting Sir R. Cecil and the House of the Howards who hated my Mother'.[24]

Many of the Scotsmen who followed James to London were granted posts. He created a new department, the Bedchamber, and staffed it almost entirely with Scotsmen. This influx caused resentment among the hopefuls whose expectations had been thwarted by those who they regarded as outsiders. Lady Anne made a sharp remark about their standards of personal hygiene, with the comment that, 'we all saw a great change between the fashion of the Court as it is now and that in the Queen's time, for we were all lousy by sitting in the chamber of Sir Thomas Erskine'.[25]

A Gentleman of the Bedchamber since 1585, Erskine was now made captain of the guard in place of Elizabeth's proud favourite Sir Walter Raleigh, who was soon to be imprisoned in the Tower on suspicion of being implicated in a treasonable plot, so quickly did the political wheel turn.

The bitterness against the Scots at court continued and in 1610 Sir John Holles commented, in Parliament, that not only did they, 'possess the royal presence, they be warm within, while the best of ours starve without'.[26] His objection was partly personal, for he had been a Gentleman of the Privy Chamber and was disappointed not to have been awarded a higher post by James. Resentment against the Scots extended beyond court circles to London's streets, where Scotsmen were roughed up by gangs known as 'swaggerers'.[27] It also reached the London stage, with *Eastward Ho!*, by Ben Jonson, George Chapman and John Marston, giving offence. Mentions of 'a few industrious Scots' and 'thirty pound knights' might have passed almost unnoticed, but the players mimicked Scottish accents. Sir Thomas Edmondes, a diplomat, wrote that, 'from the highest to the lowest, all men's parts were acted of two diverse nations; as I understand sundry were committed to Bridewell'.[28] Indeed, following a complaint to the king by one of his Scottish entourage, the play was banned and Jonson and Chapman imprisoned, Marston having made good his escape. The playwrights had touched a raw nerve and there was even talk that Jonson and Chapman might have their noses and ears lopped as punishment, but the king relented and ordered their release.

Another significant change at court was the creation of subsidiary households, those of the queen, Anna of Denmark; Henry, heir to the throne, installed as Prince of Wales in 1610; and, after his death in 1612, his brother Charles. Such households had not existed under the unmarried Elizabeth and, according to Naunton, 'by time was worn out of memory and without the consideration of the present times'.[29] They increased the crown's expenses, but also created new posts and opportunities, and could provide a centre for patronage and influence that rivalled the king's court at Whitehall Palace. By 1610 Henry's entourage, centred on St James's Palace, was said to consist of nearly 500 men. The queen's court was at Somerset House, informally referred to from 1606 as Denmark House, after the visit of her brother, Christian IV, and given that name formally in 1619. Niccolò Molin described it as, 'the most splendid house in London, after the Royal palace'.[30]

Yet not all members of the gentry who came to London did so to be near the court, looking for positions, patents or monopolies that could provide an income. Some did so because it was the customary thing to do and so was expected of them. Edward Herbert of Montgomery recalled that, as a young man, 'publique duty did not hinder mee to follow my beloved studies in a Countrey life for the most part Though sometimes also I resorted to Court without yet that I had any Ambition there'.[31] Surprisingly, given the costs of accommodation and provisions, some went to London to economise, for living in the metropolis for part of the year could reduce the costs of maintaining a large household in the country. In a period of inflation such an economy measure appealed to those whose rental incomes had not kept pace with rising prices, and so, according to James Dalton, the county gentry, 'do fly and flock to this city; the younger sort of them to see and show vanity, and the elder to save the cost and charge of hospitality and house-keeping'.[32]

This point had been raised in *A Discourse of the Commonweal of this Realm of England*, written in 1549 but not published until 1581, which was critical of the fact that to reduce their household costs, gentlemen from the provinces, 'give over their howseholds and get them chambers in London or abowte the courte, and there spend there time, some with a servaunte or 2, wheare he was wounte to kepe 30 or 40 persons daily in his house'.[33] By the late sixteenth century it was generally accepted that London was drawing off those who should have been providing political leadership and executing the law in their communities.

A proclamation issued by James I in 1608 criticized those who came to London:

> thereby leaving the reliefe of their poore neighbours, as well for food, as for good Rule, and with covetous mindes to live in London, and about the City privately, and so also in other Townes corporate, without charge of company.

The king ordered them not to break up their country households to go to London or another city, and those who had done so should return home.[34] When that policy was restated in another proclamation, in 1614, Sir Francis Bacon described it to James as being:

> for the better government of the several counties of your Kingdom and the maintenance of hospitality and relief of the poor... and likewise for the inconvenience which redoundeth to the Cities themselves by the surcharge and overflow of so many gentlemen.

The proclamation itself complained of 'a great repair and confluence, as well to the Cities of London and Westminster, and the Suburbs of them... of Noblemen and Gentlemen'. This not only led to neglect of local government and administration of justice in the counties, but to increased demand for food in the cities, and so higher prices. It was a counterpart to the policy of excluding the poor from London, but when the king ordered another proclamation reiterating the point, in 1617, the Privy Council was reluctant to issue it. Sir Ralph Winwood wrote that, 'they had withheld it because they found it needless' and the proclamation was issued only after the king, 'broke into a great choler' and insisted that he must be obeyed.[35] As with the orders against new buildings, masterless men and lodgers, this became an established policy, with similar orders repeated from time to time.

Many gentlemen had begun their connection with the capital as young men, when they spent some time at one of the four Inns of Court – the Inner Temple, the Middle Temple, Gray's Inn and Lincoln's Inn – or at one of the eight smaller Inns of Chancery. The legal quarter in which the Inns stood was concentrated around the west end of Fleet Street and east end of the Strand, and off Chancery Lane and High Holborn. In a letter of 1600 to the Privy Council, the corporation mentioned the 'divers officers of the Court of Chancery, the Court of Wards, the King's Bench, and Common Pleas, inhabiting houses within the liberties of the City, especially Fleet Street'.[36]

The Inns of Court trained men for the law, but were also attended by young gentlemen and members of the aristocracy, typically for no more than two years, to study the common law and as part of their general social and intellectual education. London was without a university until 1828, but the Inns of Court were described as England's third university. In *The Description of England*, William Harrison wrote that 'there are three noble universities in England, to wit, one at Oxford, the second at Cambridge, and the third in London... in the latter the laws of the realm are only read and learned'. The lawyer Sir Edward Coke, in 1602, praised the Inns as 'the most famous university, for the profession of law, or any one humane Science, that is in the world'.[37]

The Inns had no difficulty in attracting students, for attendance there conferred status; according to Sir Thomas Smith, in 1583, 'Whosoever studieth the lawes of the realme... shall be taken for a gentleman.' A generation later, the soldier and writer Barnaby Rich concurred: 'it skilles not what their Fathers were, whether Farmers, Shoomakers, Taylers or Tinkers, if their names be inrolled in any Inne of Court, they are all Gentlemen'. The numbers admitted to the Inns of Court increased fourfold during the sixteenth century and by the 1610s averaged 280 per year. By the early seventeenth century roughly ninety per cent of those admitted were ranked as the sons of peers, esquires or gentlemen; only ten per cent of them were Londoners. In 1598 John Stow wrote that Lincoln's Inn was 'lately increased with fair buildings, and replenished with gentlemen studious in the common laws'.[38] It contained 104 chambers and *c.*200 members during term time. The Inn became noted as the most Puritan of the Inns of Court, while Gray's Inn gained the reputation of being the most aristocratic.

The Inns of Chancery gave initial training to lawyers who were then called to the bar and progressed to one of the Inns of Court. They prospered during the period. In 1586, Barnard's Inn had 112 members, Furnivall's Inn had 80 members, and Staple Inn contained 145 students in term time and 69 out of term. All three were in Holborn. Staple Inn was the largest Inn of Chancery and was flourishing. Sir George Buck, Master of the Revels under James I, wrote that its new 'fayre hall of bricks' and other new buildings made it 'the fairest inn of chancery', and John Stow commented that the inn, 'of late is a great part thereof fair built, and not a little augmented'.[39]

In Shakespeare's *Henry IV Part II*, Clement's Inn, north of the Strand, is where Robert Shallow, an elderly Justice of the Peace in Gloucestershire, had received his legal training: 'I was once of Clement's Inn, where I think they will talk of mad Shallow yet'. Shakespeare's character tells of the fighting and whoring which he and his fellow-students had indulged in. London audiences would have recognized the type. Harrison wrote of the students of the Inns that:

> They have also degrees of learning among themselves and rules of discipline, under which they live most civilly in their houses, albeit that the younger sort of them abroad in the streets are scarce able to be bridled by any good order at all.[40]

However wayward their behaviour as students, those who administered the counties and boroughs had a link with London, beginning with their time spent at one of the Inns, and in many cases continuing when they attended Parliament or one of the law courts.

The connection between the government and the administration of London was much closer than between it and the counties. Not surprisingly, the large and expanding city so close to the court was a cause for concern, in terms of disease, disorder and implementation of the crown's policies. The corporation was consulted on issues which concerned the city, such as the action taken to restrict its expansion and the plague regulations. The Privy Council expected co-operation in the steps taken to improve the city and so took a close interest in the enforcement of its orders, reprimanding the corporation when its efforts were unsatisfactory.

Such measures increased during James's reign, for he was ambitious to enhance London's appearance, acting through the corporation and justices. As the capital of the three kingdoms within the British Isles, it had become, 'the greatest, or next the greatest Citie of the Christian world', according to the preamble of a royal proclamation of 1615. This commended 'all Edifices, Structures, and workes which tend to publique use and ornament... which have bene erected and performed in greater number in these twelve yeeres of Our Reigne, then in whole ages heretofore'. It cited a number of examples, including the landscaping of Moorfields in 1606, when the area was laid out with gravel paths lined with trees, creating London's first public park; the paving of Smithfield in 1614–15; the water supply brought from Hertfordshire to Clerkenwell by the New River Company, in 1613; and the conversion of Howard House, on the site of the former Charterhouse, to an almshouse and school, in 1613–14.[41]

But these were piecemeal improvements and the king had a much grander vision of how his capital should look, achieved through the use of brick and the uniformity of house fronts. This had been mentioned in proclamations since 1605, when it was laid down that:

> the forefront of any House in any new building... be wholly made of Bricke, or Bricke and stone. And the forefront thereof in every respect shall be made of that uniforme order and forme, as shall be prescribed unto them for that Streete where such Building shall happen to bee, by the chiefe Magistrates of the same Citie... and being out of the Citie by such Justices of the Peace or other Magistrates, as have the government in that place.[42]

The Court of Star Chamber acted to enforce this order, with five offenders convicted in February 1607, fined between £30 and £100 each, and their new buildings ordered to be demolished. But in the following year another proclamation admitted that these had been made an example of and that, in truth, 'the offenders were in great multitude'. They were to be let off with fines, but should realize that their offence and excuses were unwarranted, 'if they looke abroad, & see what is done in other well polliced Cities of Europe'. The phrase summed up James's aspiration, to create a dignified, modern European capital city, in the Classical style. Uniform street frontages of brick or stone would 'grace and beautifie' London and Westminster, 'the principall places of this Kingdome, for the resort and intertainment of

forreine Princes, which from time to time doe come into this Realme'.[43]
To achieve uniformity, windows and upper storeys projecting over the
streets were forbidden.

As well as creating a finer city, the policy could be justified by the
resistance to fire of brick and stone, and the conservation of stocks
of timber, needed for shipbuilding and, as many feared, being rapidly
depleted. A policy which could be implemented only gradually, as
existing buildings were replaced, would take a long time to effect,
even if it could be adequately enforced. Yet the proclamations show a
determination that it should bear fruit, and that of 1615 clearly stated
James's ambition:

> that as it was said by the first Emperour of Rome, that he had found the
> City of Rome of Bricke, and left it of Marble, So that Wee whom GOD
> hath honoured to be the first King of Great Britaine, mought bee able
> to say in some proportion, That Wee had found Our Citie and Suburbs
> of London of stickes, and left them of Bricke, being a Materiall farre
> more durable, safe from fire, beautifull and magnificent.[44]

James evidently wished to draw attention to the parallels between
himself and the emperor Augustus, also the founder of a new dynasty.
But while Augustus was able to boast, in the *Res Gestae Divi Augusti*,
of the public buildings which he had erected and restored, James
could undertake little building work.[45]

The Banqueting House was the major improvement at Whitehall
Palace, although the queen spent £37,500 improving Somerset
House, already more than half a century old. The crown's income was
insufficient to permit the king to indulge in large-scale building, such
as reconstructing Whitehall Palace in the fashionable Italianate style
shown in the background of Hendrijk van Steenwijk the younger's
portrait of Prince Charles, painted around 1620.[46] The painting
illustrated the ideal palace, not the reality.

The leading courtiers were those with the means to erect new
buildings. In the Strand, the Earl of Northampton built Northampton

House (known as Northumberland House after the Earl of Northumberland bought it in the 1640s), between 1605 and 1609, and Sir Robert Cecil erected Salisbury House and the New Exchange. The house was largely complete by December 1602, when the queen was 'verry royally entertained, richly presented, and marvelous well contented, but at hir departure shee strayned hir foote'.[47] The New Exchange was built slightly later, on the street frontage of Durham House, the London palace of the bishops of Durham. Cecil used his position to acquire the site, held on lease by Tobie Matthew, whose father was Bishop of Durham from 1595 until appointed Archbishop of York in 1606. Matthew had converted to Roman Catholicism while in Italy and on his return was imprisoned, in 1607, when he refused to return to the Church of England. Cecil arranged for his release, on condition that he went into exile and sold Cecil the outstanding period of the lease, for £1,200. James I and Queen Anna, accompanied by Prince Henry, opened the new building on 10 April 1609, when the king declared that it should be known as Britain's Bourse. It imitated the Royal Exchange, with a bourse and shops, aimed at those members of fashionable society who increasingly were living to the west of the City. The corporation was displeased, seeing the bourse as a competitor to the Royal Exchange, and the Lord Mayor petitioned against it, without success. This was a small matter in the overall scheme of things, but indicative of the City's sensitivity on commercial issues and the potential rivalry between it and the court.

Any capital city can cause problems for its government, as a focus for political opposition, backed by a turbulent population providing larger numbers of protesters than a state without a standing army could match. London also had considerable influence through its wealth, which the government drew on through taxation and loans. As the Venetian ambassador Marc Antonio Correr explained, in 1610: 'As the whole government of this City is in the hands of the merchants, they have acquired great power on account of the need which the King and his Ministers always have of them in realising the revenue and the subsidies.'[48]

More overtly, the Lord Mayor controlled the citizens' militia, known as the Trained Bands. In September 1618 a Venetian described them at a recent muster as consisting of 'all unpaid artisans, commanded by merchants, in the presence of the Lord Mayor, their chief. They numbered rather more than 6,000, including musketeers and pikemen, all fine fellows and in very good trim.'[49] They could be quickly assembled and were a force which the government could not match. London's latent power was acknowledged by James Dalton: 'I confess that London is a mighty arm and instrument to bring any great desire to effect'. But he went on to comment that, 'as London hath adhered to some rebellions, so hath it resisted many, and was never the author of any one'. It did not exist as a distinct political entity: 'London is but a citizen and no city, a subject and no free estate, an obedienciary and no place endowed with any distinct or absolute power'.[50]

But Londoners were well aware of affairs, domestic and foreign, and reacted to them. They held opinions on policy, which they expressed by insulting foreign ambassadors and throwing stones at their coaches as they passed. The French and Spanish envoys were particularly at risk, as representatives of the most menacing continental powers. As the capital, London would be the focus of any threat to the government, an assassination, invasion, or attempted coup. The Catholic powers were seen to employ assassination as an instrument of policy. An attempt on the life of the Huguenot leader Admiral Coligny was the prelude to the St Bartholomew's Day massacres in Paris and across France, in 1572, which appalled Protestant Europe. William the Silent was shot dead in his house in Delft in 1584 by a lone assassin and Henri III of France was killed by Jacques Clément, a monk, in 1589. The extent to which such political murders made an impression on the minds of Londoners is revealed in a letter by John Chamberlain in 1602:

Yesterday here was a running report that the Frenche Kinge was slaine by a friar. It was very current, and took fire like a traine or a squib: I never knew any newes spread so sodainly; for in lesse than three howres it was all over the towne; but this day it cooles again, and we cannot learne how it shold rise.[51]

The tale was false, but he admitted that it had disturbed him more than any news or rumour of public affairs over the previous seven years. And Henri IV was indeed assassinated, eight years later, by François Ravaillac, a devout Catholic.

Should Elizabeth fall victim to an assassin, her sudden death, without an obvious heir, could lead to a period of uncertainty, even chaos. In 1583 John Somerville, of Edstone in Warwickshire, set off towards London with the avowed intention of shooting the queen. He was an incompetent potential assassin, and probably was mentally unstable, freely talking of his intentions at an inn on the way. He was arrested and executed. Plots against the queen by Francis Throgmorton in 1583, William Parry in 1585 and Anthony Babington in 1586 were also uncovered in time. Such schemes revolved around plans to place Elizabeth's cousin Mary, Queen of Scots, on the English throne and return the country to Catholicism. Mary was being held under house arrest by Elizabeth, who finally agreed to her execution in 1587.

Londoners reacted with relief verging on elation when these plots were uncovered, removing the danger. After the Babington plotters were arrested the citizens lit bonfires in the streets and gathered together to celebrate and sing psalms. They were equally jubilant at the news of Mary's execution, according to Emanuel Tomascon, writing to the Fugger business at Augsburg: 'the citizens... lit bonfires on all sides and rang the bells, because they were rid of the danger in which they had lived so long. It looks as if the populace believed that a new era had begun in which they hope that all will remain at peace.'[52] Their reaction was generated by relief that a potential cause of a usurpation or civil war had been removed.

The bells of St Christopher-le-Stocks church were rung when Babington's conspiracy was uncovered, and when Mary, Queen of Scots was declared a traitor. They were rung again 'on the daye of execution of ye Skotts queene', and the bell-ringers at All Hallows,

Staining, were paid one shilling 'for Joye of the execution'. The churchwarden at St Alphage, London Wall, made a fuller entry in the accounts on that occasion:

> we did ringe at oure parish churche the ix day of Febrarie in ano 1586 [1587] and was for joye that the Queene of Skotts that ennemy to oure most noble Queens Majesty and ower contrie was beheaded for the wch the Lorde God be praysed and I wold to God that all her confederates weare knowne and cut of by the lyke means.[53]

Yet her execution increased the danger of foreign invasion, with Spain making preparations for the Great Armada. London was organized for defence, with the city's trained bands mustered and increased to 10,000 men, the streets patrolled, suspicious foreigners kept under surveillance, and posts and chains put up in the streets, to obstruct invading troops. The apprentices enthusiastically joined the search for Spanish sympathisers among London's stranger community. When the danger had passed, on 24 November the queen attended a thanksgiving service in St Paul's, accompanied by the nobility, the Privy Councillors, heralds, judges, and the French ambassador. From the royal box she heard a sermon delivered at Paul's Cross by the Bishop of Salisbury.

The defeat of the Armada greatly lessened the threat of invasion, but did not end it. Spain sent further fleets towards Ireland in 1596 and 1597, neither of which reached its destination, and the English fleet countered with attacks on Spain. In the summer of 1599 the Privy Council received intelligence of another threatened invasion, with the capture of London part of the operation. Extra forces were raised, the streets were again blocked by chains, and householders were ordered to hang lights outside their doors overnight. Fears were raised of fifth columnists, with the Lord Mayor writing to the Privy Council on 9 August that: 'There are lately crept into this city diverse recusants, who... may prove very dangerous to the state and city.'[54] The citizens were extremely tense; just four days earlier, according to John Chamberlain:

came newes (yet false) that the Spaniardes were landed in the Ile of Wight, which bred such a feare and consternation in this towne as I wold litle have looked for, with such a crie of women, chaining of streets, and shutting of the gates, as though the ennemie had ben at Blackewall.[55]

He added that he was 'sorry and ashamed' of such a reaction. The fleet had not existed, but an enemy force did appear in the English Channel towards the end of the month, once more putting London on its guard. This small flotilla, under the command of Federico Spinola, consisted of half a dozen galleys, unusual craft in north European waters. Towards the end of August it made its way along the Channel to Sluys, evading the English and Dutch warships. This posed nothing like the threat of the Great Armada of 1588, yet it contributed to what had been an anxious summer in London.

Even without a credible danger from abroad, the citizens remained concerned, for assassination plots were uncovered from time to time, and uncertainty over the succession grew as the queen got older. The leading factions at court polarized around the Cecils, father and son, accomplished politicians, and the queen's favourite, the brilliant young courtier and soldier Robert Devereux, Earl of Essex. Sir Robert Cecil took a leading role in policy making after the death of his father, William Cecil, Lord Burghley, in August 1598, while Essex, who had expected more from the redistribution of Burghley's offices than he obtained, needed a striking success to maintain his position with the queen. A defeat of the royal forces in Ireland required a military response and provided him with an opportunity. Essex was appointed Lord Lieutenant and took command there in the spring of 1599, but he failed to defeat the rebels and even agreed a truce with their leader, the Earl of Tyrone, exceeding his instructions in doing so. The queen responded angrily and Essex returned to court precipitately, without permission, to explain his conduct and confront his opponents. He rushed into the queen's private apartments and burst in on her before she was ready to receive visitors. Despite this unfortunate blunder, he did recover some ground with Elizabeth, although his conduct was censured by the Privy Council and he was forbidden to attend court.

As his position weakened over the following months, some of his supporters, including Henry Wriothesley, third Earl of Southampton (to whom Shakespeare had dedicated his poems *Venus and Adonis* (1593) and *The Rape of Lucrece* (1594)), planned a desperate throw, using force to regain his influence at court. This culminated in an attempted coup on Sunday, 8 February 1601, when Essex led a motley group of about 300 of his armed supporters from Essex House in the Strand along Fleet Street into the City. He hoped to rouse the citizens to support him in overthrowing Cecil and his allies, which effectively meant most members of the Privy Council. Essex was a popular figure. Londoners had lined the streets to cheer him when he returned victorious from Cadiz in 1596 and as he left for Ireland in 1599. But they would not join him now. Rumours that most of the Aldermen supported his cause also proved groundless.

Essex spoke to Sir Thomas Smythe, the Sheriff, outside his house in Gracechurch Street, although to no good purpose. Meanwhile, a scratch force was assembled on Ludgate Hill by the Earl of Cumberland and the Bishop of London. Sir John Leveson happened to be riding by on his way to his house in Blackfriars. He was stopped and asked to take command of this force, which he did. Essex's followers began to melt away and when those who had stayed with him tried to retrace their steps, they were confronted by Leveson's men at Ludgate, which was closed against them. Negotiations failed and a sharp skirmish ensued, in which Sir Christopher Blount, at the head of the insurgents, was knocked to the ground, Essex's pageboy was shot dead and several of his men were wounded. Unable to force his way through Ludgate, Essex returned to Essex House by water and surrendered soon afterwards. He was executed on 25 February and Blount on 18 March; Southampton, also condemned to death, was spared after his mother pleaded with Cecil.

Two or three days before the insurrection, some of Essex's entourage asked Shakespeare's company, the Chamberlain's Men, 'to play the deposing and killing of King Richard II' at the Globe. The players were afraid that because it was an old play they, 'should have small or no company at it', but were given £2 over and above the receipts and they overcame their scruples. The performance of Shakespeare's play went ahead on the day before Essex's ill-judged attempt, and it did not go unnoticed. The actor Augustine Philips had to explain the company's actions, but no lasting harm was done and the company played before the queen on the day before Essex's execution. In his account of the affair, Sir Francis Bacon mentioned the performance when describing the role of Essex's steward, Gilly Meyricke, referring to it as, 'that tragedie which hee thought soone after his lord should bring from the stage to the state'. Elizabeth was well aware of the play's significance, making the petulant remark to the antiquarian William Lambarde a few months later: 'I am Richard II, know ye not that?'.[56]

With Essex's removal from the political stage and Sir Robert Cecil's smooth assumption of the reins which his father had held, domestic affairs seemed stable. The campaign in Ireland and the war with Spain continued, without having a direct effect on London. Yet uncertainty over the succession remained. Londoners could not know of the negotiations with James VI of Scotland and they were apprehensive of what might happen when Elizabeth died. James's cousin Arabella Stuart also had a strong claim, and there may not be a consensus among the political nation. Put succinctly, the situation was that, 'This crown is not like to fall to the ground for want of heads that claim it, but upon whose head it will fall is by many doubted.'[57]

In March 1603 Elizabeth's health began to fail and, as she lay dying in Richmond Palace, 'a strange silence descended on the whole city, as if it were under interdict and divine worship suspended. Not a bell rang out.'[58] The Countess of Warwick sent word to Lady Anne Clifford's mother in Clerkenwell that her family should move to her house in Austin Friars, 'for fear of some Commotions'. According to John Manningham: 'There was a diligent watch and ward kept at every gate and street, day and night, by housholders, to prevent garboiles [disorders]: which God be thanked were more feared then perceived.' Indeed, all went smoothly and on the morning after the queen's death:

> About 10 at clocke the Counsell and diverse noblemen, having bin a
> while in consultacion, proclaymed James the 6, K of Scots, the King of
> England, Fraunce, and Irland, beginning at White hall gates, where Sir
> Robert Cecile reade the proclamacion, which he carried in his hand and
> after reade againe in Cheapside.[59]

As well as the Privy Councillors, members of the aristocracy, churchmen, knights and gentlemen, the reading of the proclamation was witnessed by a 'huge number of common persons'.[60] Lady Anne Clifford wrote that:

> King James was proclaimed in Cheapside by all the Council with great
> joy and triumph... This peaceable coming in of the King was unexpected
> of all parts of the people. Within 2 or 3 days we returned to Clerkenwell
> again.[61]

There had been, 'Noe tumult, noe contradicion, noe disorder in the city.'[62] This peaceful succession was not only a surprise in London, but across Europe. The French writer Thomas Pelletier wrote that Europeans had anticipated that England would become 'a theatre filled with the most horrible and bloody tragedies which one could expect in an entirely disordered and ravaged state'.[63]

Once again, a potential crisis had passed, leaving London unscathed. Yet James's policies were to produce a much more dangerous threat. The peace treaty with Spain in 1604 had not been followed by the easing of restrictions and penalties on Roman Catholics that some expected, partly because two plots uncovered in the summer of 1603 had heightened his suspicions of Catholics. And so a group of disaffected Catholic gentry from the south Midlands plotted to blow up the king and the Houses of Parliament when the sitting was resumed in October 1605. This was postponed until 5 November, by which time the plotters had their powder barrels in place within the buildings. Acting on a warning, the Council ordered searches during the night before the king was due to address Parliament, when the cache of gunpowder and the man who was to light the fuse, Guy Fawkes, were discovered.

The news spread quickly. Thomas Winter, one of the conspirators, suspected that the plot had failed and this was confirmed when he overheard a conversation in the Strand, that, 'There is a treason discovered, in which the King and the Lords should have been blown up'.[64] Edward Herbert, Member for Merionethshire, was lodging near Charing Cross and would have attended the House that day: 'Sir Walter Cope coming the 5th of November about six of the Clocke tould mee how the designe was discovered wishing mee not to goe out of my house untill Businesses were better setled'.[65] It produced a stunned reaction, with the realization of how close disaster had been. Not only would the royal family and most of the leading figures of the state have been killed, but many others could have been slain or injured, and the damage would have been immense.

Discovery of the Gunpowder Treason could only fuel James's morbid fear of assassination and did nothing to pacify his subjects' anxiety. An incident one morning in the following March illustrates just how tense Londoners were. While the king was away from Whitehall on a hunting trip, a rumour began to circulate that he had been murdered at Woking, with some courtiers. The Privy Council met and took appropriate precautions, in case this was a plot, as did Sir William Waad, Lieutenant of the Tower. The Council issued a proclamation contradicting the report, describing it as 'a seditious rumour', but could not prevent panic sweeping through the city, as Zorzi Giustinian, the Venetian ambassador, described:

> The news spread to the City, and the uproar was amazing. Everyone flew to arms, the shops were shut, and cries began to be heard against Papists, foreigners and Spaniards, and had not the contradiction

arrived some terrible accident would have happened to us all. The tumult did not last such a short time either, for his Majesty, who was in the country and knew nothing about it, did not hurry his arrival, until some courtiers went and reported all to him.

The king's return to Whitehall that afternoon was greeted with huge relief by the citizens, who welcomed him 'as one risen from the dead. He was seen and acclaimed by the populace with extraordinary signs of affection. There were fireworks and fetes, and bells were rung in the City.'[66]

Such a strong and emotional reaction no doubt owed much to the Gunpowder Treason a few months earlier. More typical were the precautions taken in London in February 1613, during the preparations for Princess Elizabeth's marriage to Fredrick, Elector Palatine. The ever-fearful James was concerned for his own safety and for that of the Elector, and so, 'Extra guards patrol the city at night. The Lord Mayor has begun to make the round; the next night, which was last night, one of the Aldermen took the duty, and so they will go on from night to night.'[67] The sense of danger felt by the monarch and his council inevitably communicated itself to the citizens, through such overt security measures.

London's role as national capital carried with it the involvement of the government in its administration, as well as giving its citizens a sense of closeness to state affairs. Union of the crowns in 1603 enhanced its position and brought to the throne a monarch with a concern for its appearance and an ambition to improve the impression which it created. The union also added to the considerable numbers of courtiers, petitioners and litigants coming to the metropolis. But the city was by no means dependent on the court and the apparatus of the state, having a distinct civic identity.

4

The World Runs on Wheels

Many aspects of the metropolitan environment were regulated by the city's authorities, including the markets, food prices, traffic, cleanliness and pollution, plague regulations and fire risks. But London's expansion and the increasing numbers at court generated a growing demand for food and fuel, changing the patterns of supply and marketing. As supplies were increased to meet that demand, the existing regulations came under pressure and had to be adapted in response. Although a run of bad harvests in the 1590s produced a difficult time for consumers, as prices rose, over the longer term food supplies were adequate and a significant development saw the growth of market gardening around the city, reducing imports of vegetables. The increasing quantities of food and fuel being transported and the use of larger vehicles, including coaches, on London's streets exacerbated the traffic congestion, requiring modification of the regulations. But the thorny question of purveyance remained, with vehicles being commandeered for royal use and so temporarily unavailable for commercial operations. The authorities also imposed and oversaw the implementation of the orders for preventing pollution and controls of fire hazards, which required increasing care, as the growing population added to the dangers.

The Lord Mayor played a vital role in managing those operations within the city, acting with the Sheriffs and Aldermen to implement the regulations and government policies. Visitors became aware of his importance, with Lupold Von Wedel in 1585 writing that, 'he is a great personage in this country and ranks next to the Queen. Princely honours are paid to him.'[1] They also acknowledged how onerous it was to hold the post. According to de Maisse, in 1597: 'The mayor is chosen from the richest merchants in the City; this office is somewhat costly to maintain and support.'[2] Baron Waldstein estimated that a Lord Mayor's outgoings were over £8,000 and his income from holding the post was only £2,000.[3] The costs included entertaining those who dined at his table, where, as Paul Hentzner wrote, 'there is always great plenty'. This warm hospitality was an obligation, according to Waldstein, 'from the moment of his election he has to hold open house to everyone and continue to do so for the whole year'.[4]

The actions of the Lord Mayor and the corporation's senior officers were overseen by the government, which used the annual inauguration ceremony for a serious purpose, informing the incoming mayor what issues he should address. In 1602 the Lord Treasurer mentioned that more hospitals were required. He also drew attention to the need to stock the City's magazines with grain, while it was plentiful and therefore cheap, in case of an emergency and as a supply for the poor when it became expensive.[5]

Harvests in the 1580s had generally been good, with the exception of 1586, and there was a run of three good years in 1591–3, but that sequence was followed by four successive poor harvests. Bad yields in 1594 and 1595 pushed grain prices up by roughly a third. In January 1594 the Aldermen asked Lord Burghley to introduce a ban on grain exports and in the following summer pointed out that, 'the poorer sorte... are cheefely pinched with the dearthe'.[6] Worse was to come and 1596 was an almost catastrophic year, with prices more than eighty per cent higher than in the early years of the decade and bread selling in London at by far its highest price for the whole of the sixteenth century. A penny loaf weighed just a quarter of what it had done in 1560. The harvest in 1597 was also bad and the price of a range of consumables reached a new peak, but there was then a respite, with average or good crop yields during the next few years. The run of good harvests was broken by a poor one in 1608, but for most of the first two decades of the seventeenth century yields were good.

Although grain prices fell after the bad years of the mid-1590s, they settled at a higher level than in the 1580s, reflecting the long-term price rise of the period. Wage earners saw their purchasing power fall by roughly a third between the 1580s and the 1610s. With an increasing supply of labour in the capital as its population grew, their power to negotiate higher wages was limited.

The corporation intervened in the market during years of hardship, acting with the authority provided by the government's dearth orders. These had first been issued by Cardinal Wolsey in 1527 and were repeated in 1586, 1594, 1595, 1608 and 1622. They authorized searches of premises where grain was suspected to be hoarded, withheld from the markets, to be released when prices rose. High prices carried with them the danger of popular disturbances and, to prevent profiteering, the Lord Mayor set the prices which should be asked. These were also adopted in Westminster. In 1615 its burgess court instructed a Mr Baker, 'to get the Orders of Newgate and Cheap side Markett under the hand of the Clarke of the Markett, for London'.[7] In addition, the corporation and livery companies maintained a store of grain to supplement supplies reaching the markets, with granaries at Leadenhall and the Bridgehouse. This ideally consisted of 10,000 quarters of grain, which was drawn upon during shortages, as in the crisis years of the 1590s. In 1594 the corporation sold grain from its stores at a little lower than the market price, but by September 1595 they were empty. It then imported wheat and rye from the Baltic, but rains across northern and central Europe made this a year of widespread shortages and high prices. In 1596 the corporation distributed 4,000 loaves weekly to the poorest households. That October twenty ships with cargoes of grain arrived in the Thames from the Baltic and the Council instructed the corporation that the poor should benefit, and not those who, 'buy great quantities to sell again at excessive prices, making thereby unlawful gains to the oppressing of the poor.'[8] The Privy Council's request that the City's grain magazines be replenished after the good harvest in 1602 was therefore a prudent precaution against future harvest failures.

In normal years London's food supply was adequate to meet demand. The price increases in 1595, however, prompted an angry response in June, attributed to apprentices. These probably were the first food riots in the capital since the 1520s. In one incident, apprentices 'took from the market-people in Southwark butter for their money, paying for the same but three pence the pound, whereas the owners would have had five pence'.[9] They also issued a demand that butter be sold in the markets, not in inns or private houses. In a similar episode, apprentices sent to buy mackerel at Billingsgate chased the fishwives who had bought the stocks and took the fish from them, selling it at the price stipulated by the Lord Mayor. In both cases they were acting conservatively, effectively enforcing the regulations by which the Lord Mayor set the price of foodstuffs. This, however, usurped the authority of the Aldermen, whose role it was to see that the market regulations and prices were maintained.

Other unrest included the pulling down of the pillories in Cheapside and at Leadenhall and a clash between a large crowd of apprentices and the City's officers on Tower Hill. In the incident at Tower Hill, 'unrulie youthes on the towerhill being blamed by the warders of towerstreete warde to sever themselves and depart from thence, threw at them stones and drave them back into Tower street'. A rumour spread that a crowd had erected gallows outside the house of Sir John Spencer, the Lord Mayor, and that the rioters were threatening that he 'should not have his head on his shoulders within one hour after'. The disturbances that summer may have been exacerbated by Spencer's unpopularity. Nevertheless, they were the kind of unrest that the government feared, and it reacted strongly. Sir Thomas Wilford, a soldier, was appointed Provost Marshal, with powers to arrest and execute those guilty of disturbing the peace; effectively putting the City under martial law. In July 1595 the treason laws were used to condemn five unruly apprentices to execution by being hanged, drawn and quartered; 'and were on the twenty foure of the same moneth drawne from Newgate to the Tower hill, and there executed accordingly'. In 1596 two more marshals were appointed, with twelve assistants, 'for the apprehending of vagrant and other disordered persons'.[10] These were draconian measures.

The corporation's actions were less fierce, as it took steps to enforce the rules governing the markets, setting up committees in 1595 and reissuing its *Laws of the markets*. The existing system for trading was based upon commodities being brought to market, where buyers and sellers met. This should have established a just price, based on supply and demand; Thomas Platter wrote that meat and fish could be bought, 'for a fair price, as good order is kept in such matters'. The principle of the open market, with deals struck openly, not privately, was applied generally; hence the phrase used in contracts of sale for many goods, that the agreement was concluded 'in open market'. The record of Richard Jones's sale of his share in theatrical property to Edward Alleyn in 1589, for £37 10s, states that he had 'bargained and solde in playne and open Market within the citie of London', even though that was a private sale.[11]

Those who traded outside these arrangements fell into three categories. Forestallers were those who bought produce from suppliers before it had reached the markets; engrossers bought in bulk to sell at a profit; and regraters bought produce for resale, either in the same market or another one close by. They were all reviled and condemned as 'people who live only for themselves', because their practices raised prices. And they were parasites, 'framing themselves to leade a more easie lyfe than by labor', according to Hugh Alley in 1598, by buying produce 'before anie the good Citizens of this Citie can come to the same'.[12] He was hopeful of obtaining a role as one of those enforcing the market regulations on the Lord Mayor's behalf. This included not only prices, weights and measures, but the markets and their buildings, the placing of the stalls and cleanliness. In 1588 the vegetable sellers in Cheapside were forbidden to wash their wares in the street, because 'it leads to great annoyance and hath byn some cause of infection'.[13] After a report in that year, the City reorganized the arrangement of the market sellers in Cheapside.

The officers in the City and at Westminster checked the quality of the meat, poultry and fish displayed, appointing those with specialist knowledge as inspectors, to judge 'whether it be wholesome or not'. Thus, the burgess court of Westminster appointed a poulterer to inspect the poultry for sale.[14] The regulations were enforced, but the number of fines fell towards the end of the sixteenth century, even though the street traders – known as huxsters, hawkers and higglers – were much complained of and, according to a mayoral proclamation of 1590, were 'of late yeres soe wonderfully encreased'. Those who were brought to court and fined for irregular selling were mostly small traders; the records of fines include such cases as 'two baskettes cheryes engroced by an huxster' and 'a quarter of veele and certain Egges hawked'.[15] Perhaps that reflected a tacit acknowledgment that the changes in marketing practices could not be stemmed.

Cheapside was one of the general markets, where poultry, butter, cheese, herbs, roots, fruit and spices were sold, together with saddlery, cloth, silks and other quality textiles. The general market at Cornhill sold a similar range of consumables as well as rabbits, poultry, game and waterfowl. Grain was sold at Billingsgate and Queenhithe, where the dock was an important one for river vessels from towns on the Thames, handling grain and malt. Other produce landed at Billingsgate included onions, oranges and other fruit; its market was just becoming a fish market, the existing fish markets were in Old Fish Street and at the Stocks market, which also contained butchers' stalls. The livestock market was held in Smithfield and the butchers' markets were at the Shambles at Newgate and in Eastcheap. By 1600 Little Eastcheap was lined with their shops and in 1618 Orazio Busino wrote that he found it, 'a marvel to see such quantities of butchers shops in all the parishes, the streets being full of them in every direction. The very fat meat is exhibited at the gratings from the top of the windows to the bottom.'[16] Animals were slaughtered on the premises and the butchers had scalding houses in Pudding Lane; one of the less salubrious streets in the City, because, according to John Stow, 'their puddings, with other filth of beasts, are voided down that way to their dung boats on the Thames'.[17] Leadenhall was a grain market and poultry, eggs, butter and cheese were also sold there. Citizens and non-citizens were allotted different sites within markets, and at Leadenhall the 'country butchers' were permitted to trade only on Wednesdays and Saturdays. They were later restricted to Saturdays only.

The City established a new meal market at Bishopsgate in 1599 and in the 1590s enlarged the market houses at Newgate and Queenhithe, and that at Southwark in 1606. This was in response to the increasing pressure being placed on markets by the amount of produce traded, caused by the growing population. Congestion was complained of at Cheapside in 1592 and in 1613 an extra market day was instituted at Southwark market. Two years later a common market place at Smithfield was considered, because 'Newgate Market, Cheapside, Leadenhall and Gracechurch Street were unmeasurably pestered with the unimaginable increase and multiplicity of market-folkes'.[18] In 1591 the City agreed that not only grain and salt could be sold at Queenhithe, but also onions, garlic, apples and other fruit. Not all food sales were restricted to the markets; women were allowed to sell oysters, mussels, salted fish and cockles in the streets, and some street sellers sold bread.

The increased quantities of produce, and the numbers of traders and consumers, combined to change the nature of the food trades. Wholesalers were taking a growing part in marketing. Deals were struck in inns and lanes. Some London bakers and brewers ensured that they received supplies at agreed prices by making contracts directly with corn dealers in the market towns. And the number of retailers selling outside the markets was increasing, such as fishmongers, poulterers, fruiterers and cheesemongers. According to Busino, 'One sees pastry cooks without end and innumerable poulterers, especially of those who sell rabbits also, of which every shop has hundreds and there are customers for all.'[19]

In 1601 counsel for the Fishmongers' Company described to the House of the Commons the way in which the fish trade was changing. It had been the practice that twelve men acted as factors, buying fish at the ports and having it shipped to London, 'to be boughte of the whole Companye, and soe sould in the market, whereby fishe was then farr cheaper than nowe it is'. The arrangement had broken down and now some sixty men were buying the whole stock for themselves, and they 'sell it at a dearer rate, by retayle to the utter undoeinge of the rest of the fishemongers, because then everye man sould for himselfe'. The consumers suffered, not only through higher prices but also because, 'the fyshe sould is seldome sweete, but ever unsavorye'.[20]

London's livery companies were part of the regulatory process, overseeing their own members' operations, but they also acted as pressure groups, to protect their interests. The brewers attracted attention, especially for charging high prices, contrary to the level fixed by the Lord Mayor. The Privy Council took an interest in this, especially in years of grain shortages. The brewers responded, for example by paying the Lord Keeper, Sir John Puckering, a bribe of £100 to obstruct a Bill introduced by the City in the Parliament of 1592 aimed at tightening the pricing arrangements.

Malt and grain were brought along the Thames from Oxfordshire and Berkshire, with Henley an important centre for the trade, and down the River Lea from Hertfordshire. The Lea navigation was authorized by an Act of Parliament of 1571, 'for the bringing of the Ryver of Lee to the northside of the citie of London'. The cost of making the cut was paid by the corporation, but it was maintained at the 'costes and charges of the countrey'.[21] Grain for London was also bought at market towns around the capital, in Middlesex, Berkshire, Hertfordshire, Essex, Surrey and Kent. Supplies were sent from the ports of Essex, Suffolk and Norfolk, and those of Kent, which supplied roughly two-thirds of grain brought to London by coastal vessels. King's Lynn shipped grain and other produce from the area drained by the rivers Ouse and Nene. Cheese and butter also came in coastal vessels, especially from Suffolk, and overland, from other counties in the South East. In his description of Middlesex (1595), John Norden wrote that the countryside was:

> so furnished with kyne that the wife... twice or thrice a weeke conveyeth
> to London mylke, butter, cheese, apples, peares, frumentye [wheat

boiled in milk], hens, chyckens, egges, baken, and a thousand other country drugges.[22]

Fish from the east coast ports included cod, ling and herring. From further afield, salmon was brought from Berwick and Chester, pilchards from Looe in Cornwall, and pilchards, hake, ling and cod from Plymouth. The range of fish available to the London housewife was described by Jacob Rathgeb, in 1592:

> Oysters are in great plenty, and are better and larger than in Italy; they are cried in all parts of the streets. They sell also cod, plaice, small white river fish, pike, carp, trout, lobster and crawfish, and in fine all kinds of sea fish, which are sold like meat in other parts, both fresh and salted.[23]

A few years later Thomas Platter mentioned that the fish sellers kept pike and tench in tanks: 'according to them fish could keep fresh for some months'. He also described how the sellers, 'kept a copper or brass needle in the tub, with a sharp knife'. When a customer considered buying a pike, the seller slit the fish open to show how fat its guts were, 'and then sewed it up again'.[24]

To supply the demand for fresh meat, lean cattle were driven from as far away as Wales and the West Country to pastures closer to London, where they were fattened. In 1618 the Venetian envoy wrote that at Bartholomew Fair he 'saw an infinite number of cattle, which filled the meadows near London, and were all disposed of in one day or a little more'. Sheep were driven from the Midlands. Travelling through the south Midlands, Rathgeb noticed, 'a fine breed of splendid large oxen, and countless number of sheep'.[25]

Fresh fruit and vegetables became available in increasing quantities. In 1652 Samuel Hartlib commented that, 'In Queen Elizabeth's time we had not onely our Gardiners ware from Holland, but also Cherries from Flaunders; Apples from France; Saffron, Licorish from Spain; Hopps from the Low-Countreys'. But market gardens were established around London from the late sixteenth century, in Hackney, Chelsea, Fulham and Kensington, and they expanded to supply the capital's fruit and vegetables, reducing the need for imports. Vegetables sold in London by the turn of the century included peas, beans, cabbages, radishes, artichokes, carrots, parsnips, turnips and onions. The Gardeners' Company was granted its charter in 1605, which gave it oversight of market gardens within six miles of London, despite opposition from the corporation. By 1617 the market gardeners claimed that they employed, 'thowsands of poore people, ould menn, women and children in sellinge of their Commodities, in weedinge, in gathering of stone, etc.'.[26]

Orazio Busino described how the ground was improved for growing vegetables, by spreading the fields:

> to the depth of four or five feet with the filth of the city, which serves as excellent manure, rich and black as thick ink and which is conveyed at small cost by the innumerable carts which are bound to cleanse the streets, so that in a very short while many spots are improved and fertilized.

On such improved ground, the gardeners 'raise a great quantity of vegetables', including cabbages of 'an enormous size', as well as 'white and very large potatoes, cauliflowers, parsnips, carrots, turnips etc.'. He was also greatly impressed by:

> their most beautiful and fine flavoured artichokes, of a sort different from ours, that is to say much larger and of a reddish tinge. Of these they gather an immense quantity during ten months of the year and sell them at a very cheap rate.[27]

Root crops were also brought from the market gardens at Norwich, shipped from Great Yarmouth. Market gardening there was begun by Dutch immigrants, who introduced carrots, turnips and parsnips. The area provided supplements to London's food supply in the dearth years of the mid-1590s. In 1593–4, 280 tons of roots were shipped from Yarmouth to London; in 1597–8 the figure was 812 tons.[28]

The Dutch had introduced commercial flower growing and London collectors were busy extending the range of flowers and edible plants grown in the city. The merchant Nicholas Lete was described as 'greatly in love with rare floures'; his factor in Syria despatched flowers to him and from Poland he was sent an orange tawny gillyflower, 'which before that time was never seen nor heard of in these countries'. He passed that on to the herbalist John Gerard, who was a member of the Barber-Surgeons' Company and was elected its Master in 1608. The first edition of his *The Herball or Generall Historie of Plantes*, was published in 1597, 'From my House in Holborn'. It included his experience with growing plants that were being sent to him from around the world, such as tomatoes from Spain, Italy and 'such hot Countries, from whence my selfe have received seeds for my garden, where they do increase and prosper'. Tiger lilies came from Constantinople and the Persian lilly was brought, 'by the industry of Travellers into those countries... [and] made a denizen in some few of our London gardens'. Potatoes were more readily available, Gerard bought 'divers roots... at the Exchange in London'. Some plants were sent to him by Jean Robin, keeper of the king's garden in Paris. Of course, not all were suited to English conditions. Ginger from North Africa and the West Indies proved to be, 'most impatient of the coldnesse of these our Northerne regions... as soone as it hath beene but touched with the first sharpe blast of Winter, it hath presently perished both blade and root'. Gerard also suggested how some of the produce could be served, for example potatoes 'as a ground or foundation whereon the cunning Confectioner or Sugar-Baker may worke and frame many comfortable delicacies Conserves and restorative sweet-meats. They are used to be eaten rosted in the ashes.'[29] From the efforts of collectors and growers an increasing range of plants became available, with the edible ones adding variety to the citizens' diet.

Food supplies were maintained even through the difficult years of the mid-1590s and the apprentices' angry outburst in 1595 was not repeated. Water supplies were also expanded to meet the growing need. The city drew its water from the Thames and its tributaries, and an increasing number of aqueducts that brought fresh water from Tyburn and Islington into the centre. Wells were dug within individual premises and some vestries maintained a parish well, many of which were converted to pumps during the sixteenth century. Public conduits and cisterns were provided from charitable donations by citizens. From there, according to Rathgeb, 'the poor labourers carry it on their shoulders to the different houses and sell it, in a peculiar kind of wooden vessels, broad at the bottom, but very narrow at the top, and bound with iron hoops'.[30] These water-bearers, commonly known as 'cobs', formed a numerous and somewhat disorderly group among the street sellers. Busino described the arrangements:

> In the heart of the city... they have fountains supplied by conduits, where the water is clear and tolerably good. Thither flock great crowds of women and porters, who for hire carry it to such houses as desired in long wooden vessels hooped with iron.[31]

But the increasing population brought rising demand and greater quantities of effluent, with the attendant risk of pollution, and so piped water was preferable to well water.

Two water wheels were built in the late sixteenth century, to raise water from the Thames. In the early 1580s the Dutchman Pieter Morice constructed 'an artificial forcier' which could deliver river water from the northern end of London Bridge as high as Leadenhall. A similar arrangement was constructed by Bevis Bulmar in 1594–5 within a ruined building at Broken Wharf, owned by the corporation. John Stow described Bulmar's work as, 'a large house of great height, called an engine... for the conveying and forcing of Thames water to serve in the middle and west parts of the city'.[32] Busino criticized the water supplied from the wheels as being 'so hard, turbid and stinking that the odour remains even in clean linen'. He was not impressed with the water supplies: 'They are very badly off for water, although they have an immense supply.'[33]

In 1602 Edmund Colthurst, a soldier, began promoting schemes to bring water to London in a channel, or aqueduct from springs at Chadwell and Amwell, in Hertfordshire. In 1604 he obtained a licence by Letters Patent from James I and started work at the Hertfordshire end. After he had cut two or three miles, he ran into financial difficulties and the corporation became involved, obtaining Acts of Parliament in 1606 and 1607 which authorized it to undertake the work. But the Court of Aldermen was unwilling to advance money to the project. Hugh Myddelton had been a member of the House of Commons committee that considered the City's Bill in 1606, and he now took an active part. A wealthy goldsmith in Cheapside, Myddelton was Prime Warden of the Goldsmiths' Company in 1610 and 1624, and MP for Denbigh from 1603. The corporation now assigned him its rights under the Acts of Parliament. He retained Colthurst as Overseer, or resident engineer, and appointed a surveyor. But when roughly a quarter of the length had been constructed the work came to halt, because of the cost and some obstructive opposition from landowners across whose land the channel was being built. With the corporation's support, Myddelton approached the king for help. In September 1611 James agreed to provide half the funds required, in return for half the profits, and also ordered those who were opposing the scheme unlawfully to desist.

The work was then resumed and the aqueduct was completed within two years. It was almost thirty-nine miles long, was 10 feet wide and 4 feet deep. On 29 September 1613 a ceremony was held at the reservoir at the New River Head near Islington. About sixty labourers marched around the reservoir, carrying their 'spades, shovels, pickaxes and such like instruments of laborious employment', and then 'the flood-gates flew open, the streame ranne gallantly into the cisterne, drummes and trumpets sounding in a triumphal manner'. From there pipes were laid around the streets in the centre and western part of the city. By March 1615 there were 384 households taking New River water, by 1618 the number was over 1,000; in 1622 the New River Company made a profit and in 1638 it had 2,154 customers.[34] This considerable achievement had been carried out by a combination of private and municipal initiative with financial support from the crown.

The growing population required increasing quantities of fuel, as well as food and water. Firewood came from Sussex and Kent, and coal from the Tyne. In 1585–6, 37,590 tons of coal were shipped from Newcastle to London; in 1591–2 the comparable figure was 54,742 tons.[35] The coal merchants and woodmongers were powerful groups, and unpopular, for selling fuel at short weights. Thomas Dekker, in 1606, mentioned them among the 'shavers' in London, those who gave short measure. In 1612 the burgess court at Westminster prosecuted two colliers for selling 'severall Sacks of Coal that wanted Measure'.[36] When William Ryder, Lord Mayor in 1600–01, undertook the reform of weights and measures, he found his attempts obstructed by the coal shippers. A dispute between the woodmongers and the wharfingers in the late 1610s produced allegations of bribery. When investigation of the matter was referred to a committee of the Common Council that included Sir Anthony Benn, the Recorder, the wharfingers claimed that Benn's wife had 'received a guilt Cup of great value from the Company of Woodmongers'. The company was subsequently accused of bribing the Attorney-General, Sir Henry Yelverton (when he was appointed Attorney-General he presented the King with a gift of £4,000), and later of offering the Lord Mayor, Sir William Cockayne, 'a bribe of great value', which he refused.[37] The dispute was part of long-running wrangles over the carriage of goods in the city. It involved the corporation and attracted the Privy Council's interest because of the problem of traffic congestion.

The corporation had oversight of traffic matters, in the streets and on the Thames. By an Act of Parliament of 1555 it regulated the watermen, specifying the minimum size of their boats, known as wherries. And, as with food and fuel, it fixed the rates which they could charge, which were fifty per cent higher for journeys against the tide, and one penny for rowing across the river. But this left the size of the tip to be negotiated between the waterman and his passengers, a process which could take some time. Although there were roughly

2,000 wherries, even with the many other vessels the river could not get clogged with traffic, unlike the streets.

John Stow included the state of the city's traffic with his list of current problems, because, 'the number of cars, drays, carts, and coaches, more than hath been accustomed, the streets and lanes being straitened, must needs be dangerous, as daily experience proveth'. Cars were two-wheeled vehicles, 12 feet long and 3 feet wide; long carts were 14 feet long and 4 feet wide. Carriers bringing goods long distances had begun to use the long wagon during Elizabeth's reign. Stow gave the precise date of 1564 and by the end of the century carriers from Canterbury, Norwich, Ipswich, Gloucester and other cities were using it. Coaches had also become more common, as members of the nobility and gentry came to London with their families, rather than riding up on horseback with just one or two servants. And people preferred to travel within the city in vehicles, when they could have walked.

Of old time coaches were not known in this land, but chariots or whirlicotes, then so called, and they only used of princes of great estates, such as had their footmen about them... but now of late years the use of coaches, brought from Germany, is taken up, and made so common, as there is neither distinction of time nor difference of persons observed; for the world runs on wheels with many whose parents were glad to go on foot.[38]

Thomas Dekker used a similar phrase when he wrote, in 1606, that, 'In every street, carts and coaches make such a thundering as if the world ran upon wheels.' Fynes Moryson attributed the congestion caused by coaches to social pretension. He wrote in 1617 that:

Sixty or seventy years ago coaches were very rare in England, but at this day pride is so far increased, as there be few gentlemen of any account (I mean elder brothers) who have not their coaches, so as the streets of London are almost stopped up with them.[39]

The carmen provided the local links in the network of suppliers involving wagoners, carters, drovers, boatmen and shipmasters who supplied London's consumers with food and fuel. Traffic congestion therefore was a serious issue. And the behaviour of the carmen gave offence, too. In 1618 the Venetian ambassador's despatch to the Doge and Senate reported the ceremony at which James I knighted the Lord Mayor. The king made a number of comments, including the instruction to take care of the great devils and the little devils. Unruly apprentices were the little devils, the great ones were the carts, 'which in passing along the streets, whether narrow or wide, do not choose to yield or give way as due to the coaches of the gentry, when they meet them'. James's concern was social precedence, rather than congestion, but later in his despatch the ambassador could not resist venting his own irritation:

> To return to the carts of London, there is such a multitude of them, large and small, that is to say on two wheels and on four, that it would be impossible to estimate them correctly. Those which circulate in the city are for the most part on two broad and high wheels like those of Rome, and serve for the conveyance of sundry articles such as beer, coal, wood etc.; but among them are some very filthy ones, employed solely for cleansing the streets and carrying manure, and it is precisely the drivers of these who are usually the most insolent fellows in the world. The other four-wheeled waggons come up from the country bringing goods and passengers higgledy-piggledy, precisely like Marghera boats, and they are drawn by seven or eight horses in file, one behind the other, with plumes and bells, embroidered cloth coverings.[40]

Commercial and social pressures combined to make regulation difficult. The carmen were members of the Fraternity of St Katherine. But the woodmongers, who operated their own carts, were numerous and powerful enough to dominate it and before the end of the century it had ceased to be effective. They and the City's officers kept the register of carts and supervised the transfer of carrooms, which were licences to operate. In 1582 the corporation intervened and gave the supervision of the carmen to Christ's Hospital, ordering that all the profits were to be 'employed onelye to the relyefe of the pore children within the same Hospitall'.[41] By 1597–8 they were considerable, with a profit of £223 that year.

In 1586 the Court of Common Council issued a detailed set of regulations. They dealt with safety, noise and traffic control, including parking and speeding. No carman or carter was to leave his vehicle in the street at night or 'ryde or drive his horse or trott in the street or otherwise in a more speedie course or pace than is usuall'. A fine of one shilling was to be imposed 'yf any Carrman or drayman shall suffer his horse to go in the streets and shall not leade him by the Coller with a special regarde always as well before him as behinde him as well for children as for aged people'. In Stow's experience that was not observed: 'The coachman rides behind the horse tails, lasheth them, and looketh not behind him; the drayman sitteth and sleepeth on his dray, and letteth his horse lead him home.'[42] Fines were also imposed on those whose wheels were shod with iron, or they creaked or squeaked, 'for want of greasing'.

The orders attempted to deal with congestion caused by a lack of courtesy and consideration for other street users:

> Thames Strete and other Narrowe lanes and places within this Cittie were pestered many tymes with longe cartes, drayes and carres by reason of the contrarie course and meetings of such carts drays and carres but soe muche the more by wilfulness of the Carters draymen and Carrmen that... will not take paynes to put back or use any other Remedie for the ease of one another.

Parked carts in busy streets also created congestion, for while the carmen with empty vehicles were waiting to be hired 'men cannot pass them without troble and danger to be hurte'. The solution was to specify places where they should wait and the maximum number at each waiting place. The number varied according to circumstances, so that fewer were allowed to wait near market places while the market was in progress, but that was increased when it had ended. And the same applied in Cornhill while the merchants were trading in the Royal Exchange. In all, seventy-seven waiting places were specified.[43]

The problem of traffic jams was not solved and the City authorities pressed the hospital to reduce the number of cars by fifty. The hospital agreed and also tightened up collection of fees. An economic recession in 1597 prompted the carmen to rebel and bring a case in the court of King's Bench against the hospital, with the support of the woodmongers, who wanted the freedom to use as many carts as they needed. As a result of the case, in 1605 the woodmongers regained the supervision of the carmen in 'one bodye Corporate and pollitique in deede and name'.[44] This did not end the litigation between the two groups within the new company, but attempts by the carmen to secede failed.

Conditions in the streets did not improve. For example, in 1613 William Wright of St Martin's-in-the-Fields, a 'tombmaker' [stonemason], was indicted at the Sessions for, 'annoying the street near Charing Cross with loading carts and turning the Judges and all other passengers into the channel'.[45] Common Council passed an act, in August 1617, designed to control the traffic, complaining of 'the disorder and rude behaviour of Carmen, Draymen and others using Cartes', which put men, women and children at risk, 'and some have loste their lives by the unorderlye stoppinge upp the streetes and passages of this Citty with Carrs Carts and drays'. Negligent leading of vehicles and 'the multitude of Carrs and Carts' caused delays for the 'Nobles and other great personages of the Realme and others occasioned to pass through the Streetes of this City'. Citizens in the busy streets, such as Thames Street, and on London Bridge, suffered because of vehicles stopping outside their premises, which was 'both a great hinderaunce to their trade and dangerous to them and their households'. As before, this was blamed squarely on the carmen's stubbornness when they came face to face in narrow streets, because they, 'are soe churlishe one to another as that they will not make waye, one for another, as conveniently they may'.[46]

The waiting places specified in 1586 had been near to the market places, as the principal need for carriage was to move goods to and from market. Over the intervening thirty-one years overseas and coastal trade had increased so much that the distribution of goods from the wharves had become a major function. New waiting places were therefore created near the river. And to reduce congestion a system was instituted which required empty carts to enter Thames Street only from thirteen specified streets, while loaded carts leaving Thames Street had to do so by St Dunstan's Hill, St Mary Hill, Garlick Hill, Bread Street Hill and the hill from Tower Dock into Tower Street. This created a one-way system, enforced by fines until at least the mid-eighteenth century. Another restriction banned carmen who had crossed the bridge from turning into Thames Street 'by St Magnus Corner Eastward'. This was designed to prevent 'the great number of Carrs which come out of Southwark and go into Thames Street from Saint Magnus Corner', causing congestion in Thames Street. Fines were levied into the eighteenth century for this transgression, known as 'coming in at St Magnus'.[47]

The problem of transport in London merged with that of purveyance, the system by which the crown acquired provisions for the royal court, and requisitioned transport. The purveyors who obtained the supplies needed set the price and the quantities, both when the court was at Whitehall and during a royal progress. The amounts required were considerable. In one year of Elizabeth's reign the court consumed 4,330 cattle, 8,200 sheep, over 4,000 quarters of wheat, and 600,000 gallons of beer and ale. And when the court went on a progress, or the queen moved between palaces, more than 400 carts were required. By the late sixteenth century many counties had compounded to pay a fixed sum to replace the purveyors, with the justices of the peace taking responsibility for supplying the court's requirements. The sums from the counties that had compounded in this way had reached £50,000 by 1604. London felt the effects of the system because of the royal palaces in and near the city. Roughly three-quarters of the provisions taken for the court were drawn from those regions which supplied London, and those obtained in the city included the bulky items such as beer, wood and coal.

When the City authorities attempted to regulate the numbers of vehicles, they had to ensure that enough were available for the royal service if needed. Yet they were also aware that this distorted prices, for those who brought goods to the city had:

> been often tymes vexed and troubeled for the unreasonable takyng of there horses and cartes by the officers of the seid Citie for the kyngs Caryage and purveaunce... [and so] they often tyme absent and withdrawe theym selves frome the seide Citie, which causyth the seid vitailles to be dere and of more excessyve price then they have bene in tymes passed.[48]

Those who were transporting goods out of London were also likely to find their carts requisitioned. In 1605 the problem was described by Robert Fletcher, yeoman purveyor of carriages and chief cart-taker to Elizabeth and James I, with the notional example of:

> an ignorant poor carter, who having loaden his cart for norwich, yarmouth, places of like distans from London, he is taken by one of thies carttakers, comanndid to unload and to load a Tune of drinck and convey the same to the court.

The cart-taker would fix the price. To avoid this inconvenience, delay and reduction of his income, the carter would be willing to pay a bribe of as much as £5 to the cart-taker, to be excused. Fletcher, as an insider, was well aware of the practice and condemned some of his colleagues. Thomas Knarisbrough was 'a notable bribing and corrupt carttaker'; Edward Coosyn he described as: 'a most sly suttle and cunninge brybing wretched fellowe, an userer verie crewel to gayne'; and John Bremell, 'his bryberyes being continewall, and his shifts in taking of bribes so artificiall as an honest man would wonder at his folly'.[49]

Fletcher also criticized those cart-takers who, 'doe dayly and overly take carts in London, whether there be cause or noe cause'.[50] This could be done just to draw a bribe from the carters, who otherwise would be kept idle and have to return without a load when the cart-taker chose to release him. Abuse of the purveyance system had become so irksome that in 1604 a petition was addressed to the king. It included the complaint that too many carts were commandeered:

> that where Two hundred, or thereabouts, would suffice for all Your Majesty's, the Queen's, and Prince's Carriages (for which only Carts are to be taken) there are taken ordinarily Eight or Nine hundred, and many times a thousand.

This kind of over-provision applied not only to a royal progress, for:

> If the King remove but for a Dinner, the Purveyor chargeth near as many Carts, as at a full Remove; and the over Number must either compound with the Purveyor for Money, to save his coming, or else travel to the Court, and go Home, as many Times he doth, empty, no Carriage being there for him.[51]

Carters who ignored the cart-taker's order to bring their carts were liable to a fine of ten shillings. A solution adopted by the wharfingers during the period when the carmen were supervised by Christ's Hospital, was to compound for £52 10s per annum for their wood wharves, which the hospital used to hire carters for the royal service in their place. But the arrangement had later broken down. Despite the system, its abuse, and its effects on supply and prices within the metropolis, attempts at reform during the early years of James I's reign came to nothing.

Carters were also liable to be commanded to carry materials for repairing the streets. Householders were responsible for the street outside their premises. In 1610 any householder in Drury Lane who 'hath not already pitched the Street before his Doore shall forthwith pitch it with Stone to the midst of the Street the breadth of his House and shall from time to time at his own Charge maintain the same'. Posts erected outside houses, to protect both the buildings and pedestrians from vehicles, should be no more than 4 feet from the wall, so as not to make the carriageway too narrow.[52]

The scavengers oversaw the rakers who cleaned the streets. The City's twenty-six wards had a total of 179 scavengers and the parishes outside its boundaries appointed their own, four in St Martin's-in-the-Fields, for example. When an outbreak of plague threatened, the thoroughness with which the surfaces of the streets was maintained attracted especial concern, because rubbish could accumulate and rot in crevices, creating dangerous miasmic air. Rubbish was to be collected, the streets were to be cleaned daily by the rakers (except on Sundays), and washed down by water provided by those householders with wells.[53] Those whose trade produced garbage could not be so clean. In 1603 Thomas Lodge recommended that the slaughter houses should be moved out to 'some remote and convenient place neere unto the river of the Thames, to the end that the bloud and garbige of the beasts that are killed may be washed away with the tide'.[54]

Paul Hentzner, in 1598, found the streets to be 'very handsome and clean'.[55] But cleanliness was achieved only with difficulty; as the number of people increased, so did the quantity of filth, human and animal. Householders dumped their garbage in the streets, where it was collected and taken in the dung carts to laystalls around the city. Among the obligations of members of the Fraternity of St Katherine was, 'to clense, purge and kepe clene all the Streetes and lanes of this Citie and Suburbes of the same of Donge and other filth'.[56] Their payment was to be fixed by the wards.

In 1613 two butchers were reprimanded for dumping 'the Soyle and filth of their Slaughter houses and hogstyes' at the end of the new churchyard in St Clement Danes parish, 'to the great Annoyance of the Inhabitants and Passengers there'. An order was issued that such rubbish should be there only for as long as it took to load it into a cart. But even when a cart was loaded, the carters did not always take it away quickly. In the following year the burgess court at Westminster instructed one Ralph Foster not to leave his 'Cart, or Dung pott to stand in the Pallace full of soyle either upon the Sunday or any other day, but [he] shall forthwith carry it away'.[57] On the other side of London, Charles and Jane Browne of Whitechapel were put in the stocks in Artillery Lane, 'for emptying a great quantity of night-work into the common sewer, to the general annoyance of all the inhabitants'.[58]

The keeping of cattle, sheep and pigs within the city added to the waste to be disposed of, hence an order in 1610 that the butchers should bring into the city only the sheep which were to be killed. And in 1613 Thomas Farmer was reported for keeping eight cows in his kitchen, 'which by his own confession he hath lately converted to a Cowhouse to the great Annoyance of the Inhabitants and Neighbours near adjoining'. The kitchen probably was a separate structure from the house and in converting it he may have enlarged the building, but even so the cows must have been tightly packed. In attempting to supply the demand for fresh dairy produce, Farmer both offended his neighbours' nostrils and created a fire risk, by keeping hay and straw on the premises. He was given seven days to remove it.[59]

Plague epidemics caused greater attention than usual to be paid to the environmental regulations. During the outbreak in 1603, Timothy Willis wrote to Sir Robert Cecil describing the area of the Savoy, where many of the plague orders were being disregarded. Among the faults was the keeping of pigs, which were allowed to roam the streets 'day and night'. Another was that many householders kept too many dogs – described as 'house curs and water spaniels' – in small houses; they wandered around without restraint, greatly annoyed the neighbours, and 'unsweeten their keeper's houses'. Dogs had attracted the corporation's attention before, as both noisy nuisances and one of the ways in which plague was thought to spread. In 1563 it had noted that the barking of 'the great multitude of dogges' disturbed the citizens' sleep and caused quarrels and disturbances. A proclamation issued by the Lord Mayor in 1592 ordered that no person should:

kepe any dogg, or bitche, but such as they will keepe within there owne
doores, withowt suffering them to goe loose in the streets, not ledd in
slippe or lyne, nor within there owne doores making howling or other
annoyaunce to there neyghbours.[60]

The drastic solution to the dog problem was to have the animals
killed, by designated dog killers, especially but not exclusively during
plague outbreaks. In 1584–6 the corporation paid for the killing of
1,882 dogs and in 1603 just one parish, St Margaret's, Westminster,
paid for 502 dogs killed. They were considered to be 'very apt cattell
to carry the infection'.[61]

Fire prevention was a continuous, not occasional, concern. Potential
hazards included the storage of larger quantities of fuel and fodder
than were required immediately, the throwing out of hot cinders, and
dangerous stoves. Offenders were instructed to remove or correct
the fault, and fined if they did not. Fire prevention also included the
requirement that chimneys were substantial and adequate, and, more
importantly, that buildings should not be thatched. After a number of
devastating fires, the London Assize of 1212 stated that 'whosoever
wishes to build, let him take care, as he loveth himself and his goods,
that he roof not with reed, nor rush, straw nor stubble, but with
tile only, or shingle or boards, or if it may be with lead or plastered
straw'.[62] Those with thatched roofs were to plaster them within eight
days or have the building demolished. By the sixteenth century, and
probably long before, that ban on thatching was effective. John Stow
was relieved to note that since it had been introduced 'there hath not
happened the like often consuming fires in this city as afore'.[63]

The fire-fighting equipment kept by the wards, parishes and livery
companies consisted of leather buckets, fire-hooks and ladders. In 1586
the churchwardens of St Mary Woolchurch Haw paid thirty shillings
'for xii lether buckites' and twenty years later the Drapers' Company
bought eighteen new buckets and paid for the repair of eighteen old
ones.[64] With the parishes and companies maintaining their allocation,
several hundred buckets were available in an emergency. Fire-hooks

were long implements like grappling irons, which were used to unroof, or even to pull down, buildings to create a fire break.

Gunpowder presented a danger, and an increasing one, as more ordnance was deployed and smaller guns came into greater use. Most large merchant vessels carried some cannon as a defence against privateers and pirates, and powder was also sold for hand guns, for self-defence and hunting. Gunpowder was imported by London merchants from Antwerp and Hamburg and stored in warehouses around the city, and the government kept its own stock in the Tower. Alarmingly, it was stored within buildings used for other purposes. In 1612 a survey of the Clothworkers' Company's hall in Mincing Lane laconically noted that the building contained two counting houses and a gallery, and on the side of the gallery 'a chimney and two gunpowder houses'.[65] A more public risk was a warehouse on Tower Hill, which in 1586 attracted the attention of Sir Owen Hopton, Lieutenant of the Tower, because over 800 barrels of powder were stored there. Hopton, understandably, wanted the government to order its removal because it was a place where, 'rogues and vagabonds oftentimes lodge in the night and burn straw to warm themselves'.[66]

Wherever it was stored and when it was being moved or transferred into smaller packages, an explosion was possible. This was neatly expressed in a letter to Sir Robert Cecil in 1595. The writer complained of the disorderly way in which the stores and gunpowder in the Tower were kept: 'Powder is an unmerciful thing, if any chimney within the Tower should take fire, and sparkes fly, or a flint stone strike fire.'[67] An explosion in a tower at the warder's gate in 1548 had killed a prisoner and 'thrown downe' the tower, and in 1560 another blast, at a house in Crooked Lane, destroyed four houses, damaged others, killed eleven people and injured sixteen more.

Through the care of those who handled gunpowder, and good fortune, there was no other major explosion in London until 1650, when the detonation of several barrels in a house near All Hallows, Barking caused sixty-seven deaths. Similarly, although fires occurred from time to time, all of them were quenched with the loss of only a few houses. Not until 1633 did a seriously destructive blaze occur, among the buildings at the northern end of London Bridge. This spread to destroy about a third of the houses on the bridge and nearly eighty more in the parish of St Magnus the Martyr. Far more destructive was the Great Fire in September 1666, which surpassed all other urban conflagrations in western Europe, destroying four-fifths of the City, and its great cathedral, although only one-fifth of the metropolis.

Until that disaster, Londoners had achieved a degree of safety from fire. And, despite the steady growth of population, the city continued to be supplied with adequate stocks of food, water and fuel, with the marketing system adjusting to keep pace with the changing conditions. Traffic congestion, the keeping of livestock and the removal of rubbish were among the environmental issues which attracted attention and regulation, but none of them became such a serious problem as to impair the life of the city. Indeed, Niccolò Molin described London as, 'full of shops and of warehouses and of all that may serve to the comfort or the use of man'.[68]

5

The Whole Trade of Merchandise

London's growth was based on its large, expanding and increasingly diversified economy, with greater specialization and new trades and industries. Both the trading companies, for those engaged in overseas commerce, and the livery companies, which regulated the City's trades, were adapted as circumstances changed. New companies were created, reflecting the changing patterns of trade and growing variety of ways in which to earn a living. Merchants, wholesalers, retailers, artisans, members of the professions, victuallers and those who provided transport formed the backbone of the workforce. But many Londoners worked outside the framework of the companies and regulated trades, taking a range of employment, and forming a pool of semi-skilled and unskilled labour. They congregated in the poorer areas, especially the suburbs, and, with the prostitutes, were viewed by the civic authorities with concern, as a potentially resentful and disruptive underclass.

Around 1580 James Dalton divided the working population of London into three categories: merchants, handicraftsmen and labourers, but subdivided the first category into three groups. Merchants were those who traded overseas, wholesalers gathered goods in the city and distributed them around the country, and retailers kept shops.[1] The trading companies defined the distinctions between these groups in order to limit their membership to those who were merchants. A member of the Merchant Adventurers Company who was 'resident in London or in the suburbes' should not 'keepe any open shoppe or shewe house of his wares'. The company's regulations also set out the minimum quantities of goods that he could sell; any member who sold smaller quantities would be classed as a retailer, and so would lose his membership. In practice, the distinction between merchants trading abroad and wholesalers was not clear cut, as Thomas Wilson acknowledged in his *A discourse upon usurie*:

> The merchant adventurer is and maye be taken for a lordes fellow in dignitie, as well for hys hardye adventurynge upon the seas, to carrye our plentye, as for his royall and noble whole sales that he makes to dyvers men upon hys retourne, when he bryngeth in our want.

Retailers, on the other hand, were small traders who were 'not worthy the name of merchaunts, but of hucksters, or chapmen of choyse... retailing small wares'.[2]

The merchants were those who operated on a large scale, and made the greatest profits. In 1607 Niccolò Molin wrote: 'It is a common opinion that the wealth of these citizens is very great and entirely the fruit of trade and commerce, which is carried on by means of companies.'[3] By the sixteenth century most of England's foreign trade was conducted through London, which handled roughly four-fifths of imports and exports at the end of the century. This dominance was much complained of by merchants in the provincial ports, such as those at Hull, who grumbled that, 'all the whole trade of merchandize is in a maner brought to the Citie of London'.[4] But the pattern was too firmly established to be altered, as the Londoners had the capital and contacts required, and the city and court provided a large and wealthy market close at hand.

In 1599, Thomas Platter watched the merchants trading in the Royal Exchange, commenting that 'several hundred may be found assembled twice daily... buying, selling, bearing news and doing business generally'. He wrote that they, 'buy, sell and trade in all the corners of the globe... ships from France, the Netherlands, Germany and other countries land in this city, bringing goods with them and loading others in exchange for exportation'.[5] De Maisse was impressed by the number of vessels on the Thames, writing in 1597 that, 'it is a magnificent sight to see the number of ships and boats which lie at anchor, insomuch that for two leagues [roughly six miles] you see nothing but ships that serve as well for war as for traffic'. Molin, too, made especial mention of the 'large number of ships from three to four hundred tons burden, which come in upon the tide from all parts of the world'.[6]

De Maisse explained that the London merchants had become dominant in England's overseas trade:

> Everything that comes from the Levant and Venice is in their hands, and they no longer allow any stranger to carry merchandise, not that they forbid it, but they so harass them with taxes and seizures on their vessels that it is not possible to endure it.

And so French merchants had stopped trading with England, for if one did try to do so, 'he is perpetually troubled'. Yet English merchants went to the Rouen fairs in fifteen or twenty vessels 'full of merchandise free without paying anything on them'.[7] He was correct in his assessment that foreign merchants had largely ceased trading with London. This was not entirely because of harassment, as he alleged. Italian merchants had almost disappeared from London after the ending of the Adventurers' arrangement with Antwerp, the Italians' base in north-west Europe.

William Harrison regarded this as a bad development, because English merchants now had a monopoly, 'and so are the high prices of wares kept up'. Writing in 1587, he commented that when foreign ships had brought in their own commodities they 'were far better cheap and more plentifully to be had'.[8] Trade had been conducted with northern and western Europe, to Spain, Portugal, France, Flanders, Denmark, Norway, Scotland and Ireland, but now:

> as men not contented with these journeys, they have sought out the East and West Indies and made now and then suspicious [exploratory] journeys not only unto the Canaries, and New Spain, but likewise unto Cathaia, Muscovia, Tartaria and the regions thereabouts.

From there the merchants 'bring home great commodities. But alas, I see not by all their travel that the prices of things are any whit abated'. And the export of goods reduced the supply of those items on the home market, raising their prices, too. It was the merchants themselves who benefited, as Thomas Wilson wrote in 1600: 'It is well known that at this time there are in London some merchants worth £100,000 and he is not accounted rich that cannot reach to £50,000 or near it.'[9]

De Maisse was aware of their developing markets, writing that, 'They trade also in Poland, Muscovy, and as far as Persia.'[10] The establishment of trading companies indicates the new areas of trade. The Muscovy Company was established in 1555, the Eastland Company in 1579 (trading with Scandinavia and the Baltic), the Turkey Company in 1581, the Venice Company in 1583 (the Turkey and Venice companies became the Levant Company in 1592), the East India Company in 1600 and the Virginia Company in 1609. Trade with Morocco began in 1551 and the Barbary Company was established in 1585, but was dissolved in 1597.

Ottoman expansion in Europe provoked the formation of an alliance by the Catholic states around the Mediterranean, which struck a mighty blow with the destruction of the Ottoman fleet at Lepanto in 1571. English foreign policy took a different course and by the end of the decade England was an ally of the Ottoman empire, opposed to the ambitions of Philip II of Spain. In 1580 William Harborne, a London merchant, obtained trading privileges for English merchants and trade developed steadily, based on Aleppo and Smyrna. In a report to the Venice authorities, Molin used the example of the Levant Company, which was affecting Venetian trade, to explain the nature of the trading companies:

> the Levant Company, and the others as well, is a close guild of men trading in the Levant, and no one who is not enrolled in the company is allowed to trade in any territory belonging to the Turk... this company and the others also, govern themselves.[11]

He added that some of its members had made large fortunes. Among them was Richard Staper, whose monument, erected in St Mary Outwich church after his death in 1608 (now in St Helen, Bishopsgate), is appropriately surmounted by a galleon. The inscription proudly records that Staper was 'the greatest merchant in his Tyme, the chiefest actor in discoveri of The trades of Turkey and East India'.

Until the 1560s exports had largely consisted of woollen cloth shipped to Antwerp by members of the Merchants Adventurers Company. They traded as individuals, not collectively through the company, which was a regulatory body dominated by around fifty London merchants. The connection with Antwerp came to an end in 1569 when the Adventurers moved their staple to Hamburg for political reasons, and it ceased to be a significant trading city after its sack by Spanish troops in 1576 and its capture by them in 1585. Other ports were used, including Stade on the Elbe, Middelburg in Zeeland and Elbing in the Baltic. In 1587–8 roughly seventy per cent of English trade was with north European ports, from Rouen to Hamburg, and a dozen years later 941 of the 1,037 English vessels that arrived at London came from ports in the Netherlands, France, Norway and Germany. The Baltic trade was harder to penetrate, as Dutch merchants obtained control over the carrying trade of the region. Only four English vessels arrived from the Atlantic, but this was to expand considerably during the early seventeenth century. After the peace treaty with Spain in 1604, trade with Spain and Portugal increased, and that with the Mediterranean also expanded, based on Leghorn (Livorno) in Italy and the Levant.

Broad cloths from the west of England formed the staple export item to northern Europe, but they were too heavy for the new markets in the Mediterranean, India and the East Indies, and the lighter cloth known as the 'new draperies' from East Anglia formed the basis of exports to those regions. Generally, cloth was exported unfinished and not dyed, described as 'in the white'. According to one estimate, by 1614 1,500 broad cloths were sold weekly in London, which cost £12,000. Finished cloth naturally commanded higher prices, but foreign merchants complained that the quality of English finished cloth was inferior and the Privy Council was told that, 'The strangers beyond sea dye and dress the cloths more truly and more cheaply, than the English do.'[12]

In 1614 William Cockayne developed a scheme to export only finished cloth. He was a wealthy London merchant and member of the Eastland Company who had succeeded to his father's business and made a fortune, chiefly in selling cloth to the Baltic. Cockayne served as Sheriff in 1609–10 and as an Alderman from 1609. He lent money to James I. Despite the difficulty of selling finished cloth abroad, he persuaded the king that it should be the principal export. The argument which he presented to the Privy Council made the point that, 'the country shall receive more benefit by dressing of cloths at home, than sending them unwrought abroad'.[13] Cloth worth £700,000 was exported yearly, bringing the crown £40,000 from customs dues, but that was declining and James saw the proposal as a way of increasing the crown's revenues. Members of the Privy Council were concerned that such a fundamental change in the country's export trade was taking a major risk. Nevertheless, the king issued a proclamation 'against the Exportation of Clothes, undyed and undressed'.[14] Because the Merchant Adventurers Company opposed the policy, the king withdrew its privileges and licensed the New Company of Merchant Adventurers, with a core membership that consisted of Eastland merchants.

The Dutch responded by banning imports of dyed and dressed cloths, to protect their own industry, 'because they will have their inhabitants employed'.[15] James then prohibited exports of wool, the essential raw material for the Dutch cloth industry. This trade war was an inauspicious beginning for the new company, which was set export targets of 6,000 finished cloths in its first year, rising by 6,000 in each of the following two years. Initially, English cloth exports to the Baltic rose at the expense of Dutch shipments, but a report made in September 1616 noted that only 1,400 cloths had been sent on the first of the two 'shippings' that year. Clearly, the target for the year would not be met. And Cockayne had to admit that the higher value cloths could not be sold in the Low Countries and so the new company was selling 'cloths of lesser value'.[16] Even without the Dutch action the export figures would have been very difficult to achieve, not least because of the time needed to develop the finishing and dyeing industries to the level required. Nor could the overseas markets for English cloth be manipulated so easily. Sales to the Baltic could not compensate for exports to Holland and Germany, which virtually collapsed, the clothiers were put out of work, the London merchants lost business and so the policy failed, having created a major trade crisis.

In 1617 the new company was dissolved and the old Merchant Adventurers Company was restored, with a Privy Council declaration that it was 'now his Majesty's pleasure and resolution not to disturb the trade of whites with any further essay, but to leave the same to the train and course of trade now in practice and according to the use before the late alteration'.[17] But this reversion to the former pattern took time and one reason given, a few years later, for 'the decay of trade' was the 'untimely project of dyeing and dressing of cloths before transportation'.[18]

Cockayne was knighted in 1616, after entertaining the king at his house in Broad Street. He retained James's confidence even after the collapse of the project and went on to serve as Lord Mayor in 1619–20. He was worth more than £72,000 when he died in 1626. Cockayne was buried in St Paul's, where a monument, with effigies of him and his wife, was erected on the south side of the choir in one of the most prominent places in the City's cathedral. His career illustrates the prominence to which a London merchant could attain, wealthy enough to lend to the crown, and having such influence with the monarch as to be able to alter a major aspect of national economic policy. He bought landed estates in Leicestershire and Northamptonshire and his eldest daughter married into the aristocracy, marrying Charles Howard, Baron Howard of Effingham.

Even without the crisis caused by the Cockayne Project, high-value imports were becoming more important sources of profit for the merchants than their cloth shipments. The range of imports greatly expanded, with pepper, currants, spices, wines, silk, cotton, indigo, calico, dyes, sugar and tobacco being brought into the port of London. Wine imports rose fivefold between 1563 and 1620. Tobacco was brought to Europe from the West Indies and Florida as early as 1560 and by the 1590s was being grown in gardens, 'where it doth prosper exceedingly... it is dispersed into most parts of London'.[19] Smoking was so well established by James I's reign that he condemned the habit in his *A Counter-Blaste to Tobacco* (1604), with the phrase 'there cannot be a more base, and yet hurtfull, corruption in a Countrey, than is the vile use (or rather abuse) of taking Tobacco in this Kingdome'. Despite his disapproval, demand was such that it became a commercial crop, not just a garden plant. Colonizing voyages in 1606 and 1607 established the colony of Virginia and after tobacco plants were introduced from Trinidad, tobacco became its major cash crop, exported to London in increasing quantities from the mid-1610s.

Merchants could obtain imports by investing in privateering. On the outbreak of war between England and Spain in 1585, the Spanish authorities seized English vessels and their cargoes. The English government's response was to license privateers, which were authorized to take cargoes from Spanish ships. Some merchants invested in such operations and reaped excellent returns. Before the war, Sir John Watts had traded with Spain, the Canary Islands and the Azores, and when those trades were interrupted by the conflict, he switched to privateering. One voyage in 1591 probably netted him £40,000. A group of London merchants invested £6,000 in the voyage in 1592 during which the Portuguese vessel the *Madre de Dios* was captured and brought to England, with an immensely valuable cargo that made it richer than 'any shypp that ever came into England'.[20] Their share of the profits was £12,000, a return of one hundred per cent. Less spectacular, but still satisfactory, was the thirty per cent which Sir Thomas Myddelton gained on an outlay of £1,500 in one voyage.

The merchants' chief market for high-value imports was metropolitan and in the expanding entrepôt trade, re-exporting goods to foreign ports. But some merchants acted as wholesalers, sending their agents to the provincial towns and fairs to sell their wares, or going themselves. George Bolles, a member of the Grocers' Company, supplied goods to the hinterland of Hull and Gainsborough. In 1596 the inhabitants of Gainsborough complained that London merchants and their agents had 'drawn away almost all the trade from the said port'. He came from a Lincolnshire family and married the daughter of Sir John Hart, Lord Mayor in 1589–90, which brought him the manor of Scampton in that county. Knighted by James I, Bolles was elected an Alderman in 1607, served as Sheriff in 1608 and as Lord Mayor in 1617–18. He died in 1621; his son John was created a baronet in 1628.[21]

At a more modest level, Robert Gray sold goods at fairs in Bristol, Exeter and Beverley between 1606 and 1618, and sent instructions to his agent Ames Baker at Chester, planning to send him on to Dublin. One of Gray's customers at Chester had bought goods worth almost £400, and he despatched to Baker 'a parsell of extreordynary good wares' that weighed two hundredweight. He also kept a shop in London, which caused him considerable anxiety while he was away. He told his wife Anne to 'be as much in the shope as well you maye and put the folks in mynde of ther besynes other wayes yt will not be well performed by them as yt should be, for they ar verye neclygent in ther besynes and doth yt by halffes'. On another occasion he mentioned that when any money was received 'praye your mother to take yt, that yt doe not lye about the shope, wherby ther should be any wantes'. He required one of his assistants, Wench, to deal with the chapmen who might call at the shop: 'I pray see that when any of our costomares com to London that Wench be verye carfull to sarve them that ar good men; and for the other lett them goe'.[22] This was clearly a business on a considerable scale, operated by the family, with employees (some of doubtful competence), in which the wholesaler traded both in person and through an agent, and from his shop in the city.

London seemed to be full of shops, with great variety, as Orazio Busino explained: 'all the houses along the streets of the city with the exception of some few palaces are shops of divers artificers of every trade, and each house has its sign or mark like an inn'. He found one district to be:

entirely inhabited by booksellers... Then there are the other streets of feather sellers, while certain mechanics make horn flowers and rosettes, as delicately wrought as if they were of the finest cambric. They paint them various colours. There is a suburb of gunsmiths; others only make bows and arrows. Some manufacture very handsome proof corslets, for the wear of the pikemen. There are several falconers' shops, whose proprietors do nothing at all but train birds of every sort for such as are fond of sport.[23]

Richard Quiney of Stratford-upon-Avon was typical of provincial mercers who bought stock in London. He was there in 1598, to petition for some respite for Stratford from national taxation. Because of devastating fires in 1594 and 1595, its citizens were unable to 'undergoe the Burthen of the subsedies and taxe impoesed uppon them'.[24] While he was there his wife sent him cheese to sell, and asked him to buy raisins, currants, pepper, sugar and other groceries 'if the price be reasonable'. Shakespeare's metropolitan audience at *The Winter's Tale* no doubt smiled at the pretentiousness of the newly-rich shepherd and his son's shopping-list for their sheep-shearing feast, which included some expensive items imported from the Mediterranean, the Levant and the East Indies: sugar, currants, rice, saffron, dates, nutmegs, mace [the outer part of a nutmeg], ginger, prunes [dried plums] and raisins [dried grapes].[25] Yet Quiney's business shows that such produce was indeed traded through the capital to the country towns, for sale to wealthy burghers and gentry.

Perhaps because of costs incurred in London on Stratford's affairs, as well as his own business, Quiney found himself deeper in debt than he would wish. He therefore wrote to Shakespeare, from the Bell Inn in Carter Lane near St Paul's, asking for a loan, although he did not send the letter:

Loveinge Contreyman I am bolde of you as of a frende, craving your helpe with xxxli uppon Mr Bushells & my securytee or Mr Mytton with me. Mr Rosswell is nott come to London as yeate & I have especiall cawse. Yow shall frende me muche in helping me out of all the debetts I owe in London I thancke god & muche quiet my mynde which wolde nott be indebeted.[26]

This episode exemplifies the connections between London and the provinces. A mercer who was in London to petition the government on behalf of his town, he bought and sold for his own business while he was there, and because his credit was stretched, approached someone known to him who had moved from that town to the metropolis, where he had prospered. His mission on behalf of Stratford was a success, for the town was excused its tax payments and granted a share in a fund for decayed and impoverished towns. And Quiney received his expenses.

Those merchants who made money from overseas trade and distribution used their profits to diversify, by trading to new destinations, investing in manufacturing and by lending, to the crown and the aristocracy. Of the 140 men who served as aldermen during the first quarter of the seventeenth century, 55 were worth more than £20,000 in goods when they died, and most of the others had personal estates of between £10,000 and £20,000.[27]

The goldsmiths, too, invested their wealth and engaged in money-lending. They fell into Dalton's grouping which he described as handicraftsmen, consisting of 'those which do exercise such arts as require both labour and cunning [skill], as goldsmiths, tailors, and haberdashers, skinners, etc.'[28] In practice, his categories were increasingly out of date, as the distinction between wholesaling, retailing and manufacture became less clear cut and the number of trades and specializations proliferated.

New industries established as a result of the growing range of imports included silk-weaving, sugar refining, and glass, vinegar, starch, pin and paper making. And, as the number of vessels rose, the shipbuilding industry grew. Between 1591 and 1618 some 317 ships over 100 tons were built on the Thames, the output being greatly increased after the East India Company established shipyards at Deptford in 1609 and Blackwall in 1614. Some of the growing, specialized, trades attempted to break away from the control of the existing livery companies by establishing their own guilds, such as the felt-makers, glovers and pin-makers. The companies struggled to prevent this and to maintain control over their trades. That was complicated by the practice, complained of by the weavers in 1595, of switching trades, that is, qualifying in one trade and joining the appropriate livery company, but subsequently practising another. In *The Customer's Alphabet* of 1608, Thomas Milles complained that, 'outrunning all the wisdom and prudence of the land, men live by trades they never learned, nor seek to understand'.[29] New trades, such as silk-weaving, were bound to draw some of their labour from other trades. This appeared to threaten the status quo, which was justified by the claim that it maintained high quality products. In reality, such switching of trades was indicative of London's dynamic economy, generating new jobs and skills.

Yet the traditional trades remained dominant, in terms of numbers employed. Clothing was the largest of the city's groups of trades, employing over one-fifth of the workforce, and the leather trades, especially shoemaking, and metal trades each employed almost ten per cent. The founders were based in Lothbury, where John Stow noted that they produced, 'candlesticks, chafing-dishes, spice mortars, and such like copper or laton works'. These were polished 'to make them smooth and bright with turning and scrating (as some do term it), making a loathsome noise to the by-passers that have not been used to the like'.[30] Some enterprises required larger sites than were available within the City and were centred in the suburbs. Bell founders were located in Whitechapel from the early fifteenth century and the Whitechapel Bell Foundry was established in 1570.

The cloth trade was difficult to regulate, if only because of the numbers involved. As well as the prominent men who were members of the companies, others were engaged in the trade. In 1612 the Merchant Taylors complained about those who were not members of the company or freemen of the city yet they, 'use dayly to kepe Chambers secretly in aleys and upon steyers & houses in corners, and cutte & make almaner of garmentes'.[31] This was a case of a trade being practised surreptitiously in small premises outside the company's control. Regulation of products was becoming less of a priority for the companies generally, because their officers increasingly came from the commercial not the manufacturing side of the trade: 'the shopkeepers growing riche doe make the workemen their underlings'. This was highlighted by the leather workers in 1619, when they complained that their company was now controlled by leather-sellers, who were 'men of other trades as braziers, hosiers, etc' and so were 'incapable to governe us through their ignorance'. They bought and sold leather 'without altering the properties of it' and their concern was their own profit, not the benefit to the workmen.[32]

Another example of the difficulty of supervision was provided by the relatively new trade of vinegar making. As a taste for malt vinegars developed, so did the industry, stimulated by Dutch refugees arriving from the 1560s onwards. It divided between those who claimed to use good ale and beer as ingredients, and the smaller makers, who produced 'corrupt vinegar, made of corrupt beer and ale'. In 1593 the makers of the 'good' vinegars attempted to get a royal grant, 'for the taking care that these Liquors should be well made, against the pretended great and dangerous Abuses commonly practised in the making thereof'. This would exclude from the trade those 'who are poor and find more sweet by making it of weaker beer or ale or of worse stuff'. Lord Burghley appointed Alderman Anthony Radclyff, 'a Person knowing in such Matters', to investigate the trade. His enquiries led him to wonder why so much of the 'Hog-wash and Dreggs' from brewing were being sold, only to be told that it quenched the thirst of felt makers and weavers. This was intended to mislead him, but after he chanced upon a brewer's drayman in the act of unloading barrels of dregs at a vinegar maker's yard, he became aware of the nature of the operation. Here was another back-street trade in which, 'the ordinary Makers of these Liquors' apparently were thriving, despite the hostile attentions of 'the substantialest men' in the trade.[33]

London's rulers at Guildhall also became concerned about abuses in the developing silk industry. When asked by the government if it should be incorporated as a company, Common Council responded that this was unnecessary because of existing statutes, it would cause unemployment, and would be harmful to the Levant and East India Companies. But because of growing awareness of such bad practices as false weaving, dyeing and weights, its members changed their minds and issued an act of Common Council to prevent the 'deceitfull Dying of Silke' in London. This was followed up by a royal proclamation of 1612 which prohibited, 'the deceitfull dying of silke, or bringing in or selling of Silk deceitfully dyed'. The problem was the illicit use of a gumming agent that increased the weight of black silk, even doubling it, so that the silk was, 'so rotted, corrupted & spoiled, that it is not fit to be worne or used'. Yet it was 'falsly made faire to the eye, to deceive the buyer and wearer thereof'. Such abuses had to be suppressed, to maintain the reputation of London's products, and in trades not effectively supervised by a livery company, both the corporation and the government felt the need to intervene.[34]

Other trades developed that produced high-value items for the luxury market. A glasshouse was established by Jacob Verzelini *c.*1570 in the former priory of the Crutched Friars, which was burnt down in 1575. He then transferred the business to the refectory of the former Augustine friary in Broad Street. In 1574 Elizabeth I granted a patent to Verzelini as:

> James Verselyne a Venetian, inhabitinge within oure cittie of London, who hathe sette uppe within oure said cittie one furneys and sette on worke dyvers and sondrie parsonnes for the makynge of drynkynge glasses such as be accustomablie made in the towne of Morano.[35]

The manufactory specialized in making wine glasses in the Venetian style. In 1592 the monopoly of glass production was acquired by Sir Jerome Bowes and in 1615 by Sir Robert Mansell.

The cutlery produced in London became known for its fine quality; in 1615 Edmund Howes wrote that 'at this day the best and finest knives in the world are made in London'. Cutlers from abroad who had settled in St Martin-le-Grand developed a reputation for the quality of their product.[36] London's coach-makers had also become well-regarded and when Breuning von Buchenbach came to Elizabeth's court on a diplomatic mission for Count Frederick of Württemberg, in 1595, he was under instructions to buy a coach for his master:

In the matter of the coach I walked all over London. I did not overlook a single coach-builder, and also saw a large number of coaches and carriages, but none that pleased me better, keeping in mind my instructions, than the one which I have bought for Your Grace.

The coach and harness cost £34.[37]

The court was the principal market for those dealing in luxury items and high-value imports. Von Buchenbach attended a function at which the Knights of the Garter were present, together with 'many other earls, lords and knights. They all wore gold and silver dress and their raiment was embroidered with precious stones and pearls. At no other Court have I seen so much splendour and such fine clothes.'[38] Extravagance at court increased after James I's accession, illustrated by the career of James Hay. The king made Hay a Gentleman of the Privy Chamber in 1603 and Master of the Robes in 1605. He lived in great style and was famous for his lavish banquets, spending £2,000 or £3,000 on an especially important one. By 1618 he had run up debts of £42,000 and after his death the Earl of Clarendon estimated that in his lifetime he had spent more than £400,000, a staggering sum. Hay set a level of sumptuousness in dress and feasting that others could not match, but nor could they be seen to behave in a niggardly way.

In addition to the annual round at court, special occasions required exceptional outlay, such as James's coronation, the visit of Christian IV, and the marriage of Princess Elizabeth to Frederick, Elector Palatine. In 1603 Henry Crosse commented censoriously that, 'every man has fallen in love with himself... his mind is set on fashions, fangles and garish clothes'.[39] Dekker wrote expressively of the tradesmen's reactions:

Now the thriftie Citizen casts beyond the Moone, and seeing the golden age returned into the world againe, resolves to worship no Saint but money. Trades that lay dead & rotten, and were in all mens opinion utterly dambd, started out of their trance... and swore to fall to their olde occupations. Taylors meant no more to be called Merchant-taylors but Merchants.[40]

For her marriage in 1613, the Princess's trousseau was assembled under Hay's direction and cost more than £10,000. The deaths of the wealthy and those of high rank also required considerable expenditure, on mourning clothes. Outlay on the funeral of Lord Hunsdon, in 1596, included payment for 1,232 yards of black cloth given to the mourners and seventy mourning gowns for poor men attending the ceremony. These 'blacks' cost £836, in a total of £1,097, paid by the queen.[41] Supplying courtiers with finery and mourning cloth was very profitable for those who were so favoured, providing they could obtain payment.

Stylish dress was not confined to courtiers. Jacob Rothgeb commented in 1592 that English women:

> go dressed out in exceedingly fine clothes, and give all their attention to their ruffs and stuffs, to such a degree indeed, that, as I am informed, many a one does not hesitate to wear velvet in the streets, which is common with them, whilst at home perhaps they have not a piece of dry bread.

This conveyed the priority which they gave to their clothes. Most visitors mentioned that English women were well dressed. Samuel Kiechel, in 1585, remarked that, 'they dress in splendid stuffs, and many a one wears three cloth gowns or petticoats, one over the other'. Another characteristic, according to Emanuel van Meteren, was that, 'they change very easily, and that every year, to the astonishment of many'. The practice of dressing finely and changing outfits regularly provided good business for those engaged in supplying fabrics and making clothes, including hats.[42]

Among those whose goods were bought for Princess Elizabeth's nuptials was Robert Baker, a tailor in the Strand. Orphaned as a boy he worked as a tailor in Taunton before moving to London, where he 'wrought as a Journeyman att Mr. Brales the Taylor'. In 1600 he married Elizabeth Nightingale at St Martin-in-the-Fields. She was described as a 'flaxwoman', and they combined their skills and opened a shop in St Martin's Lane. Within a few years they moved to 'a flax shoppe' in the Strand, which was much better placed for attracting the custom of courtiers and members of the gentry. There they specialized in making 'Pickadillys for most of the Nobilitie and Gentrie' in their workshop, where about sixty people were employed. A piccadill or piccadilly was a decorative high collar, or ruff, then much in fashion. The word was used by Thomas Dekker and John Webster in *Northward Hoe* (1607): 'A short dutch wast with a round cathern-wheele fardingale: a close sleeue with a cartoose collour and a pickadell.'[43]

The Bakers had a stroke of good fortune, because their shop was next to the site where the New Exchange was built in 1609, which drew a regular stream of wealthy customers past their door. Elizabeth died in 1614 and Robert remarried in 1615. He had bought land in St Martin's parish, where he erected a house, which by September 1614 was known as Pickadilly Hall, from the item of clothing which had made his fortune. He died a wealthy man in 1623, with land worth £200 a year, but the small estate which he had acquired was broken up later in the seventeenth century. Nevertheless, Piccadilly came to be the name of a district, a street and Piccadilly Circus, set out in 1819, which became one of London's best-known landmarks. Robert and his wife used their skills and business acumen to exploit the demand for a fashionable article of dress, providing a notable rags-to-riches story of the Jacobean period.[44]

Those who bought Baker's fashionable ruffs would have included prosperous lawyers from the nearby legal quarter, one of the professions increasing in numbers and wealth. Their business came not only from cases heard in the courts at Westminster, but from land sales, marriage settlements and money lending. Scriveners wrote out the documents and also became involved in financial business. Posts were available in the bureaucracy, with the government and the City. Clement Edmondes served in both. An Oxford graduate, he had settled in St Alphage's parish by 1598. In 1601 he became assistant to the Remembrancer of the City of London, Dr Giles Fletcher, receiving half the fee, and when Fletcher resigned in 1605 Edmondes succeeded him, at an annual salary of £100. Four years later he was appointed one of the four clerks to the Privy Council, for life, and was knighted in 1617. There were also administrative posts in the households of the leading statesmen and members of the aristocracy.

Most graduates aspired to a career in the church, but London's small parishes provided low stipends. Many of the livings were poor and so were held in plurality, and the curates' stipends were notoriously low, although opportunities were increased with the creation of lectureships. Other graduates became schoolmasters. The grammar schools provided few posts, with four at Merchant Taylors' and two at Charterhouse, for example. But there were many private schools run by the master himself or, as in Southwark, by the parish. After serving as the first headmaster of the Merchant Taylors' School for thirty-five years, from 1561 until 1586, Richard Mulcaster kept a school of his own, in Milk Street, before being appointed to a post at St Paul's School, in 1596. Thomas Farnaby's school in Cripplegate was so successful that, according to Sir John Bramston, a former pupil, 'he had 2, sometymes three, ushers besides himselfe'.[45] And the aristocracy and gentry employed tutors for their children. London provided a greater concentration of teaching posts than any other city, but they were not well paid and offered a fragile living.

London was also the centre of the medical profession, with the hospitals of St Bartholomew and St Thomas, the Bethlehem hospital, outside Bishopsgate, for the mentally ill, and the College of Physicians. The college was founded in 1518 by Royal Charter, on the advice of Thomas Linacre, the King's Physician. It had powers to license and regulate medical practice, and to punish unlicensed practitioners and prevent them from practising. Its licensing powers originally applied only to London, but in 1523 were extended to the rest of the country. The college's first premises were in Linacre's house in Knightrider Street, south of St Paul's, enlarged in 1583 with the addition of an anatomy theatre. In 1614 it acquired a new building in Amen Corner. Its most distinguished member during the period was Sir William Harvey, discoverer of the circulation of the blood.

The physicians were the élite of the medical profession. The more numerous surgeons were members of the Barber-Surgeons' Company, and

Above left: 53. The corner of Chancery Lane and Fleet Street, shown in an etching of 1789 by J.T. Smith. The large building was erected in the mid-sixteenth century and was typical of those built in the principal streets in Tudor London. The corporation demolished it in 1799, to widen the entrance to Chancery Lane.

Above right: 54. Jacobean houses at the corner of Hosier Street and Smithfield, which narrowly escaped the Great Fire and were demolished in 1809. They are shown on an etching by J.T. Smith of 1795.

Above left: 55. Houses with plaster fronts on the south side of London Wall, which dated from the early seventeenth century. They are shown in an etching by J.T. Smith of 1808.

Above right: 56. Early seventeenth-century houses on the south side of Leadenhall Street, which escaped the Great Fire, from an etching by J.T. Smith of 1796. The building at the right was the Cock tavern.

Above: 57. The Elizabethan range of Staple Inn, facing Holborn, is the best surviving half-timbered group in London, erected in 1586. Staple Inn was the largest of the Inns of Chancery. The photograph was taken c.1920.

Left: 58. Inigo Jones (1573–1652) was born in Smithfield and gained prominence as a designer of court events and as an architect. He was appointed James I's Surveyor General in 1615 and designed the Queen's House at Greenwich, begun in 1616, and the Banqueting House of Whitehall Palace, built in 1619–22. He was one of England's outstanding architects and was highly influential in his employment of the Classical style.

59. Paul's Cross, a pulpit adjoining the cathedral where open-air services were held, which were attended by large crowds. The galleries behind the congregation are the royal box and the corporation's gallery, for the Lord Mayor and Aldermen.

Above left: 60. The interior of Hatfield House shows the ornate style adopted in the aristocracy's building projects during the reign of James I. It cost Sir Robert Cecil almost £39,000 between 1607 and 1612, and he also erected Salisbury House and the New Exchange, in the Strand.

Above right: 61. Sir Walter Raleigh, soldier and courtier under Elizabeth I, imprisoned in the Tower of London by James I, from 1603 until his execution in 1618. His major work was *The History of the World*, published in 1614.

Left: 62. Richard Tarleton, drawn by John Scottowe. Tarleton was a jester at Elizabeth I's court and from the 1570s he became the most celebrated theatrical clown of the period, from 1583 as a member of the Queen's Men. He died in 1588.

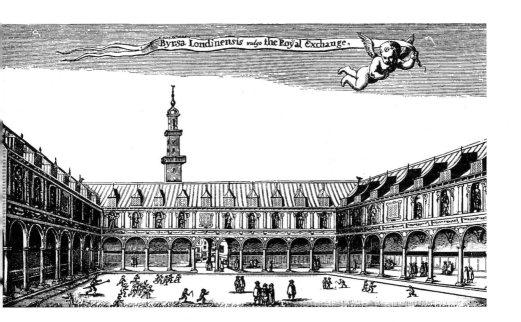

Byrsa Londinensis vulgo the Royal Exchange.

Above: 63. The courtyard of the Royal Exchange, looking south, drawn by Wenceslaus Hollar in 1644. The Exchange was founded by Sir Thomas Gresham and completed in 1568. It quickly became the focus for London's merchant community, for trading and the exchange of news and information.

Right: 64. Monument to John Stow (1525–1605) in the church of St Andrew, Undershaft. His magnificent history of London was published in 1598. His wife Elizabeth arranged for the monument, which shows him writing at a table in an alcove which has marble books on its inner walls. It has the inscription: 'He exercised the most careful accuracy in searching ancient monuments, English annals, and records of the City of London. He wrote excellently and deserved well both of his own and subsequent ages.' The quill is changed annually by the Lord Mayor, at a service held to mark the anniversary of his death.

STAT SCRIBENDA AGERE · STAT LEGENDA SCRIBERE

65. This section of Anthonis van den Wyngaerde's pen-and-ink drawing of c.1544 shows St Paul's Cathedral, with its tall spire, rising above the huddle of buildings. In the foreground is Southwark, with the frontage of two-storey houses in its High Street

broken by the Earl of Suffolk's house, Southwark Place, which was to be demolished in the following decade. To the west of St Mary Overy church and close to the river is the Bishop of Winchester's palace.

Above: 66. Cheapside in the early seventeenth century. This was the city's principal street, lined with imposing buildings. Cheapside Cross was one of the Eleanor crosses, where the body of Edward I's queen lay overnight on the journey from Harby, Nottinghamshire, where she died in 1290, to Westminster Abbey. It was demolished in 1643. Beyond it is the fountain known as the Standard.

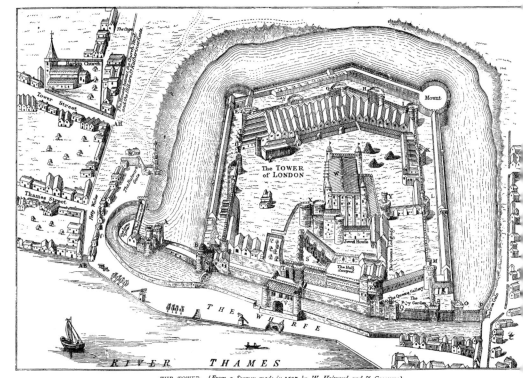

THE TOWER. (*From a Survey made in* 1597 *by* W. Haiward *and* J. Gascoyne.)

A Middle Tower.   B. Tower at the Gate.   C. Bell Tower.   D. Beauchamp Tower.   E. Devilin Tower.   F. Flint Tower.   G. Bowyer Tower.   H. Brick Tower.   I. Martin Tower.   K. Cons
Tower.   L. Broad Arrow Tower.   M. Salt Tower.   N Well Tower.   O. Tower leading to Iron Gate.   P. Tower above Iron Gate.   Q. Cradle Tower.   R. Lantern Tower.   S. Hall Tower.   T. B
Tower.   V. St. Thomas's Tower.   W. Cæsar's, or White Tower.   X. Cole Harbour.   Y. Wardrobe Tower.   A B. House at Water Gate, called the Ram's Head.   A H. End of Tower Street.

Above: 68. St Paul's and the Blackfriars district in the mid-sixteenth century. The cathedral is shown after its spire had been destroyed by fire in 1561. On the riverfront is Baynard's Castle, rebuilt by Humphrey, Duke of Gloucester, in the mid-fifteenth century. A scene of Shakespeare's *Richard III* is set there, in which the Duke of Buckingham offers the throne to an outwardly reluctant and pious Richard, Duke of Gloucester, in the presence of the Lord Mayor, Aldermen and citizens. To the west is Blackfriars. In 1613 Shakespeare bought the gatehouse of the former priory precinct; other parts of the buildings were adapted as theatres, in 1576 and 1596.

Opposite below: 67. The Tower of London as surveyed in 1597. It remained a fortress and an arsenal, and contained the Royal Mint and the royal menagerie. State prisoners were incarcerated there.

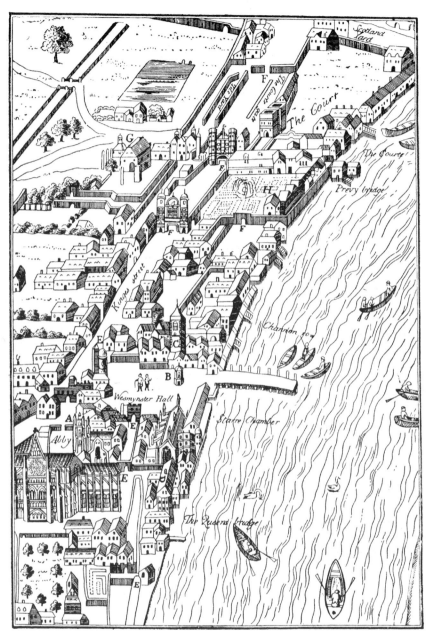

A, St. Margaret's; B, Fountain; C, Clock Tower; D, Parliament House (St. Stephen's Cha
E, Palace Gates; F, Gates; G, Cockpit; H, Queen's Garden.

69. This plan-view of Westminster and Whitehall in the mid-sixteenth century
shows St Peter's abbey in the foreground, with Westminster Hall, and Whitehall
Palace beyond. King Street was the public road from Westminster to Charing
Cross and ran through the palace. The river wherries provided convenient
transport into the city.

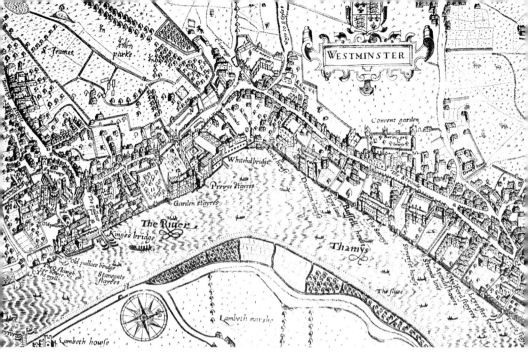

70. John Norden's plan of Westminster of 1593. St Peter's Abbey, the cluster of nearby buildings and those in Tothill Street mark the edge of the city. North of Westminster is Whitehall Palace, with Charing Cross beyond. The Strand runs from the Cross to Temple Bar at the boundary of the City. This was the aristocrats' quarter of London, containing their palaces and the courtiers' houses.

71. The Star, or Starred, Chamber, was built by Edward II as part of Westminster Palace and survived the fire which destroyed much of the palace in 1512. It gave its name to the court which sat there. This drawing was made in 1836.

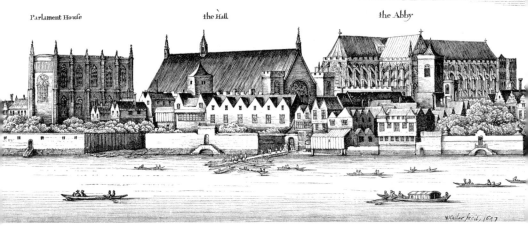

Parlament Houſe the Hall the Abby

W. Hollar fecit, 1647

Above: 72. Westminster from the river, by Wenceslaus Hollar, 1647, with its three prominent buildings: the Parliament House, Westminster Hall and St Peter's Abbey. St Peter's Abbey, early in the eighteenth-century, became known as Westminster Abbey.

Left: 73. King Street Gate, Whitehall Palace, built as part of Henry VIII's remodelling of the former York Place as a royal palace, after 1529. The gate was demolished in 1728. Engraving by George Vertue, 1725.

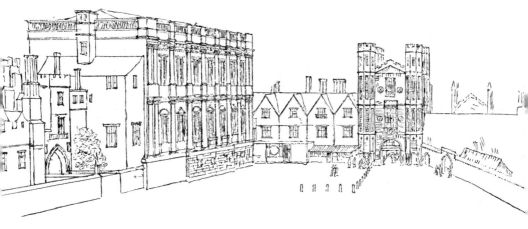

Above: 74. Wenceslaus Hollar's drawing shows the approach to Whitehall Palace, with the Holbein Gateway and, to the left, the Banqueting House, designed by Inigo Jones and completed in 1622. It replaced the banqueting house erected by James I in 1606 and destroyed by fire in 1619.

Right: 75. The Holbein Gate of *c.*1532, which served as a bridge connecting the two parts of Whitehall Palace over King Street, a public road between Westminster and Charing Cross. Although described in 1708 as 'an extraordinary beautiful Gate, considering its Antiquity', the gate was demolished in 1759. Engraving by George Vertue, 1725.

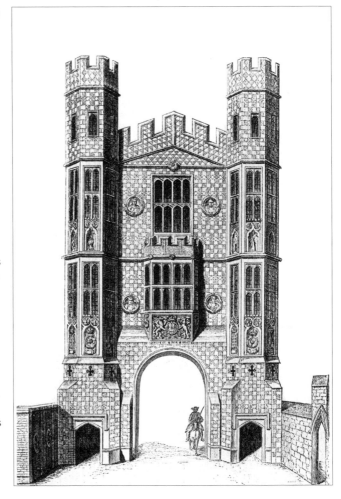

my Lord out of the loue i beare to some of youere frends i haue a caer of youer preseruacion therfor i would aduyse yowe as yowe tender youer lyf to devyse some excuse to shift of youer attendance at this parleament for god and man hathe concurred to punishe the wickednes of this tyme and thinke not slightlye of this advertisment but retyere youre self into youre contri wheare yowe maye expect the event in safti for thowghe theare be no apparance of anni stir yet i saye they shall receyve a terrible blowe this parleament and yet they shall not seie who hurts them this councel is not to be contemned because it maye do yowe good and can do yowe no harme for the dangere is passed as soon as yowe haue burnt the letter and i hope god will giue yowe the grace to mak good use of it to whose holy protection i commend yowe

76. A group of Catholic conspirators were so far advanced in their plan to blow up James I and Parliament, in 1605, that they had a cache of gunpowder in place below the Parliament House. The government was warned of the danger in this anonymous letter, sent to Lord Monteagle the day before the king was due to open Parliament.

77. The gunpowder plotters, by an unknown engraver, from *The Gunpowder Plot Conspirators* (1605). It shows, from the left: Thomas Bate, Robert Winter, Christopher Wright, John Wright, Thomas Percy, Guy (Guido) Fawkes, Robert Catesby and Thomas Winter.

Right: 78. The Gunpowder Plot was foiled when Guy Fawkes was caught, with the cache of gunpowder. He was questioned and tortured and gave this confession, naming his co-conspirators, to the Commissioners who investigated the origins of the plot.

Below: 79. This print shows the execution of the Gunpowder Plot conspirators at the scaffold in St Paul's churchyard in January 1606, watched by a large crowd. Some are being executed at the gallows, suffering the fate of traitors of being hanged, drawn and quartered. Others are being dragged to the place of execution on hurdles.

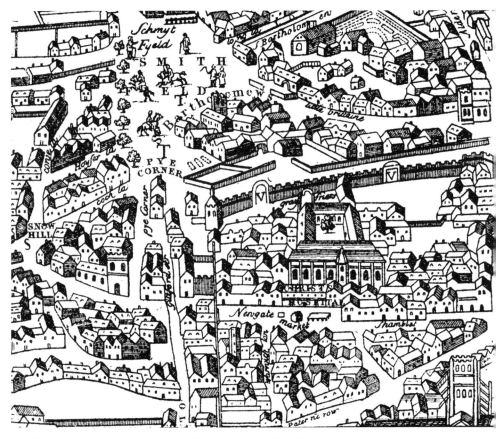

80. The area around Smithfield and Newgate, including Christ's Hospital, shown on the 'Agas' plan of mid-sixteenth century London. Smithfield was a livestock market and the annual Bartholomew Fair was held there. It was also one of the places where public executions were carried out.

81. In 1586 Anthony Babington and his fellow conspirators plotted to execute Elizabeth I and place Mary, Queen of Scots on the throne. Their plans were discovered and fourteen men, including Babington, were executed in St Giles-in-the-Fields, where the plot was laid.

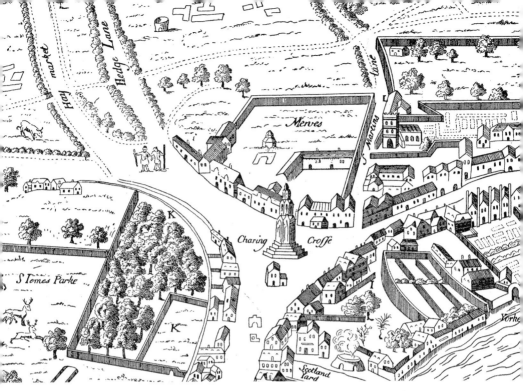

82. The area around Charing Cross, in the mid-sixteenth century. The street running eastwards is the Strand and that running south leads to Whitehall Palace. The church of St Martin, alongside St Martin's Lane, is still literally 'in the fields'. The figures in the fields are stretching newly made cloth out to dry.

83. The royal barge and its guard of smaller barges are shown passing the riverfront, between the Savoy and Whitefriars.

84. Anthonis van den Wyngaerde's drawing of *c*.1544 shows the palaces along the Thames between Charing Cross, in the west, and the Temple. Following the Reformation those palaces which belonged to the church were acquired by members of the aristocracy and were subsequently rebuilt.

Aula Domus Arrundeliana Londini, Meridiem versus,

85. The courtyard of Arundel House, in the Strand, drawn by Wenceslaus Hollar, showing a miscellany of buildings of differing periods and styles, which contrasted with the smart Classical style to which the courtiers of the early seventeenth century aspired for their London palaces.

86. Northampton House in the Strand was erected in 1605–9 by Henry Howard, who gained favour with James I and was created Earl of Northampton in 1604. He died in the house in 1614 and the property passed to his nephew Thomas Howard, Earl of Suffolk. The house then became known as Suffolk House and was shown by Wenceslaus Hollar on his Long View of London of 1647.

87. The Savoy was the London Palace of John of Gaunt and retained the status of a peculiar, outside the jurisdiction of the Middlesex Justices. During the epidemic of 1603 a complaint was made that many of the plague orders were not being implemented there.

Above: 88. London west of the city wall, including Smithfield in the north, and the prominent streets of Holborn and Fleet Street, which contiues west of Temple Bar as the Strand. From Georg Braun and Franz Hogenberg's *Civitatis Orbis Terrarum* (1572).

Left: 89. Public executions were carried out at Tyburn, in Smithfield, or where the crime had been perpetrated. This illustration from 1586 shows prisoners being executed for treason, with hanging followed by disembowelling. Those who suffered this gruesome form of execution included those convicted of plotting against the monarch, and also Roman Catholic priests.

the apothecaries part of the Grocers' Company until their own company was established in 1617. Control by the grocers was inappropriate, according to a report to the king, partly because of the 'dispositions incident to marchants and tradesmen rather to favour the Lucrative part of the trade of undersellinge than the true use thereof, by utteringe that, that is perfect and good'.[46] And while physicians and surgeons were members of the professions, 'the business of an apothecary is a mystery [craft]', according to James I.[47] This was no bar to wealth and influence and some apothecaries thrived. The royal apothecary Gideon Delaune - who was instrumental in the founding of the new company - was worth approximately £90,000 on his death. Busino wrote that in London, 'There is one particular quarter full of apothecaries' shops on either side of the way, besides others scattered here and there about the city.'[48]

London also contained numerous quacks, lacking professional qualifications and experience but dispensing a wide range of nostrums claimed to cure almost all ills. They were widely condemned. One writer at the end of the sixteenth century described them as people, 'who having run away from their occupations and trades learne in a corner to kill men'. They were nothing less than:

> simoniacall and perjured shavelings, shifting and out cast Pettifoggers, Trasonial Chymists, light-headed and trivial Druggers and Apothecaries... base Mechanickes, Stage players, Juglers, Pedlers, Prittle-pratling barbers, filthie Grasiers, curious bath keepers, common shifters, cogging cavaliers, lazy clowns, toothless and tatling old wives, chattering char-women, long-tongued midwives, Dog leeches and such like baggage.

This comprehensive denunciation suggests that quackery was something which members of other occupations dabbled in, rather than a distinct livelihood. One certain thing was their dishonesty: 'You shal sooner finde a blacke Swan than an honest man in this Bunch.'[49] But the college could not suppress them, for they supplied a demand, from those who were not wealthy enough to pay for professional care, and not ill enough to be treated in the hospitals. And they could reach a large number of customers by selling in the market places and distributing fliers advertising their wares.

Quacks probably fell into Dalton's third category, which consisted of the semi-skilled and unskilled, who provided services and labour. He described those in this group as, 'Labourers and hirelings... of which sort be porters, Carmen, watermen, etc.'.[50] Many of these were gainfully employed, although subject to periods of underemployment, both seasonally and with the swings of the metropolitan economy. The vestry of St Botolph, Aldgate in 1618 reported that the parish contained many poor people:

> most having nether trades nor meanes to live on but by their handy labour, as porters, carmen, waterbearers, chimney sweepers, servants in silk mylls, brewers' servants, the rest carpenters, bricklaiers, plaisterers, coopers, smiths, butchers, chandlers, keepers of silk mylls, priests, schoolmasters, vitulers, and brokers.[51]

This would have applied to many of the districts fringing the City and away from the river. The members of the vestry clearly regarded clergymen and schoolmasters as falling within this category. Those communities along the Thames contained a similar range of semi-skilled workers, with watermen and others with occupations servicing the wharves and shipping.

The 3,000 or so watermen were engaged in a regulated business, with their own company under the oversight of the city corporation. They had a high profile, being used by the majority of visitors to London, as well as its citizens, because the river offered a relatively easy way of moving upstream and downstream, and a speedier way of crossing the river than by negotiating the narrow and congested bridge. Their wherries were admired, as 'charmingly upholstered and... extremely pleasant to travel in', but they had a reputation for being noisy, loudly calling for business, and of giving a sharp response to those who did not tip them enough. The company admitted that its members were prone to 'abusive and unreverend speeches'.[52] Sir

Thomas Overbury penned a sardonic description of a waterman: 'When he is upon the water he is fare-company: when he comes ashore he mutinies and contrary to all other trades is most surly to gentlemen when they tender payment.'[53] Such a lack of respect for rank was deplorable, but more subversive were some watermen who objected to those who governed their company. A committee of the Court of Aldermen described them, in 1622, as 'a great company of unruly and stubbern watermen... [who have] become turbulent, malicious and troublesome against the said Rulers'.[54] But they could at least be placated by the corporation, acting through their company.

In contrast, a shadowy and ill-defined category of people lived in London, which the authorities viewed with greater unease. It included those whose skills were no longer in demand, and apprentices expelled from their masters' service before completing their term. According to an official of Christ's Hospital, it also contained unemployed soldiers, 'serving men whose lords and masters are dead... masterless men whose masters have cast them off... idle people, as lusty rogues and common beggars'.[55] Between 1597 and 1608 almost three-quarters of vagrants of London origin whose occupations were recorded had been servants and apprentices.

The poorer people congregated in the suburbs, living in shoddy housing. In *Lanthorn and Candlelight* (1608) Thomas Dekker wrote that a city without suburbs would be a happy city, because, 'they serve but as caves, where monsters are bred up to devour the cities themselves!'. Busino was also most uncomplimentary about the suburbs and their inhabitants:

> Around the liberties of London there is such a patchwork of suburbs that they look like so many monsters who have been converted after being lured by the goddess Circe, the greater part being inhabited by an inept population of the lowest description.[56]

The suburbs drew censorious comments in another respect. In 1592 Thomas Nashe asked, 'London, what are thy suburbs but licensed stews?' and, sixteen years later, Thomas Dekker wrote that in the suburbs 'the doors of notorious carted bawds like Hell gates stand night and day wide open, with a pair of harlots in taffeta gowns, like two painted posts, garnishing out those doors, being better to the house than a double sign'.[57] Nashe intimated that every second house in Shoreditch was a brothel and referred to, 'our unclean sisters in Shoreditch, Southwark, Westminster and Turnbull Street'.[58] Turnbull Street (now Turnmill Street) was in a particularly seedy part of Clerkenwell. The writer George Wilkins, who collaborated with Shakespeare in the writing of *Pericles*, had opened a tavern there by 1610, which may also have been a brothel. He was repeatedly in trouble with the law and lost his victualler's licence for a time. In 1616 a mob wrecked part of his house, which strengthens the suspicion that he was keeping a brothel, for apprentices occasionally targeted bawdy houses during their traditional Shrove Tuesday rampages.

Some prostitutes were based in such bawdy houses, concealed within businesses, others attracted clients by street walking. Their clients ranged from apprentices and servants, the largest group, to craftsmen and tradesmen, gentlemen and foreign merchants, and ambassadors and members of their retinues. Sporadic attempts were made to control prostitution by inflicting public chastisement on the women, parading them through their district and whipping them. Contemporaries linked prostitution and criminality. According to Dekker, in *The Belman of London*, 'the companion of a Theefe is commonly a Whore'. Yet, according to Thomas Platter, 'although close watch is kept on them, great swarms of these women haunt the town in the taverns and playhouses'.[59] Prostitutes were among those punished at Bridewell, the City's house of correction. Its governors were authorized to:

> search, enquire, and seek out idle ruffians, tavern haunters, vagabonds, beggars, and all persons of evil name and fame whatsoever they be, men or women, and then to apprehend and the same to commit to Bridewell, or by any other way or means to punish or correct them as shall seem good to their discretions.[60]

The corporation could claim to have made efforts to bring some of the unruly areas under its control. Alderman Stephen Soame told the House of Commons in 1601 that the City had acquired the liberty of St Katherine Cree from Lord Thomas Howard, assuming that it could then suppress its privileges, which allowed residents to evade the law. But it discovered that this was not the case, and so it introduced a Bill into the House. This he justified with the statement that the areas with such privileges:

> are the very sincke of sinne, the nurserye of nawghtie and lewd places, the harbors of theives, roagues and beggers, and mayteyners of ydle persons; for when our shoppes and howses be robbed thether they flye for releife and sanctuarie, and we cannot helpe our selves.[61]

The connection that he made between those areas, the 'idle persons', and crime was a common one. So was that between soldiers and law-breaking. John Manningham recorded an anecdote doing the rounds in 1602, concerning a soldier who did not want peace with Spain, which would put him out of work. If that happened he would be sure to 'take a purse' and so be hanged. For him, peace meant death. In 1597 Elizabeth I told de Maisse that her troops serving in France 'were but thieves and ought to hang'.[62]

Soldiering was an irregular form of employment, often involuntary and unwelcome, and sometimes brief. Most working Londoners were engaged more conventionally, in one of a whole range of businesses and trades, from merchants to labourers. The rewards were equally wide. A few became enormously wealthy, others made an adequate living, some fell into debt and so were imprisoned, while many poor people required charitable assistance. The great city was the setting for a variety of experiences within the cycle of life.

6

The Time of Life is Short

The variety of life and experience within the bustling and growing city made it difficult to summarize London's society. Those wealthy and comfortably-off citizens, who lived and dressed well, naturally attracted more attention than the majority of Londoners. Visitors were understandably curious about those aspects of London which they could compare with conditions in their own countries, such as education, religion and the role of women. They gave little attention to some aspects of London life, such as the level of child mortality and sickness, which have to be traced from other sources.

For the children who survived infancy, education provision at elementary and secondary level was good, and literacy in London was high enough to support a thriving publishing industry, producing a range of material, including contributions to religious debates. This period saw the Battle of the Bibles, culminating in the publication of the Authorised Version, in 1611. Sparring between Protestant and Catholic writers included debates about the effectiveness of poor relief and charitable giving in the aftermath of the Reformation, and concern about the extent of begging and abject poverty. The problem of poverty was addressed both by the Elizabethan poor law and private charitable giving.

A common remark of the time described England as, 'the Hell of Horses, the Purgatory of Servants, and the Paradise of Women'. Jacob Rathgeb explained this with the comment that, 'the females have great liberty, and are almost like masters, while the poor horses are worked very hard'.[1] Emanuel van Meteren wrote that they 'commonly leave the care of the household matters and drudgery to their servants'.

English women, he wrote, 'are not kept so strictly as they are in Spain or elsewhere. Nor are they shut up, but they have the free management of the house or housekeeping... [and] go to market to buy what they like best to eat.' But he introduced a note of censure into his account, commenting that they were, 'fond of taking it easy... They sit before their doors, decked out in fine clothes, in order to see and be seen by the passers-by.'[2] Women passed their time walking and riding, playing cards, visiting and entertaining friends, and attending child-births, baptisms, churchings and funerals. But artisans' wives commonly helped with the business and supervision of servants and apprentices, although few were able to participate in business on their own. Only roughly two per cent of apprentices were enrolled with women.

Almost all visitors from abroad commented how beautiful and well-dressed English women were, not only those at court and members of the gentry, but also the citizens' wives. And they were treated with respect when they attended banquets and other events. Rathgeb thought that English women, 'have much more liberty than perhaps in any other place'. Lupold von Wedel witnessed the swearing-in of the new Lord Mayor in 1585, and seems to have been surprised that women were present, noting that there was, 'a mighty throng consisting not alone of men, but also of women, for the womenfolk in England wish to be in at everything'.[3] The mingling of the sexes also surprised Orazio Busino, when he visited a playhouse in 1617: 'many very honourable and handsome ladies come there very freely and take their seats among the men without hesitation'.[4]

This freedom did not apply to young women before marriage, who, according to van Meteren, were, 'kept much more strictly than in the Netherlands'. They could be distinguished in the streets because they did not wear hats, unlike married women.[5] Fynes Moryson explained that:

Gentlewomen virgins wear gowns close to the body, and aprons of fine linen, and go bareheaded, with their hair curiously knotted and raised at the forehead, but many, against the cold (as they say) wear caps of hair that is not their own, decking their heads with buttons of gold, pearls, and flowers of silk, or knots of ribbon. They wear fine linen, and commonly falling bands and often ruffs, both starched, and chains of pearl about the neck.[6]

Bachelors were not so easily distinguished by their garb, but their behaviour marked them out. The old shepherd in *The Winter's Tale* implied that adolescence and early manhood lasted until twenty-three, the age at which apprenticeships usually came to an end: 'I would there were no age between ten and three-and-twenty, or that youth would sleep out the rest: for there is nothing in the between but getting wenches with child, wronging the ancientry, stealing, fighting.'[7]

Such irritation with their conduct was not unusual, for apprentices who were at a loose end formed a conspicuous and intimidating group within the population. Etienne Perlin complained that groups of them, perhaps fifty or sixty at a time, stood around the streets, and Jacob Rathgeb described how, 'the street-boys and apprentices collect together in immense crowds and strike to the right and left unmercifully without regard to person'.[8]

They should have been under the control of their masters, and could be subjected to strict discipline. The fear which that engendered was illustrated by a tale told by John Chamberlain: 'I shold tell you that a prentise, pursued by his master to be beaten, lept out of a garret by Holbourne Bridge, and fell upon a porters necke and got away without harme.'[9] The youth must have been very afraid of his punishment to have jumped out of an upper window.

Harsh treatment was one reason for apprentices failing to complete their term. Whipping was an approved form of physical chastisement, but they could be mistreated in other ways. In 1614 a bricklayer's apprentice in St Margaret's, Westminster, who had been transferred from one master to another 'by some indirect meanes', was then neglected, not being given 'sufficient maintenance in meat drink and apparell as was fit for him to have and in that case he ought to have'. He received a sympathetic hearing, but an apprentice who left his master's service before the completion of his term would be ordered to leave the city, or risk punishment as a vagrant.[10]

With marriage came responsibility and the establishment of a household independent of both sets of parents. Women married in their early twenties, while men typically were a few years older when they married for the first time. Young men who had completed an apprenticeship and then established themselves in work would hardly be able to marry before their mid-twenties. Some marriages were broken by a premature death, but many Londoners whose spouse had died remarried, sometimes within a few months of the death, and usually within a year. Between a third and a half of brides were widows. Childbirth and the complications which ensued were common causes of death among young women. Families in the Cheapside area had an average of four children; in Clerkenwell, a much poorer area, the average was lower, at two-and-a-half children. The disparity in terms of prosperity was also reflected in the levels of infant mortality, which was roughly twice as high in Clerkenwell as in Cheapside. And across the city the mortality rate among babies and children was shockingly high, with perhaps as many as fifty per cent dying before they reached their fifteenth birthday.

The interval between births in Clerkenwell was longer than in Cheapside. This may partly have been due to the practice of wet-nursing; women who were not breast feeding because they had entrusted their child to a wet nurse were more likely to become pregnant. Wet nursing became quite common in well-to-do families, despite the high death rate among the children sent to live with wet-nurses in villages around the capital. It was unusual for them to be wet-nursed at home. In the parish register of Mitcham, between 1589 and 1591, burials were recorded of children from London who had been wet-nursed locally, such as: 'a fleminge sonne being a Norschilde [nurse-child] from Loundoun'; 'Elizabeth Beresley a Nurschild of Londoun her father being a Joyner borne in St. Olife's parishe'; 'Mary Porter a Norschild of Loundoun being a habbardasher daughter'.[11]

At the other end of the social scale, some poor mothers abandoned their babies, perhaps because they were so ill themselves, or were too poor to care for them. Some foundlings were illegitimate, such as the child mentioned in St Botolph, Aldgate in 1617, in a censorious note referring to, 'a single woman who was delivered in the street, and like a Base Strumpet kame away and left hir child behinde hir . . . and the father of this Child also, who hath an honest wife of his owne, is runne away from hir, like a base varlet'.[12] The fortunate ones were picked up while still alive, and cared for.

The City was well aware of the scale of the problem of abandoned children and after the dissolution of the Franciscan monastery of the Grey Friars, Henry VIII granted the buildings to the corporation. The grant was confirmed by Edward VI, when he established an orphanage designated Christ's Hospital, for 'poor fatherless children'. This was one of the three royal foundations in 1552, the others being Bridewell and St Thomas's Hospital. The monastic buildings were quickly adapted and the initial intake of 340 was soon increased to 400, and within a few months the institution became a school as well as an orphanage. By 1599 there were 700 children, according to Thomas Platter, who noted that within the hospital, 'reading and writing are taught in special schools'.[13] Only a few girls were admitted; in 1601 the number was set at thirty. At first the children wore a russet-coloured costume, but within a few months this was replaced by a blue one, with yellow breeches and stockings, and the institution duly became known as the Blue Coat School. Governors and individual citizens added to the endowment through gifts and bequests, further income was received from the poor rates, the profits from the corporation's management of the cloth market at Blackwell Hall, and from 1582 the fines and rents arising from its oversight of the carts and carmen.

As their parents were unknown, many orphans were given the name of the place or parish where they were found. An entry in the register of St Dionis Backchurch in 1585 records that a boy was left, 'at Sir Edward Osbourne gate and was christned the xxiii of Aprill named Dennis Philpot, and so brought to Christes [h]ospitall' (Philpot Lane was a street in the parish). In 1618 the baptism was recorded in St Nicholas Acon of a child:

found in the streete at one Mr. Wythers dore in St. Nicholas lane upon the nynteenth of this presnt moneth of October being as it was supposed some two monthes old but we not knowing whether it was baptized before or no, baptized it by the name of Elizabeth Acon after the name of this p'she.

In that year a girl was baptized at St Dunstan-in-the-West as Mary Porch, doubtless because she was found in a porch. Much more unusual was the naming of a boy found in St Helen, Bishopsgate, in 1612, as explained in the parish register: 'Job Rakt-out-of the Asshes, being borne the last of August in the lane going to Sir John Spencer's back gate, and there laide in a heape of old cole asshes, was baptized the First daye of September following, and dyed the next day after.' His mother had attempted to leave the child with some warmth by covering him with ashes, although that did not save him.[14]

Those children who avoided such a fate and survived the hazards of early life could enjoy a school education, at both elementary and grammar-school level. Monsieur de Maisse, in 1597, wrote that there were, 'several fair colleges where the children are taught... and there is no youth in the world, poor or rich, that has greater chance of learning'.[15] Some 219 new grammar schools were founded in England during the reigns of Elizabeth I and James I. So many were in existence by 1612 that Sir Francis Bacon, in a submission to the king, could say, 'I do subscribe to the opinion of one of the wisest and greatest men of your kingdom: That for grammar schools there are already too many, and therefore no providence to add where there is excess'.[16] He was afraid that so many were being educated to that level that suitable posts would not be available, and they would be unwilling to take more menial ones. This could create a group of able men who were potentially disappointed with their lot, and reduce the numbers who would undertake manual labour.

As well as Christ's Hospital, places for poor boys were available at the Merchant Taylors' Company's school in Suffolk Lane, established in 1561. The statutes limited the number of pupils to 250, of whom

100 were to be 'poore men's sonnes', who could have a free education. The first headmaster was the distinguished classical scholar Richard Mulcaster, who included music, drawing and drama in the curriculum; for ten years from 1572 the school's troupe of boys performed before the court. In 1573–4 they also performed in the Merchant Taylors' hall, and could be seen by the public, at a charge of a penny. But in March 1574 the company intervened to ban them, because of the lack of social regulation in the seating arrangements, objecting that 'everye lewd persone thinketh himself (for his penny) worthye of the chiefe and most comodious place withoute respecte of any other either for age or estimacion in the comon weale [commonwealth]'.[17] Those performances are the earliest recorded by a boys' theatrical company in a private theatre.

Thomas Sutton's foundation at the Charterhouse, opened in 1614, consisted of an almshouse for eighty men and a school for forty scholars, between nine and fourteen years old, and the sons of poor parents. The king's authorization for the foundation specified a 'Free-School for the instruction, teaching and maintenance of poor Children or Scholars, &c. And... a learned School-master and Usher to teach and instruct the said Children in Grammar'.[18] They were to be 'well entered in learning' for their age and should be taught, 'none but approved authors, Greek and Latin, such are read in the best esteemed free schools'. The Scholars undertook weekly exercises and on Sundays those in the highest form presented, to the Master or 'any stranger', four Greek and four Latin verses on the second lesson for that day.[19]

Scholarly rivalry existed between the pupils of St Paul's School – established in 1509 by John Colet, the Dean, for 153 children – and those of St Anthony's, founded in Threadneedle Street in 1440. John Stow (born in 1525) recalled that when he was a youth St Anthony's 'commonly presented the best scholars, and had the prize' when competing with the other City schools. The pupils of St Paul's school provoked them by calling them 'Anthonie pigs'. The brothers of St Anthony's of Vienna had occupied the site until the dissolution and they depended on charity, notably pigs that were unfit for human consumption, which were slit in the ear and had a bell hung around their neck, and could wander around the city until they were fat enough to kill. St Anthony's boys responded with shouts of 'pigeons of Paul's', a reference to the pigeons that bred around the cathedral. 'And so proceeding from this to questions in grammar, they usually fell from words to blows with their satchels full of books, many times in great heaps, that they troubled the streets and passengers.' But this rivalry fell away during the sixteenth century, as St Anthony's endowment was lost and it declined 'both in numbers and estimation'.[20] Among its pupils had been John Whitgift, Archbishop of Canterbury from 1583 until his death in 1604. Westminster School, on the other hand, was re-founded, in 1560, by the queen, for 40 scholars. Like the Charterhouse, it also admitted fee-paying 'day boys'.

Academically gifted pupils were sent to one of the two universities, supported by a scholarship. Sir Thomas White created a connection between the Merchants Taylors' school and St John's College, Oxford, by making provision for forty-three scholarships there for boys from the school. Less scholarly pupils were also provided for, those at the Charterhouse who were to be enrolled as apprentices, not sent to university, were taught arithmetic and preparing accounts. Lady Dacre's foundation at Tothill Fields, Westminster, was established in 1595 with the building of 'a meete and convenient house with rooms of habitation for twentie poor folks, and twentie other poore children', who were to learn a trade.[21]

Adult education in non-classical subjects was provided at Gresham College, from 1597. The college was the foundation of Sir Thomas Gresham. He died in 1579, but his wife was opposed to the use of part of his legacy for the purpose, and so it was not until after her death that the college came into being. There were Professorships in seven subjects, with the lectures to be delivered successively, one on each day of the week. The subjects, chosen by Gresham, were divinity, astronomy, geometry, music, law, physic and rhetoric. By the terms of his will, 'none shall be chosen to read any of the said lectures so long as he shall be married, or be suffered to read any of the said lectures after that he shall be married'.[22] The first appointments were made in March 1597 and the lectures began in the Trinity term following. The college was based at Gresham House, his mansion between Old Broad Street and Bishopsgate, where the lectures were delivered and the professors had lodgings. It was administered jointly by the City Corporation and the Mercers' Company, to which Gresham had belonged.

The number of schools was the major reason for the high level of literacy in London, which was higher than elsewhere in England. Roughly three-quarters of adult men were literate. The proportion of tradesmen, craftsmen, apprentices and servants who were literate was only a little lower than the average, at around seventy per cent. Perhaps a quarter of women in London were literate by the early seventeenth century.[23]

Such a well-educated population provided a large market for the publishing industry, which was centred in the metropolis. Mary I granted the London Stationers' Company a charter in 1557 and two years later a licensing Act was passed. The company acquired powers to control the book trade, with the right to confiscate copies of any book not licensed by a warden of the company and to track down and seize illicit publications. Printers of heretical and subversive material could be brought before the company's court and fined. Legitimate publications were entered in the Stationers' Company Register.

Regulation of the trade included limiting the number of printers in London to twenty-five, in 1586. The Archbishop of Canterbury and Bishop of London were empowered to license all books and their approval was required before a publication was registered by the company. In 1587 the company fixed the number of copies in an edition at either 1,250 or 1,500, while school-books, prayer-books and some catechisms were allowed four annual impressions, each of 2,500 or 3,000 copies. Almanacs were free from such restrictions. In 1603 James I granted the company the right to print books of private prayers, primers, psalters and almanacs.

Books covered a wide range of topics and cost typically between sixpence and a shilling, although finely-produced ones were more expensive. Books on travel and topography, histories, chronicles and biographies, cookery books, music books, collections of classical quotations, or of dreams, books giving practical help on household matters, or how to write letters, competed for space on the booksellers' stalls in St Paul's churchyard with penny broadsheets and ballads. These were printed in large numbers, typically on a single sheet, with an elaborate title and woodcut illustration, describing news of a dramatic occurrence such as a fire, gale or flood, or a lurid account of a portentous event, or less dramatic material, such as a rhyme or song. No incident was too minor or seemingly insignificant for the broadsheet writers, who invariably claimed to have printed the news as soon after it happened as possible, with the assurance of authenticity by eyewitnesses, or those who could be trusted. It provided work and a small income for writers, provoking the jibe that, 'every red-nosed rimester is an author, every drunken man's dream is a booke, and... scarce a cat can look out of a gutter but out starts a half-penny chronicler'.[24]

Some printers targeted the wealthier end of the market and published handsomely printed and relatively expensive books. The original edition of William Camden's *Britannia* (1586) cost 5s, with four enlarged editions following by 1600. Raphael Holinshed's *Chronicles of England, Scotland, and Ireland*, used by the dramatists, including Shakespeare, for historical source material, cost £1 6s in 1577 (a second, enlarged edition was published in 1587). Another source which Shakespeare drew upon was Sir Thomas North's translation of Plutarch's *The Lives of the Noble Grecians and Romanes* (1579), which sold for 14s. Richard Hakluyt's influential work *The principal navigations, voiages, traffiques and discoveries of the English nation* first appeared in 1589 and cost 11s 11d. It describes the explorations of English sailors; Hakluyt included, 'the navigations onely of our owne nation'. A second edition in three volumes followed in 1598–1600. Another major and influential work was Sir Walter Raleigh's

History of the World, written while he was imprisoned in the Tower and published in 1614, four years before he was executed.

John Speed was a member of the Merchant Taylors' Company, through patrimony, and worked as a historian and cartographer, producing in 1611 his *Theatre of the Empire of Great Britain*, which contained sixty-seven engraved maps of England, Scotland, Wales and Ireland. The county maps have insets of plans of seventy-three of the principal towns. He included that of London on the map of Middlesex, apparently regretting having to do so, for in the attached comment he wrote, 'The large circuit with multitude of streets besydes the beautifull & stately buildings in this fayre, and most famous Citie London can no wise be demonstrated in soe little compasse, as here I am inforced to shewe.' Westminster was drawn separately. Speed's engraver was Jodocus Hondius of Amsterdam, but his printers were John Sudbury and his nephew George Humble, of Pope's Head Alley, between Cornhill and Lombard Street. Three new editions appeared before Speed's death in 1629. The alley also contained the workshop of John Wolfe, who in 1598 published the first edition of John Stow's *Survey of London*.

Browsers could pick up bargains among such highly-priced elegant volumes, the cheap broadsides and ballads, and books in other languages (although in 1598 John Chamberlain wrote that 'Spanish bookes are hard to come by').[25] On 12 June 1593 Richard Stonley, one of the four tellers of the Exchequer, browsed among the books on a stall in St Paul's Churchyard and noted his purchases in his diary: 'For the Survey of Fraunce, with the Venus and Adhonay pr Shakespere, xii.d.'[26] *Venus and Adonis* had been entered in the Stationers' Register on 18 April, the first of Shakespeare's works to be published. *The Rape of Lucrece* was published in 1594 and the *Sonnets* in 1609, and some of the plays were published in quarto format, beginning with *Titus Andronicus* and *Henry VI Part II* in 1594. But when Shakespeare died, in 1616, only a half of his plays had been published. His friends and fellow actors John Hemming and Henry Condell set about to remedy this and in 1623 a folio volume of thirty-six of the plays was published, containing all of the plays recognized to be by Shakespeare, except *Pericles*, which was a collaboration. Eighteen of them had not been published before and could well have been lost without Hemming and Condell's loyal efforts. And they stressed that some of the earlier editions of the individual plays were imperfect, so that readers had been, 'abus'd with diverse stolne, and surreptitious copies, maimed, and deformed by the frauds and stealthes of injurious impostors, that expos'd them'.[27]

This work, known as the First Folio, was published by Isaac Jaggard and Edward Blount at Jaggard's printing house at the junction of Aldersgate Street and the Barbican. The cost of publication was roughly 6s 8d per book, and it sold for 15s unbound and £1 for a bound copy. The print run of *c.*750 copies was sold out within nine years. It proved to be one of the most influential books ever published.

Many play-texts were not published. The acting companies did not wish to make their own material available to their rivals, and the receipts from publication were small compared to that received for performances. But in 1616 Ben Jonson published his works, in folio, including his poetry. This was the first time a writer for the popular stage had been recognized in this way and it provided a precedent for Hemming and Condell to follow.

Such works gave the censors no problems, but others did, and control of book publishing was less than complete, for only about sixty-five per cent of those printed were registered. Printers with small presses could work in premises ostensibly given over to other functions. Some publications were subversive, such as the satirical 'Martin Marprelate' pamphlets of 1588–9, which were witty and irreverent pieces on religious themes, attacking episcopacy. They angered the queen and provoked determined attempts by the Stationers' Company to track down the author. Job Throckmorton of Haseley near Warwick, and eight miles from Stratford-upon-Avon, was suspected of being the author and was tried for the offence in 1590 but not convicted, after protesting: 'I am not Martin, I knewe not Martin' (which was undeniably true, as a single writer, 'Martin', did not exist).[28] Others involved in producing the Marprelate pamphlets were not so fortunate. The premises of Robert Waldegrave, who had printed in London for ten years, were raided in 1588 and his press was destroyed. He was able to save his type and sought safety with Elizabeth Crane at her house in Aldermanbury, but later went into exile. She was fined £500 and imprisoned for keeping the type. The Welsh religious controversialist John Penry was also suspected of involvement with the Marprelate pamphlets and other puritan publications. He was captured in Stepney in 1593 and executed later that year. In the same year Henry Barrow and John Greenwood were hanged at Tyburn. Both had been active in separatist groups in London. Barrow was one of twenty-two people arrested in 1587 in a raid on a separatist meeting in the parish of St Andrew-by-the-Wardrobe and Greenwood was detained when he visited him in prison. Both men were executed for treason.

The execution of puritans such as Barrow and Greenwood in the 1590s was part of an attempt to clamp down on Puritanism within the English church, overseen by John Whitgift, Archbishop of Canterbury. After his death, Niccolò Molin described him as, 'always a bitter foe to the Puritans, the most pestilent sect in this kingdom'.[29] Some Puritans, including Barrow's followers, chose to leave London and move to Amsterdam in search of religious toleration. But in 1612 Thomas Helwys returned from Amsterdam to London and formed the first English Baptist church, which met at Pinner's Hall. Back in London he published *A Short Declaration of the Mystery of Iniquity*, a plea for religious toleration. On the flyleaf of one copy he wrote a note, intended for James I, that included the declaration that, 'The king is a mortall man, & not God, therefore has no power over the immortall soules of his subjects, to make laws and ordinances for them, and to set spirituall Lords over them.'[30] He was arrested and imprisoned in Newgate and was dead by 1616.

The attempts to achieve conformity naturally extended to control of the available versions of the prayer book and the bible. This produced the battle of the bibles. During Mary I's reign (1553–8) a number of Protestant exiles settled in Geneva, a French-speaking republic which had achieved independence from Savoy in 1535 and become allied with Berne, one of the Swiss cantons. Under the guidance of John Calvin, Geneva emerged as an influential Protestant republic and was an obvious refuge for the exiles. Some of them decided to produce a new translation of the bible, which would provide an explanation of the text to guide the reader, especially to clarify some of the more obscure 'hard passages'. The translation was produced under the leadership of William Whittingham. By the time that it was ready for publication Elizabeth had succeeded her sister, and indicated that England would once again be a Protestant country. This cleared the way for the publication of the Geneva Bible, in 1560.

The Geneva Bible was attractively produced in a quarto format, with illustrations, and printed in a roman typeface. This had been used by printers of bibles in Geneva since 1534 and made the text much easier to read than earlier versions, which had been printed in black letter typefaces that were modelled on handwriting. The Geneva Bible also followed the practice, established in that city in 1553, of dividing the whole of the bible into chapters and verses, with the verses numbered and each beginning on a new line. More importantly, it achieved the translators' intention of interpreting the text by the use of marginal notes explaining the meaning of the passages or terms. It was this which gave the Geneva Bible its distinctive character, and aroused the ire of the anti-Puritan elements in the English church.

Its convenient size and easy-to-read typeface, with the quality of the translation, made the new bible a publishing success. But some of its annotations were seen to differ from the theological stance of the church as established under Elizabeth. Matthew Parker, her first Archbishop of Canterbury, objected to the 'diverse prejudicial notes' and commissioned a new translation, which appeared in 1568. Parker blocked attempts to print the Geneva Bible in England, hoping to secure a monopoly for the 1568 version, known as the Bishops' Bible. His successor, Edmund Grindal, appointed in 1575, relaxed the ban, with the influential support of Sir Francis Walsingham, one of the Principal Secretaries of State and a Privy Councillor. From 1577 smaller duodecimo editions of the Geneva Bible were printed in England, as well as the quarto and folio editions. Whitgift's appointment as archbishop in 1583 produced another change of policy, with the Bishops' Bible issued in quarto editions, in an attempt to make it a viable rival to the Geneva Bible, and an order that only the Bishops' Bible could be used in public services of the Church of England. But the attempts of the church's hierarchy to supplant the Geneva Bible failed. Between 1583 and 1603, fifty-eight editions of the bible were published in England, of which fifty-one were of the Geneva Bible and only seven of the Bishops' Bible. The Geneva Bible was the most widely used and influential bible of the period, and was the one familiar to Shakespeare and his contemporaries.

As a Protestant brought up under the supervision of Calvinist clergymen, James I might have been expected to favour the Geneva Bible. In fact, his judgement was a political one and he regarded it as potentially subversive, with some notes seeming to encourage disobedience and defiance of kingly authority, even to justify the killing of monarchs who behaved as tyrants. The note on the passage in which King Asa is described as sparing his mother's life, even though she had usurped his authority, was that, 'she ought to have dyed both by the covenant and by the lawe of God, but he gave place to foolish pity'.[31] James was very sensitive to such entries, given his mother's fate and his own insecurities. He described the Geneva Bible as the worst English translation he knew of and as being, 'very partial, untrue, seditious, and savouring too much of dangerous and traitorous conceits'.[32]

Despite this, a new translation was not on the agenda when, early in 1604, the king convened a conference at Hampton Court to discuss the future direction of the English church. The proposal came during the conference, from the Puritan delegation, and was opposed by the anti-Puritan Bishop of London, Richard Bancroft, but, not surprisingly, was supported by James. And so the conference agreed that:

A translation be made of the whole Bible, as consonant as can be to the original Hebrew and Greek; and this to be set out and printed, without any marginal notes, and only to be used in all churches in time of divine service.[33]

The translation was done by six teams of scholars, and the final editing and collation of their texts was undertaken at Stationers' Hall by an editorial committee of representatives from each team. A contemporary described how 'they went daily to Stationers' Hall, and in Three quarters of a year, fulfilled Their Task'.[34] The result was the King James Bible, or Authorised Version, published in 1611. The Geneva Bible continued to be sold and used, but the Authorised Version swung the battle of the bibles in favour of the church's hierarchy.

To outsiders, the Church of England's doctrines and forms of worship could be confusing. According to de Maisse, 'Religion in England regarding its doctrine is like that of Geneva except for certain differences in the Lord's Supper... and indeed they take their communion on their knees and with some sort of adoration.' A little further on in his account he added that, 'As for their ceremonies, they retain many, as vestments, bells and organs.' Services were conducted in English and the psalms were sung in English, but:

one can still recognise a great part of the Mass, which they have curtailed only in what concerns individual communion, which they only make publicly, and in what is contrary to the doctrine that they hold; for they still keep the Epistle and the Gospel, the *Gloria in Excelsis Deo*, the Creed... The canons wear the amice and surplice, as also the others, and have copes.

He modified his impression of a Calvinist church, concluding instead that, 'there is little difference between their ceremonies and those of the Church of Rome'. Thomas Platter drew a similar conclusion after attending a service in St Paul's, where he 'saw and heard the canons, in white surplices and square birettas similar to the Papists at home, conduct the service in English, with music and organ accompaniment just as if they were celebrating mass'.[35] But any brief summary of the position was difficult because not all London parishes conformed to the same practices, although the pressure to do so grew after James's accession.

Puritan influence in London had increased during Elizabeth's reign. One way in which this was achieved was through the creation of lectureships by the laity, who were frustrated by their inability to influence the appointment of parish clergy. In the City, the right of appointment was largely in the hands of the church and the crown. Sir William Dugdale later wrote that such parish lectureships were introduced into most corporate towns and 'especially into the City of London'.[36] The process gained momentum in London from the 1570s and 1580s, with roughly fifty parishes having lectureships by *c*.1590 and there were 121 lecturers by 1628, financed by collections among the parishioners and from bequests.

Bancroft was translated to the Archbishopric of Canterbury on Whitgift's death in 1604, and his successor as Bishop of London was Richard Vaughan. He arrived with the reputation of having been active while Bishop of Chester in suppressing Catholic recusants. At London he was expected to enforce conformity among the Puritans within the diocese, although his sympathies lay with the nonconformists and so he, 'permitted the godly ministers to live peaceably and enjoy their liberty', according to the Presbyterian clergyman Richard Rogers. Although twenty Puritan lecturers were brought before the church courts between 1604 and 1606, only one was permanently suspended.[37] Vaughan's successor, Thomas Ravis, found himself in the same situation and reacted differently, telling Rogers that, 'I will not leave one preacher in my dioces that doth not subscribe', but the actions against Puritan lecturers and beneficed clergymen were hardly any stronger than before.[38] Ravis participated in the translation of the bible for the Authorised Version, but died in 1609, before its publication. George Abbot was appointed Bishop of London in 1610 and Archbishop of Canterbury in 1611, to be succeeded as bishop by John King. Both Abbot and King were evangelical Calvinists who had been lecturers in the 1590s and as bishops conscientiously fulfilled their preaching obligations. King, in particular, was a fine preacher. But the theology of their bishops did not necessarily reflect the convictions of many Londoners. The capital was a centre of Puritan learning and publishing, and services by Puritan lecturers and preachers were well attended.

Catholic services, too, attracted worshippers, despite the risk of harassment. Catholics were liable to recusancy fines, which James did not ameliorate, but they could worship in London, at the embassies of the Catholic countries. These should have been secure from disruption, because of diplomatic privilege, but that did not extend to English people attending mass in them. One Sunday in 1576, William Fleetwood, the Recorder, went with the two Sheriffs and a party of men to the Charterhouse, which was being used by the Portuguese ambassador, Francisco Giraldi, as his residence, and interrupted the service. Confronting the worshippers, Fleetwood asked that, 'all suche as were Englishemen born and the Queene's subjects to come forth of that place', at which 'all the straungers' moved towards him, some threatening to draw their daggers and swords. They were pacified by one of the Sheriffs, but then he, 'with all the masse-hearers, with Seigneur Girraldie's wife, and her maydes, were all in a heape, forty persons at once speaking in several languages'. When calm returned, the members of the household were allowed to go free and the Englishmen in the congregation were arrested. Giraldi and the Spanish ambassador, who was also present, both made furious complaints to the queen, who apologised. Fleetwood paid the price for her discomfiture with a spell in the Fleet Prison, from where he wrote to Lord Burghley: 'This is a place werein a man may quietlie be acquainted with God.'[39]

This remained an issue and in 1611 the Venetian ambassador reported that the Spanish embassy, 'has been frequently surrounded by the officers of the Bishop and the Sheriff of London, in order to arrest those who frequent it at time of mass'. When the Spanish ambassador complained, the Privy Council pointed out that, 'the Bishops and Magistrates of the City were greatly scandalized at his toleration of the English who frequented mass in the Ambassadors' houses'. He was told that he should take responsibility for those who attended mass at the embassy, and if he did not, then 'we shall send and arrest them in your chapel'.[40]

Other services did not have diplomatic protection and were liable to interruption. In February 1600 John Chamberlain reported a raid on, 'a great assemblie of men and women of this towne at the Marshalsee to heare a Scottish Frier Capuchin preach; where they were staide and kept all night, to the number of three or fowre score'. Some were fined and released, others were imprisoned. Two years later he mentioned that, 'ten were taken at a masse in Newgate'.[41]

Protestant and Catholic writers engaged in theological controversy, through the printed word, with books of Catholic propaganda and argument being available in London. The Privy Council had attempted to restrict this at the outset of James's reign, when it ordered, 'that no Bookes, Libells or Pamphlettes Concerning matter of Religion or State shalbe printed, brought into the Realme, or solde hereafter', unless approved by the king's Licensers of the Press, who included the Archbishop of Canterbury and Bishop of London, as before. The order banned many kinds of publications, in a wide sweep:

Bookes of erroneus exercise of Religion as Missalls, Portases, Pope the Prymers superstitious Prayer Bookes legentes and suche like are in no wise to be suffered, Bookes also written beyond Seas by ffugitives and Ennemyes, or at home by Schismatiques, Sectaryes and evill affected persons Concerning State matters and publique ordinance are likewise to be reiected, as also all kynde of scandalous libells, defamatory Pamphlettes and hurtfull Ballades. And generally Bookes & Pamphletts Concerning Religion written by Papistes and adversaries are not Comonly to be suffred.[42]

This did not deter debates between the writers of the two sides, which were sometimes furious and could become very personal and pedantic. Sir Edward Hoby, Gentleman of the Privy Chamber to James I, wrote to a friend with a list of errata for a book which he had sent earlier. He was afraid that any errors would be seized on: 'the papisticall malice being such, as they wilbe glad of the least hole, to give fuell to their depraveing humors'.[43] Direct debates were also engaged in, such as one reported by the publisher Edward Blount, in 1621, which he described as, 'the private Conference between our englishe divines and ministers and that dangerous Champion Muskett [a Catholic priest]'. This went on for four days and should have continued on the fifth, but the 'many Cartholick gentlemen and learneder priests than Muskett' who had argued the Catholic case 'refused to come, and made excuses forsooth'.[44]

Not all points debated were theological or doctrinal. One topic disputed between Catholic and Protestant writers was the availability of poor relief and care for the needy in post-Reformation England. Catholics alleged that the dissolution of the monasteries had removed a major source of assistance for the poor, which had not been adequately replaced by Protestant philanthropy. As a result, the poor, the disabled and the elderly were not adequately provided for.

Beggars constituted both a problem and a threat, according to Sir Francis Bacon: 'it is that kind of people that is a burden, and eye-sore, a scandal, and a seed of peril and tumult in the state'.[45] The scale of the problem could be seen from the number of beggars in London's streets, according to John Howes: 'the streates swarme with Beggers', and they were 'furnyshed with ydell people'. The problem was so bad that, 'no man can stande or staie in any churche or streate, but presently tenne or twelve beggers comme breathing in his face'. Howes, a member of the Grocers' Company, was writing in the aftermath of the bad harvest of 1586, not from a Catholic standpoint but with the avowed intention of exposing, 'a Nomber of Abuses Comytted in the Governemente of the Poore within this Cittie'.[46]

London's streets also yielded a grim harvest of poor people who had died without shelter, from malnourishment or exposure. This was an especial problem in the mid-1590s, when food prices were high. During those years the registers of St Botolph, Aldgate, recorded the burials of a number of people who died in the streets of the parish. Edward Ellis was described as 'a vagrant who died in the street'. He was known by name, others were anonymous: 'A young man not known who died in a hay-loft'; 'A cripple that died in the street before John Awsten's door'; 'A maid, a vagrant, unknown, who died in the street near the Postern'; 'A young man vagrant having no abiding place... who died in the street'; and a young man distinguished only by his 'white canvas doublet', who also, 'died in the street'.[47] These and many others had failed to benefit from the poor relief system and had not been able to persuade passers-by to give them enough alms even to survive.

Such scenes aroused the righteous indignation of Philip Stubbes, who, in 1583, challenged the comfortably off who were well dressed:

> Do they think that it is lawfull for them to have millions of sundry sortes of apparell lying rotting by them, when as the poore members of Jesus Christ die at their doores for wante of clothing? God commaundeth in his law, that there be no miserable poore man, nor begger amongest us, but that every one be provided for and maintained of that abundance which God hath blessed us withal.[48]

Yet two visitors from abroad during the difficult years of the 1590s formed a different impression. The Venetian Francesco Gradenigo commented, in 1596, that, 'personally I have not seen a beggar yet', and in the following year de Maisse wrote, 'one hardly sees a beggar'.[49] Philip Julius, Duke of Stettin-Pomerania, in 1602, drew a similar conclusion after a visit to the Royal Exchange:

> It is a pleasure to go about there, for one is not molested or accosted by beggars, who are elsewhere so frequently met with in places of this kind. For in all England they do not suffer any beggars, except they be few in number and outside the gates.[50]

Such visitors may not have seen the places where the poor usually begged, or they travelled through the city by coach, and so were unaware of their presence. But beggars stationed themselves where the well-to-do passed. Begging in the wealthier streets was more likely to produce alms than in those places where the citizens had nothing to spare, and so the beggars could not have been entirely hidden from visitors.

The number of poor reduced to begging fluctuated considerably, according to the amount of casual work available, the price of food, and the season. And those drawn to London did not necessarily stay. In January 1582 William Fleetwood organized a trawl throughout the city for vagrants. This lasted for a week and was so thorough that when the process was completed he, 'went to Polls [St Paul's] and in other places as well within the liberties as els where, and I founde not one rouge stirryng'. Over three days 134 vagrants were apprehended, and on another day more than 100 'lewed people'. His figures imply that several hundred were seized in all, only a few of whom were Londoners. He commented that, 'I dyd note, that we had not of London, Westm. nor Sowthwarke, nor yet Midd. nor Surr. above twelve'. The others were from outside the metropolis and few of them had been in London for more than three or four months.[51] This suggests that the majority of those classed as vagrants had come to the city for the winter. The proportion implied by Fleetwood may have been far too low, however, for during the period 1597–1610 roughly a half of vagrants taken into Bridewell were from the London area.

Other estimates included one by the Lord Mayor, in 1594, which put the number of beggars in London at 12,000, and another by Sir William Peryam, Chief Baron of the Exchequer, who in October 1602 told the new Lord Mayor, in no uncertain terms:

> that their might be some monethly strict searche be made in the Cytie for idle persons and maisterles men, whereof there were, as he said, at this tyme 30,000 in London; theise ought to be found out and well

punished, for they are the very scumme of England, and the sinke of iniquitie.[52]

Peryam probably was referring to all those he classed as undesirables, not just beggars. And those dealt with at Bridewell were, according to Howes, 'ydell lustie Rogues and strompets'.[53] The annual figures for those who passed through Bridewell increased from 209 in 1578–9 to 555 in 1600-01, although at any one time the number who were being kept there was roughly 150. During Sir Thomas Middleton's mayoral year, in 1613–14, he claimed to have freed the streets from 'a swarm of loose and idle vagrants', indicating that the number of beggars was at least manageable.[54] The scale of the problem was uncertain, but beggars do not seem to have formed a significant proportion of the total population.

Vagrants were those poor who did not deserve assistance, for they were able to work. Middleton incarcerated beggars in Bridewell, yet 'not punishing any for begging, but setting them on work, which was worse than death to them'.[55] They were distinguished from the deserving poor, who were those 'aged, decayed and impotent poore people', who 'of necessitie be compelled to lyve by almes'.[56] That was the Lord Mayor's definition in 1572, and neatly summarized those intended to benefit from the system created after the Reformation. London was the first English city to institute a system of local taxation to provide funds for poor relief, when the corporation made an order in 1547 that, 'the Citezeins and inhabitantes... Shall Furthwith Contrybute and paye towardes the Sustentacyon, maynteynyng and fyndyng of the said poore personages'.[57] The principle of a rate for the purpose was not adopted by the government until 1572. This was administered by the justices of the peace and the parishes, which appointed overseers of the poor to supervise collection and distribution. The Poor Law arrangements were confirmed by legislation in 1598 and 1601.

Private charity made a much larger contribution to poor relief than did the rates, and the contemporary view was that 'charitie ought to be free and not forced or compulsory'.[58] In the mid-1590s, money raised on the poor rates provided roughly one-quarter of charitable funds, but two-thirds came from individuals' donations. The remainder was paid by the livery companies in assistance for their members, and by the corporation, which maintained the hospitals and Bridewell. Howes noted that St Bartholomew's and St Thomas's hospitals together treated roughly 850 people each year, at a cost of £1,600.

Much help to the poor was informal, and so difficult to trace, with food given to relatives or neighbours and money to beggars or donated through collections in churches. But the corporation disapproved of beggars in churches, even when they had licences, in case donations to them, 'would prevent the citizens from contributing to the support of the Hospitals for the poor'.[59] Some collections were made in response to charitable briefs, usually as the congregation left church after a service, but also by collectors going from house to house. Briefs were issued by the Lord Chancellor and authorized collections for the victims of fire, flood, plague or other calamity. This was one way in which Londoners provided help for those outside the city. Another was by bequests to create bread charities or provision for gifts of money on the principal feast days for the poor in their place of origin. In the 1590s almost one-quarter of Londoners left bequests to non-London poor in their wills.

Residential care for the elderly was provided in almshouses, in London and across the country, in the benefactor's place or county of origin, or where they had invested in a landed estate. Sir Baptist Hicks, Viscount Campden, built almshouses in 1612 for twelve pensioners at Chipping Campden in Gloucestershire, and William Goddard, a member of the Fishmongers' Company, who died in 1609, bequeathed funds for an almshouse for forty poor people at Bray, in Berkshire. The livery companies, too, established almshouses, within the City, and by the mid-1590s they were supporting roughly 200 alms-people. Almshouses typically had accommodation for a dozen elderly people. But Thomas Sutton's foundation at the Charterhouse was for eighty elderly men, and so was spectacularly large for its time and was accommodated in a grand and prestigious mansion, adapted for the purpose. With the school, his foundation was the largest charity created between the Reformation and the establishment of Guy's Hospital in the 1720s. This provided a significant contribution for those anxious to demonstrate the strength of Protestant giving, and Sutton was hailed as 'the right Phoenix of Charity in our times'. Andrew Willet, the chronicler of Protestant giving, poured lavish praise on the charity, which he described as, 'the greatest gift that ever was given in England, no abbey at the first foundation thereof excepted'.[60] The qualifying age for admission to an almshouse was commonly set at fifty. This suggests that those who were in their fifties, or older, were regarded as elderly. Sutton's Hospital set fifty as the minimum age for admission, but permitted the disabled to enter when they were forty years old.

Shakespeare was baptized on 26 April 1564 and by tradition is held to have been born on the 23rd. If so, he died on his fifty-second birthday, 23 April 1616. His brother Edmund, also an actor, was twenty-six when he died, in 1607. Of a sample of forty of William's contemporaries within the theatre world, chiefly actors and playwrights, fourteen died before they were fifty and a further fifteen before their sixtieth birthday, six were in their sixties when they died and five in their seventies. The longest lived was the actor John Lowin, son of a leather-worker in St Giles, Cripplegate, who was seventy-six when he died in 1653. Their average life expectancy was their mid-fifties; even for members of the gentry and higher social ranks who reached the age of twenty-one, it was only sixty-three. For a man who had turned fifty, it was no exaggeration to say, 'the time of life is short!'.[61]

Sutton's generosity was contrasted with Sir John Spencer's meanness, for he made no provision for the poor in his will. Both men were immensely wealthy and died within a short time, Spencer in March 1610 and Sutton in December 1611, inviting a comparison. Yet Spencer did contribute to the poor, through his funeral, 'where some thousand Men did assist in Mourning Cloakes or Gowns', including

320 poor men, each given a basket containing a black gown and provisions. Despite protestations by contemporaries and directions by testators that funerals should be modest and inexpensive, not taking money that could be spent on more worthy causes, large-scale funerals for wealthy citizens were common. Sutton was, 'conveighed to his Grave with all the Pomp and Solemnity, which might become the Funeral of so great a Man: Six thousand people attended his Corps through the City, whose passage lasted six hours'.[62] It cost £1,673, equivalent to more than forty per cent of his new foundation's annual revenue. Orazio Busino described the arrangements for Sir William Craven's funeral at the church of St Andrew Undershaft, in 1618:

> He left directions for a funeral to cost 20,000 crowns, a part being for the dress of 600 mourners. Each of these had a black cloak of fine cloth, with silk braid three fingers deep, hanging from the shoulders and falling nine inches below the cape, a mourning custom which is usual throughout the whole country. The remainder of the sum was spent in a banquet for the multitude which took part in the ceremony, in addition to those invited, and in alms.

But Craven's charity had its limits and he instructed that, 'nothing be given to idell persons in the streates on the day of my funerall'. He was a merchant who had served as Lord Mayor in 1610–11; his estate was worth roughly £125,000 at his death.[63]

To raise funds for the Blue Coat School, its children attended funerals as 'mutes', walking in the funeral processions of 'persons of consequence'. Other groups performed the same role. Leading Elizabeth I's funeral procession were 'two hundred and sixty poor women, four in a rank, apparelled in black, with linen kerchiefs over their heads'.[64] It was also common for there to be a dole at the funeral, when food or money was distributed. In November 1601, the dole at the funeral of Lady Ramsey, when sixpences were distributed to the poor at Leadenhall, ended in tragedy. John Chamberlain described how, 'the number of beggers was so excessive and unreasonable that seventeen of them were thronged and trampled to death in the place, and divers sore hurt and bruised'.[65] This suggests that such a large number arrived to collect the dole that they overwhelmed the arrangements for distributing it.

Andrew Willet set out to resolve the question of whether charity after the break with Rome matched the assistance provided before the Reformation, by compiling a list of charitable gifts. He proudly wrote that those donations, 'doe glister as pearles, and the workers thereof, doe shine as starres amongst us'. His conclusion, in 1614, was that, 'more charitable works have beene performed in the times of the Gospell then they can shew to have been done in the like times of Popery'. The deserving benefited, while those who could work were not allowed to draw upon charity and were set to work, or punished. Between 1550 and 1620, Londoners gave almost £800,000 for charitable purposes. Willet's figures did not entirely settle the debate, but do show the extent to which Londoners provided help for the poor and needy.[66]

Writers continued to castigate the wealthy, with their tendency to hoard money until death, rather than donating it during their lifetime, when arrangements for its proper distribution could be set in place and supervised. Charity should be given throughout life, as it was needed, not concentrated at its end. But the evidence suggests that the problem of poverty was tackled and the city's streets were not teeming with beggars. Londoners were aware of the needs of their fellow citizens and contributed to their welfare. And their gifts were targeted at those most in need, especially the young and the old: sickly infants, orphans, children requiring an education, the disabled, and the elderly poor unable to maintain themselves.

7

A Quick Eye & a Nimble Hand

The routines of work and patterns of life did not necessarily generate a feeling of security. Londoners' lives could be disturbed by many things and changed by events over which they had no control. The city's streets and the daily round of life might bring accidents, dangers to life and health, sudden death, violent assaults that were casual or premeditated, the loss or theft of property, goods or livelihood. All of these contributed to the citizens' worries, as did losing their freedom, by imprisonment for debt, or enlistment as soldiers. Such concerns affected the entire social range. Assaults occurred in New Palace Yard as well as in alehouses. Criminals were not respecters of status; the properties of the wealthy offered better spoils than did the average citizens' houses, and swindlers targeted well-to-do young men, as providing the richest pickings. Crime was both opportune and organized, as the authorities discovered, as they probed into London's underworld. And those Londoners who did not have first-hand experience of misfortunes or crimes would surely hear about them in the alehouse, tavern or Paul's Walk, or read about them in broadsheets and pamphlets.

Accidents could occur at the wharves, in the home or workshop, at public gatherings, and in the streets. In 1613 a carman was indicted for failing to secure his horse and cart, which injured a child. A porter threw a pulley into the cart 'so negligently that he hit the cart-horse, which thereupon ran away and hurt the said child somewhat dangerously'. The justices were told of another serious case involving a carman of Whitechapel, who was accused of leading 'his cart over the neck of a young woman child about the age of eight years, so that the said child is thought to be in danger of death'. In 1615 Roland Merricke of Holborn, a brewer, broke a child's leg by 'leading a brewers dray' over it, and was fined 3s 4d. Others were indicted 'for hurting and maiming' with their carts and two men were fined for 'riding over' one Walter Kidd, with a horse.[1]

Streets were potentially dangerous areas, but places of entertainment also carried risks. In 1587 the lawyer Philip Gawdy attended a performance by the Lord Admiral's Men and described how they had, 'a devyse in ther playe to tye one of their fellowes to a poste and so to shoote him to deathe, having borrowed their callyvers one of the players handes swerved his peece being charged with bullet missed the fellowe he aymed at and killed a chyld, and a woman great with chyld forthwith, and hurt an other man in the head very soore'. Whoever prepared the props for that performance was at fault for loading the firearm with a ball as well as a gunpowder charge, and the actor tied to the post had a very lucky escape, albeit at the expense of members of the audience. John Chamberlain recorded a particularly bad accident of a different kind in August 1599: 'last weeke at a puppett play in St Johns Street, the house fell and hurt betweene thirty and forty persons, and slew five outright, whereof two (they say) were goode handsome whoores'.[2]

A much greater loss of life from a similar cause occurred at Hunsdon House, in Blackfriars. Roman Catholics attended services there, after it became the French ambassador's residence. On 26 October 1623 roughly 300 were at a service conducted by two Jesuits. So many were packed into the room that the floor joists gave way and many people fell through into the room below. About ninety-five of them were killed, including the two priests, and others were injured. This was dubbed the 'Fatal Vespers'. Protestant propagandists interpreted the incident as a sign of God's disapproval. According to the clergyman Thomas Goad, it showed that, 'both their Doctrine and Sacrifice are weakly and slenderly supported, and that God was displeased as well with their Pulpits, as altars'. Catholic writers countered with dark allegations that Protestants had 'secretly drawne out the pins, or sawed halfe a sunder some of the supporting Timber'. Others were more rational in attributing the disaster to the age of the building and the bad state of the beams, recognizing that such accidents were 'indifferently incident to mankind'.[3] They acknowledged that this was simply a particularly destructive example of the many accidents that could occur from time to time.

Wilful violence, as well as accidents, was a danger in public places, and one which could not always be anticipated. Quarrelling was dangerous in a society in which many men habitually carried weapons. Disputes could develop and lead to beatings and even murder, in tavern-room brawls or arguments in the streets, among acquaintances or with strangers. The most notorious murder during the period was that of Christopher Marlowe, in 1593, among a group of men socialising together. He was resting, after a meal, in a house in Deptford with three others, when a dispute broke out about the payment of the bill. Marlowe leapt from the bed on which he was taking a rest after the meal, grabbed the dagger of one of the men, Ingram Frizer, and hit him on the head with it, wounding him slightly. The two men 'offered one to another divers malicious words' and a struggle ensued, during which, 'the said Ingram, in defence of his life, with the dagger aforesaid of the value of twelve pence, gave the said Christopher a mortal wound above his right eye, of the depth of two inches and of the width of one inch.'[4] The wound was fatal. Frizer was detained, but received a royal pardon within a month and was released.

The quarrel in which Marlowe was killed may have been deliberately provoked, but even an apparently convivial session in a tavern could lead to murder. Robert Kilpatrick and John Jemison were among a group of people drinking together in the Prince's Arms tavern in St Martin's Lane one February evening in 1614, when 'because of divers opprobrious and contumelious words between the said Robert and John, a great discord arose between them'. Jemison left, but Kilpatrick pursued him, 'with his drawn sword in his hand, saying these words to the said John "Turne thy selfe slave", upon which the said John turned back and drew his sword and attacked the said Robert, and wounded him with his sword upon the left part of the belly.' He died the following day. Jemison was condemned to death, but later was reprieved.[5]

Other murders were committed in the streets. In 1583 William Fleetwood told Lord Burghley of a case in which, 'Mr. Nowell of the Court... caused his man to geve a blowe unto a carrman. His man haithe stricken the carrman with the pumell of his sword and therwith haith broken his skelle and killed hym.' According to Fleetwood, both men were likely to be indicted for the crime, which he anticipated would cause him trouble, 'as in the verie like case heretofore I have byn even with the same man'.[6] The implication is that Nowell had been charged earlier for another murder. Crowded streets caused disputes and one such quarrel over the right of way, in 1598, had a fatal outcome, related by John Chamberlain: 'Mr. Parker, brother to the Lord Morley, was slaine the last weeke by a man of Sir Thomas Gerrards, about a brabble for the way, whereof the fellow is acquitted, being found he did it in his owne defence.'[7]

Three years later Chamberlain made a laconic mention of a killing:

Yesterday a sonne of Harry Butlers of Hartfordshire stabd one Russell (a kinsman of my Lord of Bedfords that married Mrs. Skidamores sister) in my Lordes yard, and he died presently. Butler escaped through the Covent Garden and is not yet heard of.

In a letter written in the following year summarizing recent events, Chamberlain reported the murder of a man by a fellow-prisoner, the execution of the culprit, and a killing during a dispute at a game of bowls, usually regarded as the most placid of sports:

Captaine Heine (Mrs. Fowlers mignon) was hangd lately in Smithfield for killing his fellow prisoner in the Fleet... much about the same time her brother Boughton, that served the Archbishop of Canterbury, was stabd and kild in a brabble at bowles by his Lords page with the bishops owne knife.[8]

Some men who had killed escaped hanging. In 1612 John Smyth assaulted Richard Scudamore, gentleman, in St Martin's-in-the-Fields, and wounded him with a sword so badly that he died the following day. Smyth claimed benefit of clergy and was released. Benefit of clergy was a legal device by which first offenders who could read the first verse of Psalm 51 escaped the death penalty. They were branded on the thumb with the letter T, to show that they had avoided being hanged at Tyburn. In the following year Philip Foote of Westminster, a yeoman, was arraigned at the Middlesex Quarter Sessions for killing a man with his rapier. He pleaded self-defence and obtained a royal pardon.[9]

Some attacks were motivated by revenge. Fleetwood himself had been assaulted by a man who he had imprisoned, and was 'sore wounded in the head'.[10] Slights, insults and a variety of wrongs, deliberate or possibly inadvertent, led to duels and assaults in a society which set great store by a gentleman upholding his personal honour. In 1598 Ben Jonson killed the actor Gabriel Spencer, who had challenged him to a duel, which was fought close to the Curtain playhouse in Shoreditch. Jonson was indicted for murder, but successfully claimed benefit of clergy.

Not all of those attempting to gain revenge or pay back a slight did so through the formal process of a duel. Some preferred to take their intended victim by surprise. Sir Robert Drury had aroused the ire of Sir William Woodhouse, who:

> accompanied with fowre hacksters... set upon him as he was comming out of his coach, and, thincking they had dispatcht him, left him for dead, but it falles out better with him, for he is like to recover; marry, his man that offred himself in his masters defence was slaine outright in the place.

In 1600 Chamberlain mentioned a gentleman, 'dead of a light hurt' inflicted during an attack by 'some servants or followers' of an Oxfordshire gentleman, who apparently did not take part in the assault himself.[11] Sir John Ayres, on the other hand, was much to the fore in an attack on Edward Herbert, provoked, according to Herbert, because he believed, '(though falsly) that I had whored his wife'. One day he lay in wait for Herbert near Whitehall Palace, 'with fowre men armed with purpose to kill mee any way'. They wounded his horse and Herbert's sword was broken when he struck at Ayres.

> Hereupon some Passangers that knew mee and observed my horse bleeding in soe many places and soe many men together assaulting mee and my sword broken cryed to mee severall tymes, Ride away Ride away; But I scorning a base flight upon what Termes soever, in stead thereof alighted the best I could from my horse.

In the melee that followed, two gentlemen came to Herbert's assistance and engaged the other assailants, while he and Ayres fought it out and wounded each other. Eventually Ayres was dragged away by his men. In Herbert's account of the affray, he wrote proudly that, 'I remayned Master of the place and weapons'. He was clear that the affair had been to his honour and that Ayres had been dishonoured by his conduct.[12]

Most citizens need not have been involved in such skirmishes, which were confined to the principles and their servants or hired men, but they could be caught up in more general tumults. Fleetwood told Burghley of two such commotions in one week in 1584. The first occurred outside the playhouses in Shoreditch, where an apprentice sleeping on the grass was disturbed by a man who described himself as a gentleman and the apprentice to be 'but a rascal'. According to Fleetwood, 'after words they fell to plain blows' and the scuffle escalated until at least 500 people were involved in a mass brawl. The apprentices were so outraged that the next day they assembled in groups and threatened to break open the prisons to release their fellow apprentices who were being held. On the following evening another tumult arose, which also developed from a quarrel between two men, described as 'both very lewd fellows', arguing over a prostitute. One was a tailor, who gathered support from apprentices and 'other light persons'. His adversary was a legal clerk and because he was thought to have run into Lyon's Inn, a crowd of around 300, 'brake down the windows of the house, and struck at the gentlemen' of the Inn.[13]

In a case of a targeted attack, rather than an uproar that developed from a personal quarrel, apprentices assaulted the Cockpit playhouse, in Drury Lane, on Shrove Tuesday 1617. As a prestigious hall theatre its repertoire was aimed at the gentry, wealthy merchants and students of the Inns of Court, rather than the City's artisans and apprentices. This was reflected in the price of admission, which may have been at least three times that of an open-air playhouse. When the Queen's Men moved there from the Red Bull playhouse the apprentices lost their favourite entertainment, which probably was the motive for the attack. The actors tried to defend the building and fired at the attackers, 'killing three of them, and hurt divers, yet they entered the house and defaced yt, cutting the players apparell all to pieces, and all other theyre furniture, and burnt theyre play bookes and did what other mischeife they could'.[14] Three men were later convicted of this 'riotous assalte and spoyle done upon the dwellinge house' of Christopher Beeston. One of them died in gaol.[15] The destruction of the playbooks for the company's current repertoire was a serious loss, for they could not be replaced. Nevertheless, Beeston was able to restore the building and reopen the theatre, with the expressive new name of the Phoenix.

Such riotous behaviour by groups drew disapproval, according to Fynes Moryson. He claimed that the English despised those who, 'quarrel and fight in the streets publicly, and do not rather make a private trial of their difference, as also those who make quarrels with men of base condition'.[16] If that was indeed the case, the apprentices were not aware of it, for they planned another raid on the same playhouse for Shrove Tuesday the following year, but the Privy Council became aware of the plan and took steps to prevent the attack.

The justices certainly did not let such outbreaks go unpunished and arrested the ringleaders, who found themselves in gaol with criminals and vagrants. According to John Stow's account, there were more than

240 constables in London, 'the one half of them each night went in the marching watch, the other half kept their standing watch in every street and lane'. This was supported by Thomas Platter, who wrote that, 'watch is kept every night in all the streets, so that misdemeanour shall be punished'. Prisoners did not necessarily remain in custody for very long. Some were quickly tried and punished. Fleetwood mentioned that ten 'horsestealers, cutpurses, and such lyke' had been tried on a Friday and nine of them were executed on the Saturday, the tenth was spared by a legal process. Another prisoner at the same hearings, a shoemaker, was found guilty of murder and was executed on the following Monday. Platter thought that some twenty to thirty people were executed every day when the courts were in session.[17]

Other convicted criminals were condemned to stand in the pillory, often in Cheapside, where they were flogged, perhaps had their ears bored through with a hot iron, or even cut off. Some were sent to Bridewell. Executions and brutal punishments were inflicted in public; such proceedings could be watched by those who wished to witness them, and they could hardly go unnoticed or ignored by passers by. One group of condemned prisoners actually drew attention to themselves by their behaviour, as John Chamberlain reported: 'I shold tell you of certain mad knaves that tooke tabacco all the way to Tibern as they went to hanging.'[18] Lupold von Wedel described an execution when:

> eighteen persons, amongst them two women and two young lads, were simultaneously bound to the gallows. They stood upon carts and chatted together; the carts were driven off and they were left hanging... Their friends went up to the gallows tugged at their legs and struck at them over the breasts in order to hasten their death.[19]

Some prisoners died in gaol, victims of the miserably unhealthy conditions. John Donne's brother Henry was imprisoned for assisting a Roman Catholic priest and died in Newgate during the plague of 1593. The priest was executed.

Those imprisoned for debt were held in a separate set of prisons, known as compters, or counters. They were detained to prevent them absconding before they had satisfied their creditors, and their period of imprisonment could be a long one, until their debts were paid. Fear of imprisonment for debt was so strong that some who were afraid of being seized in the streets carried handguns. Elizabeth's government banned the carrying of pistols, because of 'great disorders... specially in and about her city of London and in the usual highways towards the said city and to her majesty's court'.[20] When this came to the government's attention again in 1613 and some of those who carried them were asked why they did so, they 'made their excuse, That being decayed in their estates, and indebted; and therefore fearing continually to be Arrested, they weare the same for their defence against such Arrests'. This was regarded as a weak excuse and, in any case, 'it is of it selfe a grievous offence for any man to arme himselfe against Justice'.[21] And creditors' agents could not be avoided for ever. In 1598 Chamberlain mentioned that Sir Walter Leveson had been arrested and imprisoned, 'being faln into hucksters handes (I meane his old creditors), who laide a traine for him and caught him at Lambeth'.[22] He died in prison four years later, with considerable debts.

The lengths to which debtors would go to avoid being detained reflected the foul conditions in the compters. In 1555 the one in Bread Street was closed and its replacement was established in Wood Street. Under the control of the Sheriffs, it was extremely unpopular, both for the number of fees taken from the prisoners and because of conditions there. In *The Compters Common-Wealth* of 1617 William Fennor, who described himself as a servant to James I, commented: 'This little Hole is as a little citty in a commonwealth, for as in a citty there are all kinds of officers, trades, and vocations, so there is in this place.' Among those incarcerated for debt was the agricultural writer Thomas Tusser, who was imprisoned in the Poultry compter, where he died in 1580. He had farmed in East Anglia and was well-known as the author of *Hundreth Goode Pointes of Husbandrie* (1557), which was enlarged until, in 1573, its title was *Five Hundreth Pointes of*

Good Husbandrie. Another author imprisoned there for debt was the playwright Thomas Dekker, in 1598, when the theatre manager Philip Henslowe paid £2 for his discharge. He was again imprisoned for debt in the following year and spent seven years in the King's Bench prison, between 1612 and 1619.

Dekker evidently lived on the edge, sometimes being able to earn enough to maintain his family, sometimes not. Others fell into debt because of an accident, such as a fire, or a downturn in trade. Chamberlain noted the bankruptcy of a mercer at Temple Bar, but was sceptical, claiming that the man's attractive wife had thirty gowns valued at £60. In 1622 things were more serious; he thought that 1,500 houses were empty within the City, 500 of them because of bankruptcies.[23] Shipwreck or capture by pirates or privateers could mean a serious loss for the vessel's owners and those who owned or had invested in its cargo. A period of sickness, when earnings were reduced, might be ruinous. In 1611 one John Harding was forced to plead for financial help, explaining:

> I am a musitian who formerly have brought upp noblemens daughters, as well as knights and gentlemens daughters, in the arte of musicke; who, through a long continuance of sycknes (my schollers, which were my only staye and sole mayntenance, beinge long sithence departed into the countrye and not yet returned), am, for wante of schollars, brought into such pinchinge penurye, as that I am not able to protect myselfe, much lesse my wife and children.[24]

Numerous diseases and conditions could prevent the victim from working and so cause financial problems. In *Troilus and Cressida*, Shakespeare gives a list of illnesses and afflictions which his audiences would recognize:

> the rotten diseases of the south, the guts-griping ruptures, catarrhs, loads o' gravel in the back, lethargies, cold palsies, raw eyes, dirt-rotten livers, wheezing lungs, bladders full of imposthume, sciaticas, limekilns

i' th' palm, incurable bone-ache, and the rivelled fee-simple of the
tetter.[25]

They would have identified the diseases of the south as syphilis, so
called because it was believed to have been brought to Europe through
Naples in 1494, by Spanish soldiers. As well as syphilis, his list can
be interpreted as referring to colic, hernias, catarrhs, kidney stones,
apoplectic strokes, paralysis, inflammation of the eye-lids, diseases
ascribed to the liver, asthma, cystitis, sciatica, psoriasis of the palm,
arthritis and ringworm.

Others lost money, by theft or fraud. The simplest form of theft was
cutting or taking a purse, which was worn against outer clothing or in
an open pocket. In 1613 a yeoman of Charterhouse Lane was indicted
for picking the pocket of Peter Vandall, a merchant of Lime Street, and
taking fourteen shillings. In another case that year, Francis Snell of
Long Lane, a haberdasher, was accused of picking the purse of Daniel
Musgrave, a brewer of St Katherine's-by-the-Tower, which contained
twenty shillings in silver. People in crowds were especially vulnerable.
Paul Hentzner's visit to Bartholomew Fair in 1598 provided an
example. After describing the opening of the fair, he added:

> While we were at this show, one of our company, Tobias Salander,
> Doctor of Physic, had his pocket picked of his purse, with nine crowns,
> which without doubt was so cleverly taken from him by an Englishman
> who always kept very close to him, that the Doctor did not in the least
> perceive it.[26]

The theft was nimbly done. Autolycus in *The Winter's Tale* comments
that, 'to have an open ear, a quick eye, and a nimble hand, is necessary
for a cut-purse'.[27]

In *The Blacke Bookes Messenger* (1592), Robert Greene described
a technique for separating a 'country gentlewoman... in a satin gown',
who was walking in Smithfield, from her 'marvellous rich purse', even
though she was accompanied by four men. Watching his opportunity

closely, the thief approached and pretended to have recognized her, 'and not only greeted her, but, as if I had been acquainted with her, I gave her a kiss, and so in taking acquaintance closing very familiarly to her I cut her purse'. When they parted the woman was quite unaware of her loss, and Greene's fictitious rogue commented that he had a 'good bung', while she had had a kiss.[28] 'Bung' was used for both a purse and a pickpocket. In *Henry IV part 2*, Doll Tearsheet exclaims to Pistol: 'Away you Cut-purse Rascall, you filthy Bung, away.'[29]

Wealthy and well-dressed people provided the most profitable potential targets, and the thief dressed accordingly in order to mingle unsuspected. An especially audacious crime was the theft of a purse in the chapel of Whitehall Palace on Christmas Day 1611, when the king was present. This attracted such attention that a pamphlet was published describing how the thief, John Selman, 'came into the Chappell in very good and seemely apparel, like unto a Gentleman or Citizen'. The purse contained forty shillings. Selman was apprehended and executed, but his fate did not deter another cut-purse mingling with the crowd at his execution and taking a gentleman's purse. He, too, was caught.[30] Selman's case attracted considerable notoriety and was alluded to by Ben Jonson in *Bartholomew Fair* (1614), in which the character Nightingale describes cutpurses plying their trade in crowds attending plays and sermons, at the sessions, even at executions, and, 'At a far better place, At court, and in Christmas, before the King's face.'[31]

An equally impudent theft was carried out in 1612, when the Spanish ambassador was the victim. As his coach was crossing Holborn Bridge a man rode up alongside, reached in and 'snatches the Ambassador's hat off his head, which had a rich jewel in it, and rides away with it up the street as fast as he could, the people going on and laughing at it'. The thief got clean away. The tale was told to illustrate how unpopular the ambassador was, but the narrator added, 'I am sorry they had so just an advantage against us to say we are barbarous in our City of London'.[32]

Farmers in London to attend a hearing in the courts would carry a purse containing £20 or £30, according to Robert Greene. Cutpurses did not necessarily act alone and Greene described a case, probably either fictitious or embellished, by which a set of thieves who had failed to separate a farmer from his purse entered an action against him for a trespass. When two sergeants tried to arrest him, in St Paul's, some of the group intervened and questioned whether they had jurisdiction in the cathedral, and a brawl was staged during which one of the thieves dragged the farmer away on pretence of befriending him. The purse was taken during the confusion. After the farmer was arrested, the thieves' accomplice who had made the charge now withdrew it because, he said, it had been based on a mistaken identity. The farmer was free to go, but only when he had paid the sergeants' fees. This he could not do because his money was gone, so a friend had to pay for him, and the farmer had earlier been overheard telling that friend that no cutpurse would ever lift his purse. This was the kind of case with which Greene regaled his readers, with the boastful countryman outsmarted by resourceful metropolitan thieves.[33]

Such well-organized groups of criminals did have a basis in fact. During Fleetwood's investigation of London's rogues and vagabonds in 1585 he inadvertently uncovered, 'a schole howse sett upp to learne younge boyes to cutt purses'. This had been established by:

> one Wotton a gentilman borne, and sometyme a marchauntt man of good credyte, who fallinge by tyme into decaye, kepte an Alehowse att Smarts keye neaere Byllingesgate, and after, for some mysdemeanor beinge put downe, he reared upp a newe trade of lyffe, and in the same Howse he procured all the Cuttpurses abowt this Cittie to repaire to his said howse.

There a pocket and a purse containing counters were hung up, surrounded by small bells, for training purposes. Those who could take the counters out of the pocket without disturbing the bells was allowed to be 'a publique foyster', and one who could rob the purse without ringing them was 'a judiciall Nypper'. Fleetwood explained that a foister was a pick-pocket and a nipper was a cutpurse, or pickpurse. In an appendix to his letter to Lord Burghley, he added further explanation, for the uninitiated:

> Note that ffoyste is to cutt a pocket, nyppe is to cutt a purse, lyft is to robbe a shoppe or a gentilmans chamber, shave is to ffylche a clooke, a sword, a sylver sponne or such like, that is negligentlie looked unto. Nota, that mylken ken is to commytt a roborie or burgularie in the night in a dwelling howse, &c.[34]

Robbery from shops or houses could be opportune, or premeditated, the thief using a hook on the end of a pole to lift items through windows. Others sent a small and lithe boy through a window to burgle the premises. Thefts from houses were common. Those of Cuthbert and Richard Burbage near the Curtain playhouse in Holywell Street, Shoreditch, were broken into one night and cloaks valued at £6 5s, a carpet, a fowling-piece, pewter and clothing to the value of over £11 were stolen. Three people were indicted for the crime; one was sentenced to death, another was branded and the third released. The aristocracy were the victims of housebreaking, as well as the citizens. Silverware worth £150 4s was stolen from the Earl of Suffolk during one burglary.[35] In 1613 two men were condemned to death for breaking into the Earl of Sussex's house near the Charterhouse and stealing a tawny cotton gown worth twenty shillings, two pairs of sheets worth ten shillings, and a saddle-cloth worth ten shillings. The house of Thomas Viscount Fenton, Captain of the Yeomen of the Guard, in St Martin-in-the-Fields, was broken into one night around midnight. The thief, a local man, got away with silverware worth £82, but he was caught and sentenced to death. In May 1614 Ann Strange, of St Martin-in-the-Fields, was charged with robbing the Spanish Ambassador. Whitehall Palace itself was burgled no less than five times between August 1613 and March 1614, when plate and linen were taken, including a collar of gold set with pearls and diamonds worth £300.[36]

Stolen goods were fenced by brokers, or broggers, who were accused of encouraging thefts. In 1601 the Lord Mayor and Aldermen wrote to Sir Edward Coke, the Attorney General, complaining that a Bill before Parliament, 'for the reformacions of abuses practised by brokers in and aboute this Cittie', had been delayed and could be lost. The issue was:

> Fellonies which the Brokers seeke by all possible meanes to abett by sellinge the stolen goods unto duchmen, Scotts and French Brokers: Whoe secretlie convey the same beyonde the seas to the great hurte and preiudice of her Maieties subiects.

They avoided registering the goods, so that many stolen items were never traced, and operated from the privileged areas in and around the City, beyond the Lord Mayor's jurisdiction. The problem had worsened because, 'those Brokers are nowe of late growen soe manie'.[37] The City had not solved its problem with 'thieving brokers or broggers, who were the receivers of all stolen goods' when Sir Thomas Middleton described his attempts to reduce vagrancy and crime during his Mayoralty in 1613–14.[38] And so an Act of Parliament was drafted in 1614, 'for discovery of thieves and punishment of retailing broggers, brokers, and other concealers of stolen goods within the City of London and within the compass of three miles of the said city'. Brokers operated as legitimate traders, as well as handlers of stolen goods, and therefore the practice was difficult to control.

Cheating and deceiving gullible men out of their money, and even their inheritance, was more sophisticated. It generated a burst of publications exploiting the public's fascination with the activities of those who fleeced, or cozened, their victims. The genre flourished between the early 1590s, when it was popularized by Robert Greene in a series of pamphlets, and the late 1610s. Thomas Dekker's descriptions of the practices of the cozeners in defrauding their victims were especially popular. In *The Dead Tearme* (1608) he asks, 'What plots are layde to furnish young gallants with readie money (which is shared afterwards at a Tavern) therby to disfurnish him of his patrimony?', and in that and later publications he explained the process.

The typical victim was portrayed as a naïve young man from the provinces, arriving in London for the first time and anxious to cut a fashionable figure. He wore fine clothes, which he was proud to display, and affected a manner and conversation that hinted at his background as a gentleman, the heir to a country estate, his wealth, and perhaps his connections at court. A figure of fun for the Londoners, he was shown to be an easy prey for the conny-catchers, who slowly entrapped him.

The process was a patient one, for the victim had to be groomed to trust the predators and not frightened off. Having identified a potential victim, they would be friendly and amenable, willing to indulge him while introducing him to the ways of the city, where he would be shown respect and given the opportunity to play the role to which he aspired. But expert players would slowly win money from him at games of cards or dice, and when he needed more, he would be introduced to an associate of theirs who could provide him with a loan. That may not have consisted of coin, however. Pleading a shortage of ready cash, the lender would offer commodities instead, which the victim could sell to raise money, or which the lender could kindly sell on his behalf. This would not raise the promised sum, but the borrower would have committed himself to repaying the original figure agreed, and be liable for a penal sum if he defaulted. To avoid that, he would take further loans, with the lender raising the stakes and demanding secure collateral as the sums increased, which often meant property. With his credit exhausted and his inheritance pledged to the lender, the gull could even be reduced to joining the conny-catchers, meeting young men from his own background when they arrived in London, to ensnare them in their turn.

The conmen's practices were alluded to by playwrights, such as Thomas Middleton and Shakespeare. In *Measure for Measure* (1604) Master Rash is described as one of the 'customers' of Mistress Overdone, a bawd: 'He's in for a commodity of brown paper and old ginger, nine-score and seventeen pounds, of which he made five marks ready money. Marry, then ginger was not much in request, or the old women were all dead.'[39] In other words, the aptly-named victim was committed to a payment of £197, having received paper – well known to be a commodity in such transactions – and ginger which he had been able to sell for no more than five marks (£3 6s 8d). The difference seems to be absurdly exaggerated, to make the point.

But the poet and playwright George Chapman actually was the victim of a fraud on a similar scale, perpetrated by two brokers, John Wolfall and Richard Adams, in 1585. Chapman, then in his mid-twenties, entered into bonds to repay a loan supplied by Wolfall and Adams, on forfeit of £100 if he defaulted. It seems likely that he did not receive the money, yet Wolfall pursued him for repayment and fifteen years later had him imprisoned for debt. After Wolfall's death, his son took up the case and in 1608 sued Chapman again for the money. Chapman's only recourse was the court of Chancery, having been pursued for more than twenty years for repayment of a loan he had not received.

Wolfall was also involved in swindling the poet Matthew Roydon, a process begun by Nicholas Skyres, who introduced Roydon to a London goldsmith, with whom he sealed a bond for £40. That was in 1582, when Roydon was a law student, and he was then drawn into further borrowing, through Wolfall, until by 1593 he owed him £150. Skyres admitted that he was Wolfall's agent, 'to draw young gents into bonds'. His victims included one Drew Woodleff who was loaned £60, but actually given, 'a certain number of guns or great iron pieces' then on Tower Hill, sold on his behalf for £30, just a half the sum for which he was now indebted. Within a short time Woodleff's pressing financial needs had led him to sign a bond in the penal sum of £200.[40] Ingram Frizer was a member of the network involved in the loans to Woodleff and he made £30 from them. Frizer and Skyres were two of the men who dined with Christopher Marlowe, before Frizer killed him. While contemporary writers cheerfully depicted the gull as an amusing figure because of his credulity, the reality for young men whose pressing need for money caused them to become ensnared by hard-nosed conmen, who were not above engineering a killing, was altogether different.

Being invited to join a game of dice or cards was not in itself suspicious. According to Fynes Moryson such games were, 'frequently used by all sortes, rather as a trade than as recreation'.[41] Those who did treat it as a source of income included the Gull-groper, described by Dekker as, 'an old Money-monger, who... comes to an Ordinary to save charges of housekeeping... yet swears that he comes thither only for the company, and to converse with travellers'. Watching the games, he would befriend a player who was running short of money, perhaps saying that he knew his father and offering to lend him a hundred pounds or two, 'then is the gold poured on the board. A Bond is made for repayment at the next quarter-day.' The gull was hooked if he took the loan, for if he lost he would be unable to repay it, and if he was winning, the gull-groper 'steals away of purpose to avoid the receipt of it'.[42] Gulls could be defrauded more swiftly if the dice were false or the cards were marked. Those who used false dice spanned the social range, for in 1613 a Robert Fuller of the Strand who was accused of cozening an apprentice 'at dice with false dice' was described as a gentleman, and Henry Raymonde of St Botolph-without-Bishopsgate, who was charged with cozening William Hurlebolte of £7 10s with false dice, was described as a poulterer.[43] Robert Dyan suffered a smaller loss, of thirty shillings, when he was defrauded by two men described as tanners, also playing with false dice.

A contemporary account listed fourteen varieties of false dice. Making them was a specialist craft, and 'Bird in Holburn is the finest workman'. The simplest form of illegal dice was one on which a number was missing.

> Sir William Herbert playing at Dice with an other gentleman, there arose some question about a cast: The other swore it was a 5 and 4: and he swore it could not be so, for it was 6:5: the other swore againe, and curst himselfe to the pitt of Hell, if it were not 5 and 4.

Herbert demonstrated that his opponent was 'a damn'd periurd Rogue' by showing that there was no 4 on the dice, so he must have been lying.[44]

Not everyone who was cheated at cards or dice lost all of the money. In December 1616 three men were indicted at the sessions, accused of waiting in the highways intending 'to deceive and defraud honest travellers of their goods and money by false arts and games'. They persuaded two millers from Canterbury to take part in a card game in a house in East Smithfield, where one of them lost £5 13s and the other £4 8s 'at decoy', which was also known as 'mumchance'. But the constable of East Smithfield apprehended two of the defrauders and recovered £9 11s of the money. This was repaid to the millers, with £1 deducted for the poor of the district.[45] Others were not so lucky, or found that the 'money' they were playing with in fact consisted of false tokens. In 1613 Henry Jeffreys was charged with 'cheating a Derbyshire gentleman with counters instead of silver'.[46]

Alehouses were believed to be at the root of these and other evils. They were generally small establishments, drawing most of their business from the poor. Taverns were somewhat grander, but still modest. John Earle wrote that, 'A tavern is a degree or (if you will) a pair of stairs above an ale-house.' It was a place to hear news, to be merry and noisy, to quarrel and yet make friends, a place to pass an afternoon or while away a rainy day.

> A house of sin you may call it, but not a house of darkness, for the candles are never out... To give you the total reckoning of it: it is the busy man's recreation, the idle man's business, the melancholy man's sanctuary, the stranger's welcome, the Inns of Court man's entertainment, the scholar's kindness, and the citizen's courtesy.[47]

An inn was a much larger and grander establishment, catering for travellers, with rooms for visitors and stabling for their horses. They were the destinations for carriers and travellers from the provinces. Thomas Platter observed that:

> There are a great many inns, taverns, and beer gardens scattered about the city, where much amusement may be had with eating, drinking,

fiddling, and the rest... what is particularly curious is that the women as well as the men, in fact more often than they, will frequent the taverns or ale-houses for enjoyment.[48]

Although they were licensed, the number of places where drink could be bought was thought to be increasing. In 1612 the Privy Council wrote to the Lord Mayor and Aldermen complaining that, 'there is almost no house of receipt, or that hath a back door, but when it cometh to be let it is taken for a tavern'. Even the best houses were being used as taverns, including those fit to be used for ambassadors' residences or those 'of the best quality'. Despite repeated warnings from the Council, the corporation had tolerated this, so that the number of taverns in London had increased, 'to far exceed the number meet in a well ordered state'. Its argument that good houses were being used as taverns was supported by a petition against the conversion of a house on Ludgate Hill. The Council passed this on to the corporation. Yet it emerged that the house had recently been bought by Sir Henry Hobart, Lord Chief Justice of the Common Pleas, who explained that, having had lost his position as Attorney General, he was opening the tavern 'for the better support of himself and family'.[49] He did not fit the profile of those whom the Council had in mind as tavern-keepers.

When Sir Thomas Middleton became Lord Mayor in 1613, he set about to ascertain the situation by conducting a survey of alehouses and victualling houses, even going into them himself, in disguise. He discovered that there were over 1,000 such premises, where strong beer was brewed and, he believed, 'much mischief... plotted'. Middleton tried to reduce both their number and the amount of beer they could brew, which, he claimed, then lowered the demand for corn and malt, and so the price of corn.[50] But the brewers stood to lose from this tightening up and 'by their indirect dealing' circumvented it by supplying the usual quantities of beer to those who kept tippling houses, 'in the night'. Prices rose again as a result.

Middleton's diligent efforts did not go unnoticed. They were mocked by Ben Jonson in *Bartholomew Fair*, which was first performed in

October 1614, just at the end of Middleton's term of office. Justice Adam Overdo, in disguise, describes the 'worthy worshipful man, sometime a capital member of this city', who masquerades as a porter, carman, dog-killer and, in the winter, a seller of tinder-boxes, and fussily enters 'into every alehouse, and down into every cellar', measuring puddings and custards, pots and cans, and weighing loaves. In other words, he enforced the regulations, and 'he would not trust his corrupt officers; he would do't himself'.[51]

This was just one phase in a continual process, in which the justices tried to restrict the numbers of alehouses and taverns, and so the amount of corn converted into malt, while those prosecuted for keeping unlicensed alehouses remained undeterred, encouraged by a buoyant demand for beer and food, and hospitable premises in which to consume it. Just a few years after Middleton's attempted curb, Orazio Busino wrote that:

> There are endless inns and eating houses, for board alone or for board and lodging, beer and wine shops, wholesale and retail for every imaginable growth, alicant, canary, muscatels, clarets, Spanish, Rhenish and from hundreds and thousands of other vineyards, all excellent, though... they are very dear.[52]

De Maisse reported the arrival of the wine ships from Bordeaux towards the end of December, commenting that, 'They discharge half their cargo and more at London, and the rest is for other places in the Realm.'[53]

The eating places that Busino referred to included ordinaries, which offered a greater range of provisions than alehouses, and they were graded socially. Some were for gentlemen. Others were for the citizens, who, according to Dekker, were typically, 'your London Usurer, your stale Batchilor, and your thrifty Atturney', where the rooms were 'as full of company as a Jaile, and indeede divided into severall wards, like the beds of an Hospital'. But George Whetstone, in 1584, identified an even less salubrious grade of ordinaries, which were 'placed in

Allies, gardens, and other obscure corners, out of the common walks of the Magistrate'. They were frequented by 'maisterless men, needy shifters, theeves, cutpurses, unthriftie servants, both serving men, and prentises'. Here could be found not only petty criminals, but someone 'who for a pottle of wine, will make no more conscience to kill a man, than a Butcher a beast'.[54] Among the prisoners sharing Barnadine's gaol in *Measure for Measure* were, 'Master Starve-lackey, the rapier and dagger man, and young Drop-heir that killed lusty Pudding'.[55]

Alehouses and low-grade ordinaries were just the sort of places where the justices went when they were ordered to recruit soldiers. Rathgeb explained that, 'when soldiers are wanted, and idlers are seen lounging about, they give them money, and then they are bound to serve whether they like it or not'.[56] London was not exempt from contributing troops, as James Dalton explained, *c*.1580: 'If soldiers must be mustered, Londoners have no law to keep themselves at home.'[57] But there were few volunteers, most soldiers did not serve willingly, and so the city's quotas had to be filled by forcible recruitment. Elizabeth's campaigns against Spain, in the Netherlands, supporting the Protestants in the French Wars of Religion and fighting the Irish rebels required more troops than could be supplied by volunteers. Men aged between sixteen and sixty were liable to serve, but those responsible for meeting the city's allocations were unwilling to enlist householders and those established in a trade, who would, in any case, be able to bribe the recruiting officers.

Single men and the poor were most at risk. In 1597 the Privy Council authorized the enlisting of vagabonds and told the Lord Mayor that 200 should be seized and offered the choice of being incarcerated in a house of correction or serving at Ostend. In 1601 the Justices in Middlesex and Surrey were instructed to, 'make perfect searches in all alehouses, inns and such places as those loose persons do lodge'. Yet their raids did not provide enough men. In the early spring of 1596 Spanish forces from Flanders besieged the French town of Calais. The prospect of the closest port to England being captured by the Spanish was so uncomfortable that a plan was hastily made to send a force to raise the siege. The need for men was so immediate and desperate that at the Easter communion services the constables in London, 'were fain to close up the church doors, till they had pressed so many men'.[58] This was in vain, Calais fell to the Spanish before an English force could be assembled.

In 1602 the shortage of men was such that the Lord Mayor's officers quite overstepped the mark. According to Philip Gawdy, a lawyer of Clifford's Inn:

> There hath bene great pressing of late, and straunge, as ever was knowen in England, only in London... they did not only presse gentlemen, and sarvingmen, but Lawyers, Clarkes, country men that had lawe causes, aye the Quenes men, knightes, and as it was credibly reported one Earle.

They were rebuked by the Privy Council, which announced that all who had a complaint would be heard. What it had intended, when it ordered the levy, was that:

> they should take out of all ordinaryes all cheting companions, as suche as had no abylyty to lyve in suche places, all suche as they cold fynd in bawdy houses, and bowling allyes, wch they never went to any but only to the bowling allyes. All the playe howses wer beset in one daye and very many pressed from thence, so that in all ther ar pressed fowre thowsand besydes fyve hundred voluntaryes, and all for flaunders.[59]

Perhaps the Lord Mayor's men had taken too literally a complaint made by the Council in 1598. Its order for 600 men from London contained the instruction that they should be 'better chosen, both for ability of body and aptitude for war service, than heretofore, and that they be well appareled'.[60] Knights, gentlemen and lawyers should certainly have met those requirements.

Men who had been impressed were resentful and unruly, but desertion was dangerous, as Chamberlain reported in October 1600: 'Here were five or sixe souldiers hangd the last weeke in divers quarters of this towne for running from their captaines'.[61] Soldiers who had been discharged were also likely to be disorderly. When a mob of 500 of them who had returned from the expedition to Portugal in 1589 became over-boisterous at Bartholomew Fair, threatening to loot the stalls, 2,000 of the Trained Bands were called out to subdue them.

Between 1582 and 1602 London sent 9,515 men to the wars. This was a disproportionate number. Although the city contained five per cent of England's population, it supplied roughly eleven per cent of its soldiers. With even those attending church or a playhouse regarded as legitimate targets for impressment, being taken to serve in the armies was a persistent source of anxiety for men without the means, or a master, to pay for a substitute, or otherwise escape the recruiters' clutches. A period of service could prove to be more than a loss of freedom for a time, for the danger of death, maiming or disease was very high. In 1589 Lord Willoughby led an expedition to Brittany that lasted for three months, and only roughly fifty per cent of the men who embarked returned. The force of 4,000 soldiers which the Earl of Essex took to Rouen in 1591 had been reduced to just 380 men by the end of the campaign.

Accidents and tumults, casual or pre-determined violence, theft, cheating and impressment were among the hazards of daily life. But the risks to be run in the streets, at alehouses and ordinaries, around the playhouses, even when emerging from Easter communion, did not deter the citizens from participating in a wide-range of entertainments and enjoying a lively social life in the city.

8

A World of People

Londoners were not totally confined by the daily routines of work and chores; they had leisure time and could afford to pay for entertainments. The amount of work available might vary, by season or as demand fluctuated, and the hours of the working day and week were flexible. The amusements available included annual pageants, Bartholomew Fair, the plays that were performed in the yards of inns, adapted for the purpose, and increasingly at the new playhouses. The playhouses attracted all social groups, while access to the masques performed at court or in the Inns of Court was restricted, by rank. But a range of informal recreations could also be enjoyed; Londoners might gaze at street entertainers and those displaying the extraordinary and the bizarre, go to see exotic animals at the Tower menagerie, or watch them being baited on Bankside. Their periods of convivial leisure were enlivened by music and dancing, at the playhouses and at home.

The inauguration of a new Lord Mayor was the major event in the civic calendar and an opportunity for display and celebration. The mayoral election was held on Michaelmas Day, 29 September, and the newly elected mayor took office on 28 October. On the following day he went in procession on the Thames to Westminster, to be sworn in by the Lord Chancellor. This was a great occasion. William Smith, in 1575, wrote that the procession passed along the Thames 'in a most triumphant-like manner'.[1] Each company had its own barge, decked out in its livery, and many other boats joined the flotilla. Von Wedel was greatly impressed by the spectacle: 'The river was covered with little boats, and the throng was so great that the number of the vessels assembled was estimated at some hundreds.' The boats carried not only the officials of the City and companies, but also 'all sorts and conditions of artisans'. This popular participation in the celebrations continued at Westminster, where, 'Although the courtyard is very large, there was no getting either in or out.'[2]

After the Lord Mayor had taken the oath he returned to the Guildhall in another grand procession, along Cheapside. This was an elaborate affair, with the theme of the pageant often adapted to the new mayor's trade, and enlivened by exotic touches, such as 'a lyon and a cammell' in 1602. From at least 1585 it was common for the pageant to be written by an established dramatist. The incoming Lord Mayor's livery company arranged and funded the event and the companies vied with each other in the lavishness of the occasion. The most expensive pageant of the period was that in 1613, which cost the Grocers' Company £1,300. In 1561 the Drapers' Company had spent just £151.

The Lord Mayors' shows drew very large crowds. Von Wedel noticed that, 'right in front walked some with squirts such as are used for quenching a fire. With these they squirted water at the crowd, for the street was full of people, so that they were forced to make way.'[3] Orazio Busino attended the inaugural celebrations for George Bowles, a grocer, for which the pageant was written by Thomas Middleton and entitled 'The triumphs of honour and industry'. Busino and his compatriots watched from an upper window in Goldsmiths' Row, in Cheapside, where the windows were 'all crowded with the sweetest faces'. And below:

> looking into the street we saw a surging mass of people, moving in search of some resting place which a fresh mass of sightseers grouped higgledy piggledy rendered impossible. It was a fine medley: there were old men in their dotage; insolent youths and boys, especially the apprentices... painted wenches and women of the lower classes carrying their children, all anxious to see the show.

At the windows, 'as far as the eye could reach, we perceived sundry gallants in attendance on fine ladies'. He saw few horsemen or coaches, and those coaches that did arrive were harassed by the crowd:

They cling behind the coaches and should the coachman use his whip, they jump down and pelt him with mud. In this way we saw them bedaub the smart livery of one coachman, who was obliged to put up with it. In these great uproars no sword is ever unsheathed, everything ends in kicks, fisty cuffs and muddy faces.[4]

Squibs and firecrackers were thrown from the windows into the crowd, which was so large that a passageway for the procession could be kept open only with difficulty. The City Marshal and two footmen paraded up and down, helped by:

> a number of lusty youths and men armed with long fencing swords, which they manipulated very dexterously, but no sooner had a passage been forced in one place than the crowd closed in at another. There were also men masked as wild giants who by means of fireballs and wheels hurled sparks in the faces of the mob and over their persons, but all proved unavailing to make a free and ample thoroughfare.

The procession included, 'lions and camels and other large animals, laden with bales from which the lads took sundry confections, sugar, nutmegs, dates and ginger, throwing them among the populace'. One of the floats carried a model of a ship, supposed to have just returned laden from the Indies. Children danced, 'with much grace and great variety of gesture, moving the whole body, head, hands and feet, keeping excellent time and performing figures, first round one tree and then another, changing their positions, so as really to surprise everybody'. As well as the Lord Mayor, Aldermen and Sheriffs, the procession included the Archbishop of Canterbury, members of the aristocracy, and perhaps as many as one thousand liverymen of the Grocers' Company. The acts, banners and floats created a spectacle which Busino found fascinating.[5]

A feast at Guildhall followed the procession. William Smith explained that, 'they dine that day to the number of 1000 persons all at the charge of the Mayor and the two Sheriffs'. He estimated the cost at £400, half of which was paid by the Lord Mayor and the remainder equally by the Sheriffs.[6] The final event of the two-day celebrations was a service at St Paul's.

Another hugely popular event in the civic calendar was Bartholomew Fair in Smithfield. That had been established in 1123 by Rahere, founder of St Bartholomew's Priory, with the tolls levied contributing to the priory's income. It was held on three days centred on St Bartholomew's Day, 24 August. The fair was a great event, combining general entertainment and trading, especially in cloth, leather, pewter, livestock, and butter and cheese. It became an important cloth market and although that declined in the late sixteenth century, in 1593, when the government proposed to ban the fair because of an outbreak of plague, the Lord Mayor objected that to do so would be economically damaging, especially for the clothiers.

The fair was opened by the Lord Mayor, who arrived on horseback, followed by the Aldermen, and a procession which von Wedel, in 1585, numbered at roughly 1,000 people. Wrestling matches followed and when the opening ceremonies were concluded, 'the Mayor again appeared to a flourish of trumpets and returned to the town'.[7] A few years later Hentzner saw, 'a parcel of live rabbits turned loose among the crowd, which boys chase with great noise'.[8]

Jonson's play *Bartholomew Fair* (1614) conveys the bustle, variety of people, range of entertainments and the incidents characteristic of a day at the fair. Attractions included puppeteers, conjurers, actors, balladeers, wrestlers, tightrope-walkers, fire-eaters, sideshows and booths for eating and drinking. As well as legitimate trading and general jollity, the fair was associated with cheating, petty crime and immorality and was roundly condemned. In 1610 Robert Cecil, Earl of Salisbury described it as, 'this filthy Fair of St. Bartholomew... continual origin of the plague'.[9]

Elizabeth I's accession was celebrated annually during her reign on Accession Day, 17 November. A special event and celebration was held to mark James I's accession. This was his ceremonial entry into the City, delayed by the plague epidemic until March 1604. When the royal party arrived at Tower Wharf, 'landing they could only climb the stairs with difficulty, owing to the crowd which had gathered to see their Majesties'. On the following day the royal party passed through the City, from the Tower to Whitehall, 'preceded by all the magistrates of the City, the Court functionaries, the clergy, Bishops and Archbishops, Earls, Marquises, Barons and knights, superbly apparelled and clad in silk of gold, with pearl embroideries; a right royal show'. The principal feature was seven enormous wooden arches topped with pageants, five erected by the city and one each by the Dutch and Italian communities in London. The first arch that the king passed through, at Fenchurch Street, was the Londinium arch, 50 feet wide and 50 feet high, surmounted, according to Thomas Dekker, with 'true models of all the notable houses, turrets, and steeples within the City'. The Dutch arch at the Royal Exchange was described by him as, 'a royall and magnificent labour', but in the, perhaps slightly biased, opinion of Niccolò Molin, a Venetian, the Italian arch, 'certainly came first, both for the excellence of its design and for the painting which adorned it'. To make and erect the arches required the efforts of eighty joiners, sixty carpenters, twelve sawyers and seventy labourers, with specialist craftsmen such as turners, smiths, moulders, carvers and painters, and plumbers for a fountain. The text was written by Dekker and Jonson, and the entertainers included musicians and actors.[10]

The citizens were enthusiastic. Dekker wrote that the City became:

a world of people. The Streetes seemde to bee paved with men; Stalles... were set out with children, open Casements fild up with women. All Glasse-windowes taken downe, but in their places, sparkeled so many eies, that had it not bene daye, the light which reflected from them, was sufficient to have made one.[11]

The king did not display quite the same enthusiasm as the spectators, showing impatience with the length of some of the speeches and being uneasy when the crowds came too close to him, as he usually was.

This was a highlight for the citizens, but they also attended more frequent events in large numbers, at the theatre and animal baiting arenas staging bear- and bull-baiting, and the cockpits for cock fighting. Theatres became increasingly popular during the second half of the sixteenth century, and their commercial success was reflected in the investment in playhouses, a new building type. Following the adaptations of the yards of inns along Bishopsgate, Gracechurch Street, in Whitechapel and at the Belle Sauvage on Ludgate Hill, purpose-built playhouses came to be erected around London. These were in the suburbs, at Whitechapel, Shoreditch, Bankside, Cripplegate and Clerkenwell. The corporation was generally hostile and from time to time tried to close down the playhouses, partly reflecting the moral repugnance to public plays among Puritan elements in the city, but partly, too, fear of disorder, crime and vice among the large numbers who congregated there. They were closed during plague outbreaks, as the corporation explained to the actors in 1584: 'To play in plagetime is to encrease the plage by infection: to play out of plagetime is to draw the plage by offendinges of God upon occasion of such playes'.[12] Objections to the playhouses also had a practical, self-interested, basis, for they, 'corrupt the youth of the Cittie, and withdrawe Prentises from their worke'.[13]

The first purpose-built playhouse was the Red Lion, erected on the south side of Whitechapel High Street in 1567. Described as a 'messuage or farme house', the building had a turret 30 feet high and tiers of galleries. The builder was John Brayne, a grocer and the brother-in-law of the actor and impresario James Burbage. They also collaborated in the erection in 1576 of the Theatre, in Shoreditch. Burbage's brother Robert was a carpenter, and he probably was responsible for the construction. The Theatre was an amphitheatre playhouse, with three galleries, and a tiled roof. It cost approximately £666. In August 1578 John Stockwood, a schoolmaster, described it as 'a gorgeous Playing-place erected in the fieldes'.[14] The venture proved to be such a success that in the following year another playhouse, the Curtain, was built just 170 yards away. John Stow, in 1598, wrote that near Holywell, 'are builded two publique houses for the acting and shewe of comedies, tragedies, and histories, for recreation. Whereof the one is called the Courtein, the other the Theatre.'[15]

The two houses came to be managed by Burbage and the profits were pooled. With an admission price of 1d for standing space in the yard, but higher charges for more select places in the galleries, Burbage succeeded in attracting large and socially diverse audiences. Annual profits were between £190 and £235. Most of the leading companies of players performed there, including the Lord Chamberlain's Men, after the company was formed in 1594. Shakespeare was one of its actors and stayed with the company throughout the remainder of his time in London. The Theatre was the better and more prestigious house and it is likely that all of Shakespeare's plays until 1597 were staged there, as well as Marlowe's *Dr Faustus* and *Edward II*. Although the Curtain was the subsidiary playhouse, *Romeo and Juliet, Henry IV part II* and *Henry V* were performed there in the mid-1590s and Ben Jonson's *Every Man in His Humour*, in 1598. Because of occasional public disorders and the character of some playgoers and those who hung around the playhouses, they drew the hostile attention of the Middlesex justices and the Privy Council. In July 1597 the Council ordered that both should be dismantled, although the order was not carried out.

The first playhouse south of the Thames was built at Newington Butts in the village of Newington, beyond Southwark, in the late 1570s. It seems not to have been a great success, perhaps because of 'the tediousnes of the waie' which led there and its distance from the river. In 1592 it was said that, 'of long time plays have not there been used on working days'. The playhouse was brought back into use for a time in 1594, but by 1599 was described as 'only a memory'.[16]

Bankside was much more advantageously placed, as audiences could be brought by the watermen to the riverside landing stages close by. It had the added advantage that bear- and bull-baiting had been well established there from at least as early as the 1540s. The Rose was built there in 1587 by the impresario Philip Henslowe and John Cholmley, 'citizen and grocer'. Cholmley received the exclusive right to sell food and drink on the premises. The playhouse was a polygon of fourteen sides, roughly 72 feet across, with three tiers of galleries. In 1592 Henslowe enlarged it, at a cost of £105, raising the audience capacity from roughly 1,950 to 2,400. In that year some actors defected from Burbage's company at the Theatre to join Lord Strange's Men at the Rose, boosting its appeal.

The Rose was followed by the Swan, erected in 1595 by Francis Langley. A member of the Drapers' Company, he had made a fortune through the fees and duties payable to him as the City's alnager, its inspector of wool and cloth. His conduct provoked such opposition that he was deprived of the post in 1599, but he had also made money as a property landlord, brothel keeper and money lender, acquiring the Paris Garden from a creditor who defaulted. A writ was served on Langley, William Shakespeare, Dorothy Soer and Anne Lee in November 1596, perhaps instigated by William Gardiner, Sheriff of Surrey and Justice of the Peace with jurisdiction over the Paris Garden area. Nothing further is known of the case, which may have been part of a legal manoeuvre against Langley and the playhouse.

The Swan was circular or polygonal, with three tiers of galleries. A Dutch visitor, Johannes de Witt, was there in 1596 and noted that the theatre consisted of a timber frame on a brick base, and that it had space for 3,000 spectators. He sent a sketch of the interior to Arendt de Buchel, who copied it into his commonplace book; a copy of it survives as the only contemporary illustration of a playhouse of the Elizabethan and Jacobean period.

In 1597 *The Isle of Dogs*, by Thomas Nashe and Ben Jonson, was performed there and provoked a sharp reaction as containing 'very seditious and slanderous matter'. Jonson and two actors were arrested and imprisoned and Nashe fled. Langley had fallen foul of Sir Robert Cecil over the theft of a Spanish diamond that should have gone to the queen, which may explain the forcefulness of the reaction to the play.[17]

A different kind of scandal occurred in 1602, when the author Richard Vennar advertised a production at the Swan called *England's Joy*, in nine scenes, and sold tickets at the high price of twelve shillings each. This was, he declared, 'To be acted only by certain gentlemen and gentlewomen of account'. According to John Chamberlain, the audience that assembled included 'great store of good companie and many noble men'. Vennar spoke only a few lines of the prologue and, as there was nothing to follow, then attempted to flee, but was arrested. The Lord Chief Justice treated his fraud as merely 'a jest and a merriment', but the audience, having been cheated, was less indulgent and 'the common people... revenged themselves upon the hangings, curtains, chaires, stooles, walles, and whatsoever came in theire way, very outragiously, and made great spoile'.[18]

In 1600 Langley sold the Paris Garden, with the Swan, but had become embroiled in another dispute involving a playhouse. This was the Boar's Head on the north side of Whitechapel, just outside the City boundary. It was first mentioned in 1557 and was one of the two inns first recorded as used for playhouses, the other being the Saracen's Head in the village of Islington to the north of the city. In 1594 a lease was granted to one Oliver Woodlife, a haberdasher, stipulating that he should build a stage and a tiring-house (changing room) here, which he did, and in 1597 he extended the galleries. The stage occupied much of the former inn yard and was surrounded with new galleries on three sides, with the existing inn gallery on the fourth. The galleries and stage were roofed.

The playhouse came into the possession of Robert Browne, an actor with the Earl of Derby's Men in 1599 while they played at the Boar's Head. By 1600 he had become the actor-lessee there and Langley was now co-landlord with Woodliffe. They attempted to dispossess him of the lease by systematically impeding his productions; hiring men to stop performances, taking the entrance money from the collectors, and enforcing payments from the acting companies. When trouble of this kind led the company to curtail its season there in 1601, Browne took them to court and the acting company counter-sued. Browne won the case and in 1602 the Privy Council licensed a joint company of members of the Earl of Oxford's company and the Earl of Worcester's company to play there as 'the place they especially have used and do best like of'. It probably ceased to be used as a playhouse at the end of that lease in 1616. Browne had died of plague in 1603, 'very pore' according to Edward Alleyn's wife Joan.[19]

James Burbage was also troubled by disputes, exacerbated by his personality; in 1584 William Fleetwood, the Recorder, described him as 'a stubburne fellow'.[20] John Brayne died in 1586 and his widow attempted to claim a share in the Theatre and the company's profits. This led to an unseemly brawl in 1590 between her representatives and the Burbages, in which James's son Richard, by now a leading actor, was alleged to have committed an assault, using his fists and a broomstick.

The lease of the ground on which the Theatre stood was due to expire in 1597, and as that came closer another problem developed. The landlord, Giles Allen, threatened to raise the rent by £10 per annum, but for only five years, claiming that ownership of the building would then revert to him. James Burbage died early in 1597, having invested roughly £1,000 creating an indoor theatre at Blackfriars, which the Privy Council prevented him from opening after protests from residents. His elder son Cuthbert continued the negotiations and eventually agreed terms for a new lease, but Allen would not accept Richard Burbage as surety. After the lease expired, the company performed at the less satisfactory Curtain, while the Theatre stood unused.

The impasse was decisively broken on 28 December 1598, a cold and snowy day, when the Burbages, with Peter Street, a carpenter, and a team of workmen dismantled the building, stacking the materials and marking the timbers so that they could be reassembled. These were taken to Street's wharf at Bridewell Stairs, and from there shipped across the river to Bankside, where they were used to construct the Globe playhouse. Astounded and outraged, Allen took the case to court, but without success.

The Globe was an open-air playhouse; a regular polygon of twenty sides, with a diameter of roughly 100 feet. Like the Theatre, it had three tiers of galleries; unlike the Theatre its roof was thatched, not tiled, despite the corporation's prohibition of thatching. It could hold up to 3,000 patrons. A description of mid-May 1599 refers to it as 'newly erected' and on 21 September the Swiss traveller Thomas Platter saw a performance of Shakespeare's *Julius Caesar* there, 'in the house with the thatched roof... with a cast of some fifteen people; when the play was

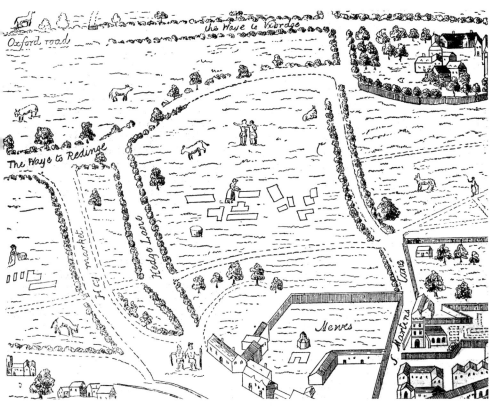

90. This mid-sixteenth century plan-view has the future Oxford Street to the north and the Haymarket along the west, with St Martin's Lane to the east. The fields shown here were to be developed as part of the West End, including Leicester Square and Soho.

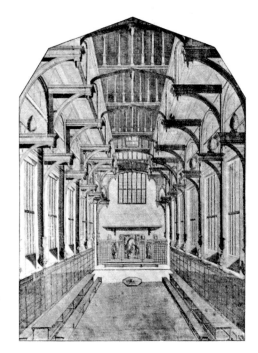

91. The interior of Middle Temple Hall, erected in 1562–70. The hall is 101 feet long and is spanned by a double hammerbeam roof.

NAVIS ECCLESIÆ CATHEDRALIS S PAVLI
PROSPECTVS INTERIOR

92. The nave of St Paul's cathedral, drawn by Wenceslaus Hollar. Known as Paul's Walk, this was a busy meeting place, where gossip and news were exchanged and business was transacted, and also a thoroughfare, between Cheapside and Ludgate Hill.

Opposite below: 95. Outdoor services were held on the site of Paul's Cross, adjoining the cathedral, where the weekly sermons delivered from the pulpit attracted large congregations. The print shows the houses on the north side of the cathedral, in Paternoster Row, a centre of publishers and booksellers.

93. Cornhill, c.1630, with the conduit house known as the tun on the right and the tower of the Royal Exchange in the background.

94. Cornhill c.1599, with the tower of St Peter's church.

Yea, becaufe of the houfe of the Lord our

God, I will feeke to do Thee good, Pf. 122. 9.

Bleffco m'y that Preacher bee, That will pray and fpeake for mee.

96. St Saviour's church, Southwark, was the church of a twelfth-century Augustinian priory, and subsequently a parish church. The fabric was much rebuilt and restored; the central tower is of late fourteenth-century date. In 1905 it became the Anglican Southwark Cathedral. William Shakespeare was a parishioner for a time and in 1911 a memorial was erected to him, with a reclining effigy in alabaster. His brother Edmund was buried here in 1607.

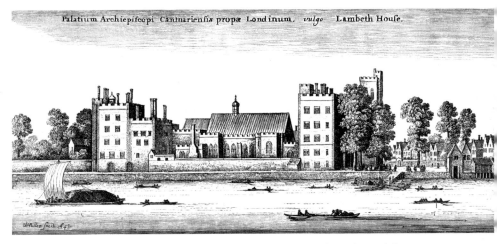

Palatium Archiepiſcopi Cantuarienſis propæ Londinum. *vulgo*   Lambeth Houſe.

97. Lambeth Palace, across the Thames from Westminster, is the palace of the Archbishops of Canterbury. It was substantially rebuilt by Thomas Cranmer, in the 1540s. Richard Bancroft (archbishop, 1604–10) directed that his book collection should remain at Lambeth and his successor, George Abbot (archbishop, 1611–33), employed it as the basis of a free public library, established at the palace in 1612. James I gave it his approval, as 'a monument of fame within his kingdome'.

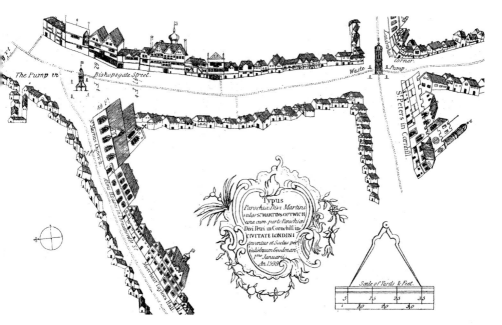

98. Plan of parts of Bishopsgate Street, Threadneeedle Street and Cornhill, drawn in 1599. It shows the churches of St Martin Outwich and St Peter's, Cornhill, and the Merchant Taylors' hall in Threadneedle Street, where the company's troupe of boy players acted in 1573–4. During the mid-1590s Shakespeare lived in the parish of St Helen, Bishopsgate, part of which appears on the left of the plan.

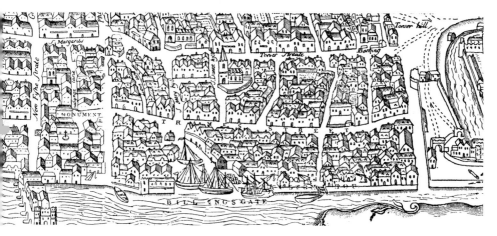

99. The Thames Street and Billingsgate area, between London Bridge and the Tower, shown on the 'Agas' plan of mid-sixteenth century London.

ESCHEAPE MARKET
from a very old Drawing. Vide Dr Combe.

100. Eastcheap Market in 1598, drawn by Hugh Alley. This was one of the butchers' markets; Alley shows livestock being driven along the street and carcasses in the butchers' shops which line the frontage. Alley had a role in enforcing the market regulations imposed by the corporation.

101. The New River brought water from Chadwell and Amwell, in Hertfordshire, to the New River Head at Islington. This ambitious scheme to supplement London's water supply was completed in 1613.

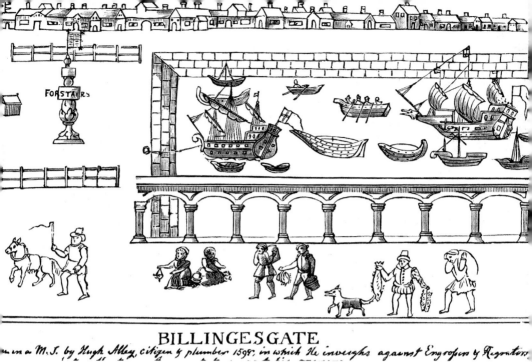

BILLINGESGATE

...an a M.S. by Hugh Alley, citizen & plumber 1598; in which he inveighs against Engrosers & Regraters

102. The dock and market area at Billingsgate, drawn by Hugh Alley in 1598. It depicts three-masted sea-going vessels, as well as smaller craft. Billingsgate was beginning to develop as a fish market, with grain, fruit and root crops also traded there. The market and the trade at the wharves caused traffic congestion along Thames Street, shown in the background, which regulations in 1617 attempted to lessen.

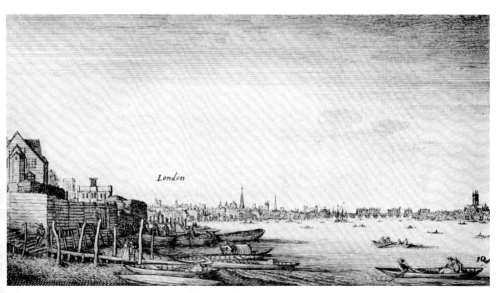

103. Milford Stairs, close to Arundel House, off the Strand, was a landing point for wherries, roughly 2,000 of which transported passengers along the Thames. On the skyline is the Tower of London, beyond London Bridge; the prominent tower to the right of the bridge is that of St Mary Overy's church, Southwark.

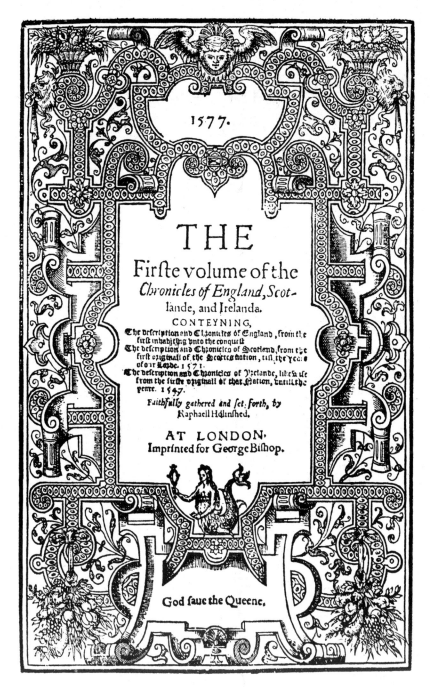

1577.

THE

Firſte volume of the
Chronicles of England, Scot-
lande, and Irelanda.

CONTEYNING,

The deſcription and Chronicles of England, from the
firſt inhabiting vnto the conqueſt
The deſcription and Chronicles of Scotland, from the
firſt originall of the Scottes nation, till the yeare
of our Lorde. 1571.
The deſcription and Chronicles of Yrelande, likewiſe
from the firſte originall of that Nation, vntill the
yeare. 1547.

Faithfully gathered and ſet forth, by
Raphaell Holinſhed.

AT LONDON.
Imprinted for George Biſhop.

God ſaue the Queene.

Above: 105. The title page of Raphael Holinshed's *Chronicles of England, Scotland, and Ireland*. This was one of the principal sources which Shakespeare drew upon for material for his history plays.

Opposite: 104. Printing was an important trade in London, with Fleet Street one of its centres from the early sixteenth century. Jost Amman's woodcut of 1574 shows a printer's workshop, with plates being inked before being put into the press, and the compositors working in the background.

106. A parish constable doing his rounds, guarding the citizens from fire and robbery, with lantern, bell, pike and dog. Shakespeare's London escaped a major fire, but burglary was among the crimes that troubled Londoners, and the house in the background has a prominent lock. From the title-page of Thomas Dekker's *The Belman of London* (1608).

107. The aristocracy and gentry increasingly travelled to London by coach, not on horseback, adding to the traffic congestion in the city. When plague threatened, they left the metropolis, such as this family depicted on the road to Hammersmith.

To cut off ones head, and to laie it in a platter,

which the iugglers call the decollation of Iohn Baptiſt.

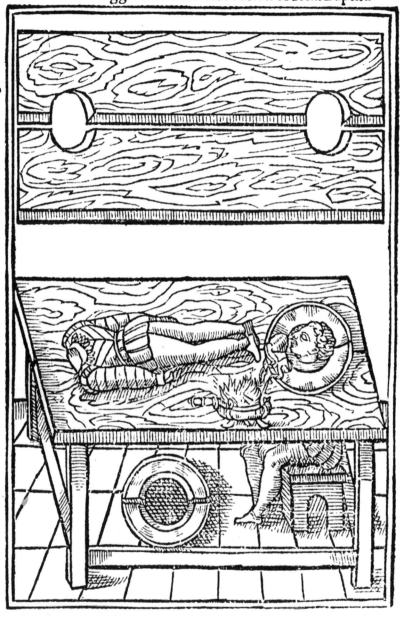

The forme of ỹ planks, &c.

The order of the acti-on, as it is to be ſhew-ed.

108. Among the many entertainers in London were conjurors, described by contemporaries as jugglers, using tricks to deceive the eyes of gullible audiences. This example was known as 'the decollation of John the Baptist', which showed an apparently decapitated body and the head alive at its feet.

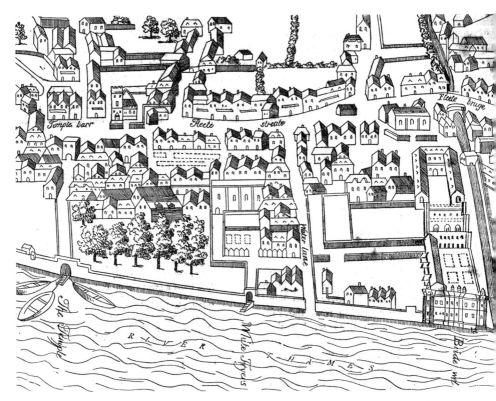

109. The Fleet Street area in the mid-sixteenth century, with the Temple between the street and the river, its gardens marked by a grove of trees. To the east is 'White Fryers', the site of the monastery of mendicant friars, dissolved in 1538. A hall theatre was created in part of its buildings in the early seventeenth century and was used by a boys' company between 1607 and 1613. The Fleet River runs north from the Thames at the eastern edge of the plan; alongside it is the former palace of Bridewell, which became the City's house of correction.

of the Plague.

A fingular and fecret Remedie the which I receiued from a worthy man of *Venice*, admirable for his learning in all Sciences, who of curtefie imparted the fame vnto me, with proteftation that he had feene wonderfull effeéts of the fame.

Take of the Rootes of Tormentil and white Diptamy, as much of the one as of the other, of Bole Armenus wafht in Rofe water, the quantitie of a great Cheffnut; of orientall Pearles one dramme : of the fharings of Iuory one dramme and a halfe, beate all thefe into a fine powder, and incorporate them with conferue of Rofes in a marble Morter, referue this confection in a veffell of glaffe well coucred. Take hereof the quantitie of a great Nut in the Morning, and drinke a fpoonefull of the Iuice of Mary-golds or Lemons with Sugar after it. The Gentleman that gaue me this, affured mé that hé had giuen it to many in the time of the great Plague in Venice, who though continually conuerfant in the houfes of thofe that were infected, receiued no infection or prejudice by them. A Remedie worthy the vfe and noting.

110. During plague epidemics the prescriptions of many preventatives were circulated. This one, described as 'a Remedie worthy the use and noting', was included in Thomas Lodge's *Treatise of the Plague* (1603) and was claimed to have been effective during the great plague in Venice in 1576.

111. The late sixteenth and seventeenth centuries was a particularly
active period in the foundation of almshouses for the elderly poor, in
response to the loss of charitable provision following the dissolution
of the monasteries and other religious houses during the Reformation.
These almshouses in Tothill Fields provided for twenty elderly women.
They were founded by Cornelis Van Dun, born in Breda in Brabant and a
Yeoman of the Guard to the Tudor monarchs. He died in 1577.

112. Charles I's mother-in-law, Marie de Medici, arrived in London in
1638 and her procession is shown passing alongside Cheapside, escorted
by members of London's Trained Bands. This was one of the wealthiest
streets in the city and was lined with large houses. The illustration is from
Jean Puget de La Serre's *Entrée Royalle de la reyne mere du roy tres-
Chrestien dans la ville de Londres* (1638).

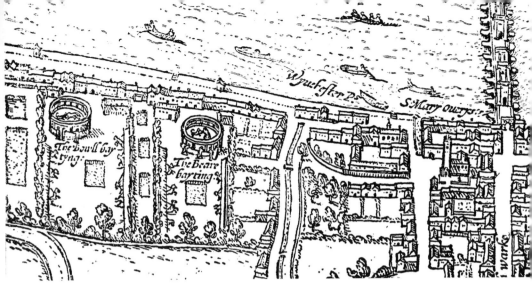

113. Bankside as depicted on the plan of London included in Georg Braun and Franz Hogenberg's *Civitatis Orbis Terrarum* (1572). The bull- and bear-baiting arenas are shown; the first playhouse in the district was built later. That was the Rose, erected in 1587 by Philip Henslowe and John Cholmley.

Opposite: 115. The Bankside area of Southwark, shown on Wenceslaus Hollar's Long View of London of 1647. The Globe Theatre is mistakenly labelled as the 'Beere bayting house'; it was the second Globe, erected in 1614 after its predecessor had been burned down. The building labelled the Globe was the Hope, erected in 1613 and used for animal baiting and as a theatre. The error was corrected in later editions.

114. The Globe Theatre on Bankside, home of Shakespeare's company, redrawn from Visscher's view of 1616. The first Globe was built on this site in 1599, with a thatched roof. It was destroyed by fire in 1613 and rebuilt in 1614, with a tiled roof. The new theatre was described as 'the fayrest that ever was in England'.

Convent garden   S. Clement

Arundel house   Pink house   Temple stayre   Temple   Blackfryers   Baynar de Ca...

The Globe

Beere bayting h

VENVS
AND ADONIS

Vilia miretur vulgus: mihi flauus Apollo
Pocula Castalia plena ministret aqua.

LONDON
Imprinted by Richard Field, and are to be sold at
the signe of the white Greyhound in
Paules Church-yard.
1593.

Left: 116. The title page of William Shakespeare's poem *Venus and Adonis,* the first of his works to be published, in London in 1593. It was followed in 1594 by *The Rape of Lucrece.* Both were dedicated to his patron Henry Wriothsley, third Earl of Southampton.

Below: 117. Warrant of James I dated at Greenwich on 17 May 1603, ordering the issue of Letters Patent authorizing the king's servants, including William Shakespeare, Richard Burbage, John Hemming and Henry Condell, to play 'comedies, tragedies, histories, enterludes, pastoralls & stage plaies... within their now usuall house called the Globe'. James had succeeded Elizabeth on her death on 24 March and had arrived in London only ten days before issuing this warrant.

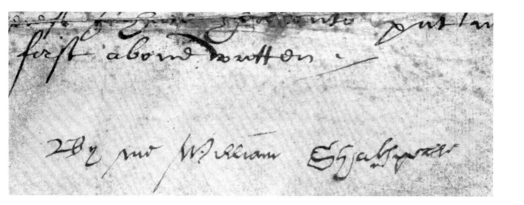

Above: 118. William Shakespeare's signature on a page of his will. The will was dated 25 March 1616, but perhaps first drafted in January, for at the head of the first page 'January' was struck through and replaced by 'March'. Shakespeare describes himself as of Stratford-upon-Avon in the county of Warwickshire, gentleman, with the conventional phrase that he is 'in perfect health & memorie god be praysed'. He died on 23 April and the will was proved by his son-in-law John Hall on 22 June.

Middle: 119. William Shakespeare's signature on a legal document of 1612.

Below: 120. Richard Burbage (1568–1619) was the leading actor of the Chamberlain's Men, formed in 1594, and renamed the King's Men after the accession of James I in 1603. This was Shakespeare's company, and Richard acted the leading roles in his plays. His father James managed the Theatre and the Curtain playhouses in Shoreditch and created a theatre at Blackfriars. After his death in 1597 Richard, with his brother Cuthbert, continued his work and in 1599 they erected the Globe playhouse on Bankside.

121. The Swan theatre, redrawn from Visscher's view of 1616. The playhouse was built on Bankside in 1595, following the enlargement of the Rose in 1592. The first Globe was to be built in the same district in 1599.

If on your man you light
The firft draught fhall you play,
If not tis mine by right
At firft to lead the way

122. A game of chess between two gentleman, with the pieces represented by letters (1614). Chess was recommended as 'one of the things, which best difcouereth the imagination'.

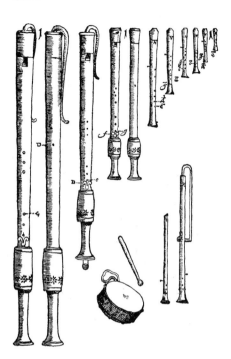

123. Woodcuts showing flutes, pipes and tabor, from the *Theatrum Instrumentorum* of 1620, by the German composer and musical theorist Michael Praetorius (c.1571–1621).

THE MASQVE OF QVEENES

Penthesilea, the braue Amazon,
Swift=foote Camilla, Queene of Volscia,
Victorious Thomyris of Scythia,
Chast Artemisia the Carian Dame,
And fayre=hayr'd Beronice, Egipts fame,
Hypsicratea, Glory of Asia,
Candace, pride of Æthiopia,
The Britane honor, Voadicea,
The vertuous Palmyrene Zenobia,
The wise, And warlike Goth, Amalasunta,
And bold Valasca of Bohemia:

124. Ben Jonson (1572–1637) wrote some of the masques performed at James I's court, collaborating with the designer Inigo Jones. *The Masque of Queenes*, performed at court in February 1609, extolled the virtues of the queen and her ladies in waiting.

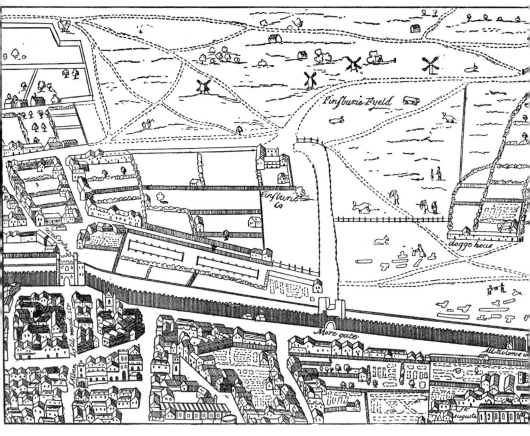

125. London Wall, Cripplegate and Moorgate in the mid-sixteenth century. Although a suburb had developed beyond Cripplegate, no development had taken place outside most of this stretch of the city wall and archers are shown in Finsbury Fields, set out as an archery ground in 1498. The subsequent growth of the extra-mural suburbs was one of the developments that attracted comment as the city's population grew in the late sixteenth century.

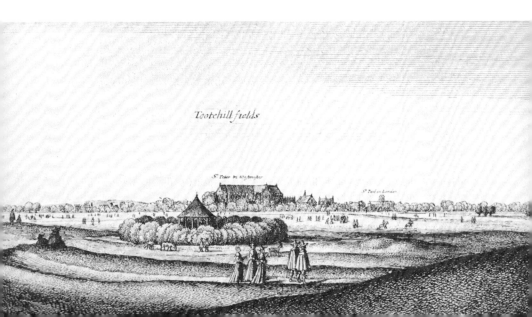

Mr. WILLIAM
SHAKESPEARES
COMEDIES,
HISTORIES, &
TRAGEDIES.

Published according to the True Originall Copies.

LONDON
Printed by Ifaac Iaggard, and Ed. Blount. 1623.

127. The title page of the First Folio edition of Shakespeare's plays, published in 1623 and incorporating his portrait, engraved by Martin Droeshout.

Opposite: 126. Westminster Abbey stood at the edge of the metropolis, with Tothill Fields beyond, which provided a place for recreation, close to Westminster and Whitehall.

over, they danced very marvellously and gracefully together as is their wont, two dressed as men and two as women'.[21] Of the twenty-nine plays known to have been written specifically for the Globe between 1599 and 1608, sixteen were by Shakespeare. Ben Jonson's *Every Man out of his Humour*, *Sejanus* and *Volpone* and Thomas Dekker's *Satiromastix* were among the other plays performed there.

Shakespeare was one of five members of the Lord Chamberlain's Men who owned, between them, one half of the shares in the playhouse; the Burbages owned the other half. The actors were replaced as they either left the company or died, but the arrangement of joint ownership continued. The Chamberlain's Men became the King's Men following the accession of James I in 1603. The company performed at the Globe during the summer and, from 1608, in the winter at the indoor theatre at Blackfriars. No company had previously attempted to run two theatres, but the Blackfriars proved to be a financial success. In 1612 it was said that in the course of a winter season the King's Men gained £1,000 more from the Blackfriars than they usually did from a summer season at the Globe, and by the mid-1630s a share in the Blackfriars was almost twice as valuable as one in the Globe. The two theatres drew a different clientele, with the Blackfriars appealing to a more affluent and sophisticated audience than the populist Globe. The lowest admission price to the Globe was 1d, to the Blackfriars it was 6d.

The Blackfriars was available because the Privy Council had relented on its earlier ruling. The theatre had been used since 1600 on a lease held from the Burbages by Henry Evans, for a boys' company, the Children of the Chapel. It was renamed the Children of the Queen's Revels after James's accession. Boys' companies performed in London, and also before the court, from the mid-1570s; the Chapel Children at an earlier hall in the Blackfriars priory buildings and the Paul's Boys at their choir school adjoining the chapter house. They performed no oftener than once a week, and around 1590 their performances were discontinued. But both companies were revived in 1600, with such success that almost all of the leading playwrights produced material for them, with the exception of Shakespeare and Thomas Heywood. Although performing only infrequently, and in small halls, the professional companies saw the boys' popularity as something of a threat. The controversy was referred to by Shakespeare in *Hamlet*, with the comment that, 'there has been much to-do on both sides'. Rosencrantz tells Hamlet that the 'tragedians of the city' are not as well followed as before, not because their own standards have fallen, but as a consequence of the 'late innovation'. This he explains as, 'an aery of children, little eyases, that cry out on the top of question, and are most tyrannically clapped for 't. These are now the fashion, and so berattle the common stages – so they call them – that many wearing rapiers are afraid of their goose-quills, and dare scarce come thither.'[22] An aery was a bird's offspring and an eyas a young hawk not yet fully trained, and so Shakespeare was describing them as inexperienced birds of prey. But their popularity did not last and the Paul's Boys' final performance was in 1606.

When the Burbages did not renew Evans's lease of the Blackfriars in 1608, the Children of the Queen's Revels were transferred to the Whitefriars, a hall theatre recently created by the poet Michael Drayton and Thomas Woodford in a former friars' refectory. In 1607 the dramatist Lording Barry, with several other investors, including Drayton, established the boys' company there, outside the City's jurisdiction. But on 30 September 1608 that exemption came to an end and in October the court of Star Chamber committed two men to Newgate for, 'suffering a stage play to be publicly acted in the Whitefriars', when all theatres should have been closed as part of the plague regulations. This gave the investors great problems and Barry, unable to meet his debts, went off to be a pirate. The boys continued to use the Whitefriars playhouse until 1613, but the company was disbanded by 1615.

By then the Burbages and Shakespeare had suffered a major crisis, the destruction of the Globe. This can be dated precisely, to the afternoon of Tuesday 29 June 1613, during a performance of Shakespeare's *Henry VIII*. When the point was reached in act I scene IV where the stage direction is 'Drums and Trumpets, chambers discharge', the chambers (cannon) fired accordingly and a spark set the roof alight. The folly of building a thatched roof, presumably for cheapness, was now dramatically demonstrated, as the fire spread to destroy the roof and then engulf the building, gutting it within an hour. The loss to the company could have been even worse, for its invaluable play-books and costumes were saved. The only injury was suffered by a man whose breeches caught fire, but they were extinguished by someone with a bottle of ale, who was prepared to sacrifice it to save the victim from further harm.

The Globe was rebuilt by the partnership of the Burbages and five members of the company, still including Shakespeare, at a cost of £1,400. It stood on its predecessor's foundations and so had the same dimensions, and presumably was similar in most other respects, but was given a tiled roof. The rebuilt playhouse was open again by the end of June 1614 and John Chamberlain described it as 'the fayrest that ever was in England'.[23]

The Bankside playhouses competed for their audiences with the animal baiting arenas nearby, which were well established there and presented other entertainments as well. In 1585 von Wedel and his companions went to 'a round building with three corridors built one above the other', where they watched as 'three bears, each larger than the other were baited one after another by some dogs'. Then a horse was baited, followed by a bull, which 'offered game resistance'. Then 'out of a mechanical contrivance there came forth various males and females who danced, sang and spoke'. A man threw bread into the crowd, which was also showered by apples and pears from 'a rosette which hung above the place', and those scrambling to pick up the fruit were bombarded with fireworks and 'were greatly scared, which was a mirth-provoking sight'. The entertainment ended with a firework display. Thomas Platter went to the Bear Garden in 1599 and watched as a blind old bear was beaten by boys with sticks. He counted 120 English mastiffs that were kept to fight the bears and complained that the stench from the animal pens and kennels pervaded the entire area.[24]

Philip Henslowe acquired a controlling interest in the Bear Garden in 1594 and bought Edward Alleyn's share in 1611. In 1613 Henslowe granted a lease to Jacob Meade, and they contracted with Gilbert Katherens to demolish the buildings and erect a playhouse. Known as the Hope, it was to be, 'bothe for players to playe in, And for the game of Beares and Bulls to be bayted in the same'.[25] Katherens agreed to complete the playhouse, with the stables for bulls and horses, by the end of November 1613, for £360. The timing suggests that Henslowe was hoping to take advantage of the fire which had destroyed the Globe, picking up its customers while it was being rebuilt. But the much lower building costs indicate a far more modest building than the Globe.

Although Jonson's *Bartholomew Fair* was performed at the Hope in 1614, the rebuilt Globe prospered and the sharing arrangement did not endure. Henslowe died in 1616, leaving his share to Alleyn, and he and the actors' company, Prince Charles's Men, quarrelled with Meade. After Henslowe's death, bull- and bear-baiting came to predominate at the Hope; in 1632 Nicholas Goodman wrote that 'wilde beastes and Gladiators did most possesse it'.[26]

When the first Globe was built, the Rose was in disrepair. Rather than spend money on refurbishing it, with the competition from the Globe so close by, Alleyn and Henslowe built a new playhouse for their company, the Lord Admiral's Men, in the City's northern suburbs at Golden Lane, Cripplegate. Although the site was approved as 'very conveneient, for the ease of People', some objections were raised, until a warrant from the Privy Council to the Middlesex justices required them, 'to Tollerate the proceedinge of the saide New howse near Goulding lane. And... theffectinge and finishinge of the same Newehowse, without anie yor lett or interruption'. Known as the Fortune, it was opened in 1600, the builder having followed the pattern set at the Globe for many aspects of the Fortune, although it was a square building. The Council then stipulated that the Fortune was to replace the Curtain as one of only two theatres permitted in London, the other being the Globe.[27]

Each side of the building was 80 feet long externally and 50 feet internally and it was 32 feet high. Built of timber, it had a tiled roof and two levels of galleries, said to be large enough to hold 1,000 people. After Henslowe's death, in 1616, ownership of the playhouse, which cost £520, passed to Alleyn, who in 1618 was leasing it to the acting company, now known as Palsgrave's Men, for £200 per year.

In December 1621 the Fortune burnt down; Alleyn made a laconic entry in his diary that, 'this night at 12 of the clock the Fortune was burnt'. John Chamberlain wrote that, 'On Sonday night here was a great fire at the Fortune in Golden-lane, the fayrest playhouse in this towne. It was quite burnt downe in two howres & all their apparell & playbookes lost, whereby those poore Companions are quite undone.'[28] The loss must have been disheartening, but Alleyn immediately began a new building and raised £1,000 for the purpose. Built on the same site, the new Fortune was polygonal, not square, and of brick.

The Fortune and the Red Bull, an inn playhouse in Clerkenwell, were 'mostly frequented by Citizens, and the meaner sort of People', according to the seventeenth-century theatre historian James Wright.[29] Other writers sneeringly described the Fortune's patrons as apprentices, apple-wives and chimney-boys. Its reputation was not helped by the behaviour of some of its clientele. In 1612 the Middlesex Justices noted that because of:

> certayne lewde Jigges songes and daunces used and accustomed at the playhouse called the Fortune in Goulding lane, divers cutt-purses and other lewde and ill disposed persons in great multitudes doe resorte thither at the end of every playe, many tymes causinge tumults and outrages.[30]

Their reaction was to issue an order banning jigs at the end of plays.

Among the Fortune's patrons was the notorious transvestite Mary (or Marion) Frith, known as Moll Cutpurse and the subject of Thomas Middleton and Thomas Dekker's play of 1611 written for the Fortune and entitled, *The Roaring Girl, or, Moll Cutpurse*. She was accused by the church's High Commission court of appearing at the Fortune, 'in man's apparel and in her boots and with a sword at her syde' and she also 'sat upon the stage in the public viewe of all the people there present in man's apparel and played upon her lute and sange a song'. She was even daring enough to challenge those who doubted her sex to come to her lodgings to discover the truth, with 'other immodest and lascivious speeches'. When the play was published in 1612 the title page carried a woodcut of her in man's clothing and smoking a pipe.[31]

The Red Bull also developed a reputation for violence and vulgarity. It had been adapted as a permanent theatre c.1605 by Aaron Holland, perhaps specifically for the Queen's Men. The last inn theatre to be adapted, it was a large, rectangular building, with galleries and a tiring house. The Queen's Men's principal playwright was Thomas Heywood, and plays by Thomas Dekker, John Ford and John Webster were also performed there. In 1616 the actor and impresario Christopher Beeston moved the company to a hall theatre, adapting a cockpit in Drury Lane into an indoor playhouse. In contrast to the Red Bull's large and rowdy audience, the Cockpit, like the Blackfriars, was smaller and aimed at a more select clientele.

Audiences at the Blackfriars may indeed have been select, but they were also numerous, which created problems for the locals, according to their petition of 1619: 'There is daylie such resort of people, and such multitudes of Coaches (whereof many are Hackney Coaches, bringinge people of all sortes) that sometymes all our streetes cannott containe them.' The congestion was so bad that Ludgate became blocked, and the coaches were a danger, for they:

> breake downe stalles, throwe downe mens goodes from their shoppes. And the inhabitantes there cannott come to their howses, nor bringe in their necessary provisions of beere, wood, coale or haye, nor the Tradesmen or shopkeepers utter their wares, nor the passenger goe to the common water staires without danger of their lives and lymmes.[32]

John Taylor estimated the numbers attending plays every day, in a petition he prepared on behalf of the watermen in 1614. Their complaint was based on a fall in trade because of the removal of some of the companies, 'the players have all (except the King's men) left their usual residency on the Bankside, and do play in Middlesex far remote from the Thames, so that every day of the week they do draw unto them three or four thousand people'. This was a serious loss for the watermen, who, according to Taylor, had increased in numbers to serve the large audiences crossing the river to the Bankside playhouses.[33]

The playhouses were thriving. Paul Hentzner, in 1598, wrote that there were performances almost every day, where the actors played, 'to very numerous audiences; these are concluded with excellent music, variety of dances, and the excessive applause of those that are present'.[34] They took place in the afternoon, 'beeing the idlest time of the day', according to Thomas Nashe.[35] Platter gave a much fuller account of the theatre at the end of the sixteenth century:

> daily at two in the afternoon, London has two, sometimes three plays running in different places, competing with each other, and those which play the best obtain most spectators. The playhouses are so constructed that they play on a raised platform, so that everyone has a good view. There are different galleries and places, however, where the seating is better and more comfortable and therefore more expensive. For whoever cares to stand below only pays one English penny, but if he wishes to sit he enters by another door, and pays another penny, while if he desires to sit in the most comfortable seats which are cushioned, where he not only sees everything very well, but can also be seen, then he pays yet another English penny at another door. And during the performance food and drink are carried round the audience, so that for what one cares to pay one may also have refreshment.[36]

The cheapness of the admission for the groundlings standing in the yard helped to make the theatre so popular. Even the Venetian ambassador was prepared to watch a play from there, according to Antimo Galli, a Florentine, reporting his visit to the Curtain in 1613. Galli described the yard as, 'an infamous place in which no good citizen or gentleman would show his face', yet the ambassador chose to stand there, 'down below among the gang of porters and carters'.[37]

Visitors commonly went to the playhouses, and they were impressed. Busino reported that:

in London, as the capital of a most flourishing kingdom, theatrical representations without end prevail throughout the year in various parts of the city, and are invariably frequented by crowds of persons devoted to pleasure who, for the most part dress grandly and in colours, so that they all seem, were it possible, more than princes, or rather comedians.[38]

The playwright Thomas Heywood wrote that:

playing is an ornament to the city, which strangers of all nations, repairing hither, report of in their countries, beholding them here with some admiration: for what variety of entertainment can there be in any city of Christendom, more than in London?[39]

Fynes Moryson summarized the situation in 1617, with the comment that London, 'hath foure or five Companyes of players with their peculiar Theaters Capable of many thousands, wherein they all play every day in the weeke but Sunday, with most strang concourse of people'. He was widely travelled, yet proudly concluded that, 'there be, in my opinion, more Playes in London then in all the partes of the worlde I have seene, so doe these players or Comedians excell all other in the world'.[40]

In 1594–5, when two playhouses were open, the weekly audience may have been about 15,000 people. Ten years later at least three playhouses and two hall theatres were presenting performances and the audience was likely to have been 21,000 people per week.[41] With such large audiences, plays ran for just a few performances, and most were not revived. This required a constant flow of new material and between 1558 and 1642, roughly 3,000 new plays were written, 650 of which have survived. That represented a period of sustained creative writing, for acting companies that were highly praised, and performed before large and socially varied audiences.

Writers also produced texts for the masques performed at court and by the lawyers' societies at the Inns of Court. The masque became firmly established as a courtly entertainment during the early years of James's reign, with one performed on Twelfth Night and at least one more during the winter months. Inigo Jones designed those produced for the court, eight of them with Ben Jonson, in an uneasy but productive collaboration. A feature of the masque was that women courtiers took the female parts, whereas in the playhouses all the parts were acted by men and boys.

According to Busino, 'after Christmas day there begins a series of sumptuous banquets, well-acted comedies, and most graceful masques of knights and ladies'. He and his fellow Venetians attended the Prince of Wales's masque at the Banqueting House of Whitehall Palace in 1618: 'A large hall is fitted up like a theatre, with well secured boxes all round. The stage is at one end and his Majesty's chair in front under an ample canopy.' Masques were performed before invited audiences of aristocrats, courtiers and diplomats, and were well attended. Indeed, Busino and the other members of the Venetian retinue in their usual box were, 'so crowded and ill at ease that had it not been for our curiosity we must certainly have given in or expired'. And the whole house was packed full, with 'such a concourse... for although they profess only to admit the favoured ones who are invited, yet every box was filled notably with most noble and richly arrayed ladies, in number some 600 and more according to the general estimate'.[42]

Masques were expensive productions. The two which were performed by the Inns of Court at the wedding celebrations of Princess Elizabeth and Frederick, Elector Palatine, in 1613, were prepared, 'without respect of charges or expenses'. Those who arranged the performances:

employed the best wits and skilfullest artisans in devising, composing and erecting their several strange properties, excellent speeches, pleasant devices and delicate music, brave in habit, rich in ornament, in demeanour courtly, in their goings by land and water very stately and orderly.

The elaborate procession that made its way from Chancery Lane to Whitehall Palace along the Strand included fifty gentlemen on horseback, two triumphal chariots, about a hundred horses, each led by 'two Moors... attired like Indian slaves', and the masquers themselves, on horseback. Also in the procession was, 'an antic or mock-masque of baboons, attired like fantastic travellers in very strange and confused manner, riding upon asses or dwarf jades, using all apish and mocking tricks to the people, moving much laughter as they passed'.[43]

The citizens could only watch these and other lavish shows as they went along the streets, but they indulged in their own popular amusements, quite separate from those of the court. After Moryson had praised the actors he added:

> Not to speake of frequent spectacles in London exhibited to the people by Fencers, by walkers on Ropes, and like men of activity, nor of frequent Companyes of Archers shooting in all the fieldes, nor of Saynts dayes, which the people not keeping (at least most of them, or with any devotion) for Church service, yet keepe for recreation of walking and gaming.[44]

In 1574 Thomas Norton complained of 'the assemblies' who were watching some women acrobats then performing in London, which he described as, 'the unchaste, shamelesse and unnaturall tomblinge of the Italian Weomen'.[45] In 1602 John Chamberlain told Dudley Carleton of 'a Sicilian juggler that workes wonders at cardes, and gets very much otherwise of our curious and credulous women'. In *The Comedy of Errors*, Antipholus mentions 'nimble jugglers that deceive the eye'.[46]

As well as such examples of street theatre, strange phenomena drew the crowds. After von Wedel left Bartholomew Fair he went into the city, where he saw 'a cow with six legs and also a porpoise and a turtle'. On another occasion he went to look at a fifty-three-year-old woman who was so small that she was 'but six thumbs long. Her legs were marvellously short being but a span in length. Her paces were no longer than those of a cock.' He also saw, 'a boy whose head was speckled red and black like a pig's'.⁴⁷ Shakespeare drew attention to the gullibility, or perhaps fascination, with the unusual or freakish. On Prospero's island in *The Tempest*, the jester Trinculo comes across the prone figure of Caliban and tries to decide whether he has found a man or a fish. From the smell he thinks it may be a fish:

> A strange fish! Were I in England now, as once I was, and had but this fish painted, not a holiday fool there but would give a piece of silver. There would this monster make a man. Any strange beast there makes a man. When they will not give a doit to relieve a lame beggar, they will lay out ten to see a dead Indian.⁴⁸

Archery and wrestling were among the popular sports. According to Busino, 'Well nigh throughout the year they have archery meetings in the fields near London', and that they, 'frequently wrestle before a concourse of two or three thousand curious spectators'. Young people amused themselves. They could throw and kick a ball:

> a great distance dexterously and well... The lads throw the ball in the streets, aiming at a mark, according to certain rules, females also taking part with them, as they also like to have a little capering on feast days. Other lads more spirited, contend with wooden swords and daggers, exchanging rough blows.⁴⁹

More rumbustious ball games did not find favour. Football was played 'within the streetes and lanes neere adioyninge to ye Citye of London'. The Puritan clergy disliked and condemned it, as they did 'any exercise which withdraweth us from godlines'. Sabbath observance and the playing of sports on Sundays were among the sources of tension between Puritans and many citizens. Philip Stubbes, in 1583, singled out football not only for that reason, but because of its pernicious influence:

> it may rather be called a frendly kinde of fyghte than a play or recreation – a bloody and murthering practise than a felowly sport or pastime.

For dooth not everyone lye in waight for his adversarie, seeking to overthrowe him and picke [pitch] him on his nose, though it be upon hard stones?

He regarded it as a pastime from which grew, 'envie, malice, rancour, cholar, hatred, displeasure, enmitie, and what not els, and sometimes murther, fighting, brawling, contortion, quarrel kicking, homicide, and great effusion of blood, as experience dayly teacheth'. Thirty years later the justices decided to act because of the 'greate disorders and tumults [which] doe often arise and happen within the streetes and lanes neere adioyninge to ye Citye of London by playinge at the footeball'. In January 1615 they instructed the constables to 'represse and restrayne all manner of footeballplaye'. But that was an unenforceable measure, given the popularity of the sport and the numbers taking part.[50]

Bell-ringing was also popular and, in contrast to football, an approved activity. The queen was said to support the practice, 'considering it as a sign of the health of the people'. Hentzner commented that the English were, 'vastly fond of great noises that fill the ear, such as the firing of cannon, drums, and the ringing of bells, so that in London it is common for a number of them... to go up into some belfry, and ring the bells for hours together, for the sake of exercise'.[51] Four years later, in 1602, Philip Julius, Duke of Stettin-Pomerania was struck by the bell-ringing in London, going on until late in the evening. He was told that 'young people do that for the sake of exercise and amusement, and sometimes they lay considerable sums of money as a wager, who will pull a bell the longest or ring it in the most approved fashion'. The parishes vied with each other to have a peal of 'harmoniously-sounding bells'.[52] In 1618, Busino was rather irritated by the bell-ringing in London, both because of the noise and the misuse of bells for recreation, not for their true religious functions:

In almost every belfry they ring seven or eight large bells in tune, just like a piece of music. It is said that some of them do it to warm themselves in the winter by pulling, since for summoning the people to sermons or to their other devotions, they touch them sparingly... They continue this pompous noise whole days and nights, without considering for what holy purpose they were sounded of yore.[53]

Serenading was much less noisy and intrusive, yet it, too, could create a nuisance, for in 1606 the corporation imposed a ban on the playing of musical instruments, 'at or under any nobleman's, knight's or gentleman's window'. More than 100 men in Elizabethan London described themselves as 'minstrels', although they were not well regarded and were bracketed with vagabonds in some legislation. They had a wide repertoire of songs, madrigals and ballads to draw on. Much of it was published; in 1575 Elizabeth I granted to Thomas Tallis and his younger colleague William Byrd the monopoly of publishing any 'songe or songes in partes, either in English, Latine, Frenche, Italian, or other tongues that may serve for musicke either in Churche or chamber, or otherwise to be either plaid or soonge'.[54] Both were organists and composers of church music, Gentlemen of the Chapel Royal and Roman Catholics.

Tallis died in 1585; according to his epitaph, 'As he did live, so also did he die, In mild and quiet sort, o happy man'. Byrd became the dominant figure in English musical life over the following generation, composing a range of music, including masses, anthems, fantasias, keyboard music, elegies and laments, and secular songs. Composers wrote for church, court and theatre, and published songs as well as formal works. The music published during the period included two sets of madrigals by Alfonso Ferrabosco, from Bologna, who worked at Elizabeth's court in the 1570s and was married at St Botolph, Aldgate, in 1578. His son, also Alfonso, composed music for the courts of Elizabeth and James I, and theatre music, collaborating with Jonson in the production of masques and composing the songs for *Volpone*, performed at the Globe in 1606. The Italian madrigal was taken up and adapted by Thomas Morley, who was both organist and singer at St Paul's cathedral, and from 1592 a Gentleman of the Chapel Royal. He and his wife lived in St Helen's, Bishopsgate at the same time as Shakespeare. His published compositions include versions of 'O mistress mine' from *Twelfth Night* and 'It was a lover and his lass' from *As You Like It*. His collection of instrumental pieces published in 1599 was, according to the dedication, suitable for the City Waits, the City of London's consort, who he described as 'excellent and expert musicians'.[55]

Music and dancing were an integral part of the entertainment provided at the playhouses. The plays themselves contained music and players had to be proficient musicians as well as actors. All of Shakespeare's plays contain music, with the sole exception of *The Comedy of Errors*. Music was also performed before and after the play. When the Duke of Stettin-Pomerania attended a playhouse in 1602, a concert before the play lasted roughly an hour and was performed on, 'organs, lutes, pandores, mandolins, violins and flutes'. Cornets and hautboys, forerunner of the oboe, were common instruments on stage, and when the Privy Council refused to permit the opening of Burbage's theatre at Blackfriars it cited the 'noyse of the drummes and trumpets' among its reasons.[56]

Ballads formed the less reverential part of the contemporary repertoire, written or adapted by writers who specialised in the form, such as William Elderton, Thomas Deloney and Richard Johnson, who described himself in 1603 as 'a poore freeman' of the City. Some were aimed at Londoners, telling of great events, celebrating famous citizens, such as Richard Whittington, or describing and praising the city's districts and buildings: Gray's Inn, Hyde Park, Maiden Lane, St Paul's Steeple, Tower Hill, the New Exchange. They could be uncomfortably topical. A ballad by Deloney issued in 1596 complained of the shortages of grain, prompting the Lord Mayor to imprison the publisher and printer, Deloney presumably having made himself scarce. Others were more light-hearted pieces.

They were circulated in large numbers and were said to have been pasted on the walls of alehouses, to encourage communal singing. In the scene in *Twelfth Night* in which Sir Toby Belch and his companions make merry in Countess Olivia's house, with songs, ballads and catches (rounds, in which singers enter at different times, with the same words), they are reprimanded by her steward Malvolio:

My masters, are you mad? or what are you? Have ye no wit, manners, nor honesty, but to gabble like tinkers at this time of night? Do ye make an alehouse of my lady's house, that ye squeak out your coziers' [cobblers'] catches without any mitigation or remorse of voice? Is there no respect of place, persons, nor time, in you?

Sir Toby did not respond to the social insult, but defended their musical abilities with the indignant retort that, 'We did keep time sir, in our catches'. In 1609 Thomas Ravenscroft, who worked with the Paul's Boys, published *Pammelia*, the earliest printed collection of English rounds and catches, partly to preserve them, for 'pittie were it, such Mirth should be forgotten of us'. Also that year he published another collection in *Deuteromelia*, which included 'Hold thy peace, knave', sung in *Twelfth Night*. He published further settings of rounds in *Melismata* (1611).[57]

Shakespeare's plays contain about forty songs, but also quotes or mentions of more than a hundred other songs of the period. Londoners could enjoy music at the playhouses and the fair, in taverns, alehouses and their homes, and in the streets, while the courtiers had their occasional masques and frequent dancing. In 1600 John Donne described the court as 'full of jollity and revels and plays'.[58] The galliard, pavan and courant were favoured at court; Shakespeare mentions those dances, as well as the measure, brawl (a brando), canary, Scotch jig and sinke-a-pace (or cinque-pace, a galliard).

Music making, the annual Lord Mayor's Show and Bartholomew Fair, and the entertainment at playhouses and in the streets, were a part of life in the busy, bustling, prosperous and growing metropolis. Such relaxations could offset the citizens' anxieties, caused by the hazards of daily life and the threats to their city. Londoners heard of repeated plots to kill the monarch – that in 1605 would have detonated an explosion on an unprecedented scale – and were aware of potential political instability, reflected in uncertainties over the succession to the throne and the Earl of Essex's armed foray into the City. Other concerns were involvement in the conflicts in the Low Countries and France, and the war with Spain, the great power of late sixteenth-century Europe, which lasted for nineteen years. This brought the danger of invasion in 1588, the year of the Great Armada, and damage to overseas trade by enemy action. And the rebellion in Ireland seemed to drag on and on. Cold winters increased the consumption of fuel and wet summers inevitably were followed by poor harvests and high prices. Even a run of good harvests could not stem the overall rise in the cost of food. As the city grew, increasing numbers of poor Londoners lived in shoddy housing and squalid, overcrowded conditions.

Yet London's economy adapted to the challenges posed by its expansion and foreign competition, and by the time of Shakespeare's death the metropolis was a wealthier city than it had been when he first arrived there. Politically and socially it was a stable community, overseen by its own corporation and livery companies, and by the government, which scrutinized the city's life in some detail. Many Londoners benefited from the city's economic success, and growing demand produced initiatives, in the supply of water, the development of food supplies, and the establishment of market gardening. A diversified economy produced greater specialization and generated a varied range of employment. Its expanding trade brought a wider assortment of merchandise to the port. And Londoners were charitable, donating help for the orphaned, the destitute and the elderly, and establishing schools and almshouses. The challenges of such a rapidly growing city were great, but most of them were met.

As London grew, so did its cultural influence within the British Isles, especially after the union of the crowns in 1603, as those who visited the capital returned to their own communities. So did some who had lived and worked there, including Shakespeare. They took with them their experiences of London's life, its fashions and commodities, and even its patterns of speech. Foreign visitors, too, absorbed what they saw and conveyed their fascination with the burgeoning metropolis and its society in their letters and memoirs. Orazio Busino typified their reactions with the admiring remark that: 'The city of London renders itself truly worthy to be styled the metropolis of the kingdom and the abode of royalty.'[59]

References

List of abbreviations

APC   *Acts of the Privy Council*

Chamberlain, *Letters*   *Letters Written by John Chamberlain during the reign of Queen Elizabeth*, ed. Sarah Williams (Camden Soc., 1861)

CSPD   *Calendar of State Papers, Domestic*

CSPVen   *Calendar of State Papers Relating to English Affairs in the Archives of Venice*

De Maisse   *A Journal of all that was accomplished by Monsieur De Maisse, Ambassador in England from King Henri IV to Queen Elizabeth Anno Domini 1597*, ed. G.B. Harrison and R.A. Jones (Nonesuch Press, London, 1931)

HMC   Historical Manuscripts Commission

Larkin and Hughes   *Stuart Royal Proclamations, Volume I Royal Proclamations of King James I 1603–1625*, ed. James F. Larkin and Paul L. Hughes (OUP, 1973)

LMA   London Metropolitan Archives

Manley, *London*   *London in the Age of Shakespeare*, ed. Lawrence Manley (Croom Helm, Beckenham, 1986)

Manningham, *Diary*   *The Diary of John Manningham of the Middle Temple, 1602–1603*, ed. Robert Parker Sorlein (University Press of New England, Hanover, New Hampshire, 1976)

ODNB   *Oxford Dictionary of National Biography* (Oxford University Press, 2004)

Platter   Clare Williams, *Thomas Platter's Travels in England* (Cape, London, 1937)

Rye   William Brenchley Rye, *England as seen by foreigners in the days of Elizabeth and James the First* (John Russell Smith, London, 1865, reprinted 2005)

Stow, *Survey*   John Stow, *The Survey of London*, ed. H.B. Wheatley (Dent, London, 1987)

TNA   The National Archives

Von Klarwill   Victor von Klarwill, *Queen Elizabeth and Some Foreigners* (Bodley Head, London, 1928)

Waldstein   *The Diary of Baron Waldstein. A Traveller in Elizabethan England*, ed. G.W. Groos (Thames & Hudson, London, 1981)

1. A Little World in Itself

1. John Donne, *Selected Letters*, ed. P.M. Oliver (Carcenet, Manchester, 2002), p.22.
2. *The Trumbull Papers* (Sotheby's, London, 1989), p.10.
3. Rye, p.7. Von Klarwill, p.314. Manley, *London*, p.108.
4. Platter, p.153.
5. Rye, p.185.
6. Von Klarwill, p.314. Giovanni Botero, *The Greatness of Cities: A Treatise Concerning The Causes of the Magnificency and Greatness of Cities*, trans Robert Peterson (1606) bk 2, sect 11. *CSPVen*, 10, 1603–7, p.502.
7. *CSPVen*, 9, 1592–1603, p.237.
8. Rye, p.7. Platter, p.174.
9. John Dover Wilson, *Life in Shakespeare's England* (Penguin, London, 1944), p.125.
10. Waldstein, p.175.
11. P.S. Seaver, *Wallington's World. A Puritan Artisan in Seventeenth-Century London* (Methuen, London, 1985), p.222.
12. Wilson, *Shakespeare's England*, p.117.
13. Stow, *Survey*, p.473.
14. Stow, *Survey*, p.115.
15. Stow, *Survey*, p.131.
16. Stow, *Survey*, p.216 n.1.
17. Stow, *Survey*, pp.74–5, 214, 24, 309, 317.
18. Stow, *Survey*, pp.162, 188, 233, 236, 262, 264, 266.
19. Stow, *Survey*, pp.126, 180.
20. Stow, *Survey*, p.116.
21. Stow, *Survey*, pp.149, 376, 378.
22. Stow, *Survey*, pp.118, 126, 176, 212, 332, 333.
23. Stow, *Survey*, p.276.
24. Stow, *Survey*, pp.210, 319, 379.
25. Manningham, *Diary*, p.154.
26. Stow, *Survey*, pp.159, 315.
27. Pamela Tudor-Craig, 'Old St Paul's': The Society of Antiquaries Diptych, 1616 (London Topographical Soc. and Soc. of Antiquaries, 2004), p.48.
28. Rye, p.8.
29. Waldstein, p.65.
30. Thomas Dekker, *The Dead Tearme* (1608), cited in Frank Aydelotte, *Elizabethan Rogues and Vagabonds* (Cass, London, 1967), p.85.
31. Chamberlain, *Letters*, pp.10, 176.
32. Chamberlain, *Letters*, p.162.
33. Rye, pp.9, 132.
34. De Maisse, p.32.
35. Stow, *Survey*, p.389.
36. Manley, *London*, p.40. Platter, p.157. Rye, p.166.
37. *The Court and Times of James the First*, II, ed. Thomas Birch (London, 1848), p.346. Gordon Williams, *A dictionary of sexual language and imagery in Shakespearean and Stuart Literature* (Continuum, London, 1994), p.458.

38. *CSPVen*, 10, 1603–607, p.503.
39. Stow, *Survey*, p.173.
40. Von Klarwill, p.318.
41. Rye, p.207.
42. Waldstein, p.62. Anna Keay, *The Elizabethan Tower of London: The Haiward and Gascoyne plan of 1597* (London Topographical Soc. and Historic Royal Palaces, 2001), p.59.
43. De Maisse, p.35. *CSPVen*, 10, 1603–1607, pp.502–3.
44. Stow, *Survey*, p.26.
45. Von Klarwill, p.314. Rye, p.9. *CSPVen*, 10, 1603–1607, p.503.
46. Stow, *Survey*, pp.154–5.
47. Stow, *Survey*, p.156.
48. S. Schoenbaum, *William Shakespeare, A Compact Documentary Life* (OUP, 1987), p.131. *2 Henry IV*, act II, sc II.
49. Stow, *Survey*, p.156. Lisa Jardine and Alan Stewart, *Hostage to Fortune: The Troubled Life of Francis Bacon 1561–1626* (Gollancz, London, 1998), p.161.
50. Stow, *Survey*, pp.359, 365, 369.
51. Stow, *Survey*, p.360.
52. Stow, *Survey*, p.274.
53. Charles Nicholl, *The Lodger: Shakespeare on Silver Street* (Allen Lane, London, 2007), pp.303–4.
54. Kate Pogue, *Shakespeare's Friends* (Greenwood, London, 2006), p.76.
55. Stow, *Survey*, p.305.
56. Richard Wilson, *Secret Shakespeare: Studies in Theatre, Religion and Resistance* (Manchester University Press, 2004), p.259.

2. A Great Multitude of People

1. Bernard Harris, 'A Portrait of a Moor', in *Shakespeare Survey Volume 11: The Last Plays*, ed. Allardyce Nicoll, (CUP, 1958), pp.89–97.
2. *St Martin-in-the-Fields: The accounts of the churchwardens, 1525–1603* (1901), pp.260, 447, 481.
3. HMC, *Calendar of the Manuscripts of the Marquess of Salisbury*, XII, p.569.
4. Rye, p.186.
5. Rye, p.7.
6. Rye, p.70.
7. Garrett Mattingly, *The Defeat of the Spanish Armada* (Cape, London, 1959), p.292.
8. *CSPVen*, 15, 1617–1619, pp.60–1.
9. Rye, p.186.
10. Rye, p.186.
11. *Letters, by John Chamberlain*, ed. Norman Egbert McClure (Greenwood Press, London, 1979 edition), I, p.531.
12. *CSPVen*, 15, 1617–1619, p.61.
13. Larkin and Hughes, pp.403–4.

14. Charles Hughes, *Unpublished Chapters of Fynes Moryson's Itinerary* (Sherratt & Hughes, London, 1903), p.474.
15. Rye, p.178.
16. Hughes, *Moryson's Itinerary*, p.474.
17. LMA, Corporation of London, Remembrancia, I, 53.
18. Paul Slack, *From Reformation to Improvement: Public Welfare in Early Modern England* (OUP, 1998), p.54.
19. Anthony Munday et al., *Thomas More* (Nick Herne Books, London 2005), pp.xviii–xix, 26–8.
20. *Proceedings in the Parliaments of Elizabeth I, Volume III, 1593–1601*, ed. T.E. Hartley (Leicester University Press, 1995), pp.138–9.
21. *Proceedings in the Parliaments*, ed. Hartley, III, pp.137–8, 143.
22. Manningham, *Diary*, p.42.
23. *CSPVen*, 15, 1617–1619, p.59.
24. LMA, Corporation of London, Remembrancia, I, 507.
25. Nigel Goose and Lien Luu, *Immigrants in Tudor and Early Stuart England* (Sussex Academic Press, Brighton, 2005), p.151.
26. Stow, *Survey*, p.187.
27. LMA, Corporation of London, Remembrancia, II, 258; III, 19.
28. M.D. George, *London Life in the Eighteenth Century* (Penguin Books, Harmondsworth, 1965), pp.331, 334.
29. Goose and Lien Luu, *Immigrants*, p.147.
30. Irene Scouloudi, 'The Stranger Community in the Metropolis 1558–1640', in *Huguenots in Britain and their French Background, 1550–1800* (Macmillan, London, 1987), p.44. Rye, p.20.
31. Goose and Lien Luu, *Immigrants*, p.152.
32. *Proceedings in the Parliaments*, ed. Hartley, III, p.144. Platter, p.156.
33. Seaver, *Wallington's World*, p.68.
34. Stow, *Survey*, p.492.
35. Stow, *Survey*, p.492. *CSPVen*, 15, 1617–1619, pp.58–9.
36. Rye, p.197. Minsheu is cited in *OED*, sub 'cockney'.
37. *Tudor Royal Proclamations, II: The Later Tudors (1553–1587)*, ed. Paul L. Hughes and James F. Larkin (Yale University Press, 1969), p.466.
38. Steen Eiler Rasmussen, *London: The Unique City* (MIT Press, Cambridge, Mass., 1982), pp.67–9. C.C. Knowles and P.H. Pitt, *The History of Building Regulation in London 1189–1972* (Architectural Press, London, 1972), pp.12–13.
39. Steve Rappaport, *Worlds within worlds: structures of life in sixteenth-century London* (CUP, 1989), pp.83, 85.
40. LMA, Corporation of London, Remembrancia, I, 495, 496.
41. Rasmussen, *London*, pp.73–4. Knowles & Pitt, *Building Regulation*, p.14.
42. Stow, *Survey*, pp.374–5, 383. Goose and Lien Luu, *Immigrants*, p.159.
43. Larkin and Hughes, p.269n.
44. TNA, STAC, 8/212/2.
45. Knowles & Pitt, *Building Regulation*, p.15.
46. Chamberlain, *Letters*, p.142.
47. Larkin and Hughes, p.399n.

48. TNA, STAC,8/30/17.
49. LMA, Corporation of London, Remembrancia, II, 263, 343.
50. W.H. Manchée, *Westminster City Fathers* (Bodley Head, London, 1924), pp.93, 94, 96.
51. LMA, Corporation of London, Journal of Common Council, xxi, f.199v.
52. J.F.D. Shrewsbury, *A History of Bubonic Plague in the British Isles* (CUP, 1970), p.355.
53. Thomas Lodge, *A Treatise of the Plague* (1603).
54. *Antony and Cleopatra*, act III, sc.X.
55. F.P. Wilson, *The Plague in Shakespeare's London* (OUP, 1927), p.191.
56. LMA, Corporation of London, Journal of Common Council, xxi, ff.285–86v.
57. R.A. Foakes, *Henslowe's Diary* (2nd edn, CUP, 2002), p.276.
58. *APC*, 1592–3, p.400.
59. *The Plague Pamphlets of Thomas Dekker*, ed. F.P. Wilson, (OUP, 1925), pp.31–2.
60. *Plague Pamphlets*, ed. Wilson, pp.34, 35, 36.
61. *CSPVen*, 10, 1603–1607, p.126.

3. The Greatest City of the Christian World

1. De Maisse, pp.27, 29.
2. Von Klarwill, p.322.
3. Waldstein, pp.36, 43.
4. Von Klarwill, p.320.
5. De Maisse, p.23.
6. Waldstein, p.51, 57.
7. *CSPVen*, 15, 1617–1619, p.111.
8. Waldstein, p.59. Rye, p.100.
9. De Maisse, p.11.
10. Von Klarwill, p.324.
11. Rye, p.95.
12. Stow, *Survey*, p.486.
13. *APC*, 1592–3, p.31.
14. Stow, *Survey*, pp.495–6.
15. Henry Ellis, *Original Letters Illustrative of English History*, II (London, 1824), p.291.
16. *The Winter's Tale*, act IV, sc.IV. John Donne, *Satyre* I.
17. Von Klarwill, p.339.
18. Robert Naunton, *Fragmenta Regalia: Or, Observations on the late Queen Elizabeth, her times and favourites* (1641), in *A Miscellany of Tracts and Pamphlets*, ed. A.C. Ward (OUP, 1927), pp.212–13.
19. Naunton, *Fragmenta Regalia*, p.215.
20. Thomas Dekker, *The Wonderfull Yeare*, 1604.
21. *CSPVen*, 10, 1603–1607, p.33.
22. Larkin and Hughes, pp.37, 45.
23. *The Stuart Courts*, ed. Eveline Cruickshanks (Sutton, Stroud, 2000), pp.3, 35.

24. *The Diaries of Lady Anne Clifford*, ed. D.J.H. Clifford (Sutton, Stroud, 1990), p.22.
25. *Diaries of Lady Anne Clifford*, p.22.
26. John Adamson, 'The Tudor and Stuart Courts, 1509–1714', in *The Princely Courts of Europe*, ed. John Adamson (Weidenfeld & Nicolson, London, 1999), p.112.
27. D.M. Loades, *The Cecils: Privilege and power behind the throne* (National Archives, London, 2007), p.236.
28. Andrew Gurr, *Playgoing in Shakespeare's London* (2nd edn, CUP, 1996), pp.280–1.
29. Naunton, *Fragmenta Regalia*, p.173.
30. *CSPVen*, 10, 1603–1607, p.143.
31. *The Life of Edward, First Lord Herbert of Cherbury written by himself*, ed. J.M. Shuttleworth (OUP, 1976), p.38.
32. Stow, *Survey*, p.496.
33. *A Discourse of the Commonweal of this Realm of England*, ed. Elizabeth Lamond (CUP, 1893), p.81.
34. Larkin and Hughes, p.188.
35. Larkin and Hughes, pp.323, 369–70.
36. *Analytical index to the series of records known as the Remembrancia*, ed. W.H. and H.C. Overall, II (London, 1878), p.172.
37. Negley Harte, *The University of London 1836–1986* (Athlone, London, 1986), pp.49, 50.
38. Wilfrid R. Prest, *The Inns of Court under Elizabeth I and the Early Stuarts, 1590–1640* (Longman, London, 1972), p.23. Stow, *Survey*, p.392.
39. George Buck, *A Discourse or Treatise of the third universitie of England* (1615). Stow, Survey, p.348.
40. Harte, *University of London*, p.49.
41. Larkin and Hughes, pp.345–6.
42. Larkin and Hughes, p.112.
43. Larkin and Hughes, pp.193, 270.
44. Larkin and Hughes, p.346.
45. *Res Gestae Divi Augusti*, ed. P.A. Brunt and J.M. Moore (OUP, 1967), pp.26–9, 61.
46. Adamson, 'Tudor and Stuart Courts', p.111.
47. Manningham, *Diary*, p.150.
48. *CSPVen*, 11, 1607–1610, p.475.
49. *CSPVen*, 15, 1617–1619, p.321.
50. Stow, *Survey*, p.491.
51. Chamberlain, *Letters*, p.165.
52. *The Fugger News-Letters: First Series*, ed. Victor von Klarwill (Bodley Head, London, 1924), p.116.
53. J. Charles Cox, *Churchwardens' Accounts from the Fourteenth Century to the Close of the Seventeenth Century* (Methuen, London, 1913), p.219. Margaret E. Tabor, *The City Churches* (Headley, London, 1917), p.26.
54. James Shapiro, *1599 A Year in the Life of William Shakespeare* (Faber, London, 2005), pp.198–9.

55. Chamberlain, *Letters*, p.59.
56. Margaret Healy, *William Shakespeare*, Richard II (Northcote House, Plymouth, 1998), pp.17, 28.
57. R.B. Outhwaite, 'Dearth, the English Crown and the "Crisis of the 1590s"', in *The European Crisis of the 1590s*, ed. Peter Clark (Allen & Unwin, London, 1985), p.23.
58. William Weston, *The Autobiography of an Elizabethan*, ed. Philip Caraman (Longmans Green, London, 1955), p.222.
59. Manningham, *Diary*, p.208.
60. John Stow, *Annales*, ed. Edmond Howes (1631), p.817.
61. *Diaries of Lady Anne Clifford*, p.21.
62. Manningham, *Diary*, p.209.
63. *Stuart Courts*, ed. Cruickshanks, p.34.
64. Alan Haynes, *The Gunpowder Plot* (Sutton, Stroud, 1994), p.96.
65. *Life of Edward, First Lord Herbert*, p.39.
66. *CSPVen*, 10, 1603–1607, p.333.
67. *CSPVen*, 12, 1610–1613, p.491.

4. The World Runs on Wheels

1. Von Klarwill, p.315.
2. De Maisse, p.34.
3. Waldstein, p.172.
4. Waldstein, pp.172, 177. Rye, p.107.
5. Manningham, *Diary*, p.113.
6. *The European Crisis of the 1590s*, ed. Peter Clark (Allen & Unwin, London, 1985), p.28.
7. W.H. Manchée, *Westminster City Fathers* (Bodley Head, London, 1924), p.49.
8. LMA, Corporation of London, Remembrancia, II, 59.
9. J. Leeds Barroll, *Politics, Plague, and Shakespeare's Theater* (Cornell University Press, Ithaca, 1991), p.231.
10. Mihoko Suzuki, 'The London apprentice riots of the 1590s and the fiction of Thomas Delony', *Criticism* (Spring 1996), 22, 24. Barroll, *Politics*, p.232.
11. Platter, p.180. R.A. Foakes, *Henslowe's Diary* (2nd edn, CUP, 2002), p.272.
12. *Hugh Alley's Caveat: The Markets of London in 1598*, ed. Ian Archer, Caroline Barron and Vanessa Harding (London Topographical Soc., 1988), p.15.
13. *Hugh Alley's Caveat*, p.90.
14. Manchée, *Westminster*, p.50.
15. *Hugh Alley's Caveat*, p.23.
16. *CSPVen*, 15, 1617–1619, p.102.
17. Stow, *Survey*, p.189.
18. F.J. Fisher, *London and the English Economy, 1500–1700*, ed. P.J. Corfield and N.B. Harte (Hambledon, London, 1990), pp.145–6.
19. *CSPVen*, 15, 1617–1619, p.102.
20. *Proceedings in the Parliaments of Elizabeth I, Volume III, 1593–1601*, ed. T.E. Hartley (Leicester University Press, 1995), p.463.

21. T.S. Willan, *The inland trade* (Manchester University Press, 1976), p.23.
22. Fisher, *London and the English Economy*, p.143.
23. Rye, p.52.
24. Platter, p.175.
25. *CSPVen*, 15, 1617–19, p.321. Rye, p.31.
26. Fisher, *London and the English Economy*, p.142.
27. *CSPVen*, 15, 1617–1619, pp.318–19.
28. Malcolm Thick, 'Market Gardening in England and Wales', in *The Agrarian History of England and Wales, V 1640–1750, pt ii, Agrarian Change*, ed. Joan Thirsk (CUP, 1985), p.505.
29. *Gerard's Herbal*, ed. Marcus Woodward (Studio Editions, London, 1994), pp.43, 47, 79, 135, 221.
30. Rye, p.8.
31. *CSPVen*, 15, 1617–1619, p.102.
32. Stow, *Survey*, p.323.
33. *CSPVen*, 15, 1617–1619, p.102.
34. A.W. Skempton, 'Colthurst, Edmund (*c*.1545–1616)' in *A biographical dictionary of civil engineers in Great Britain and Ireland, 1500–1830*, I, ed. Sir Alec W. Skempton, R.W. Rennison and R.C. Cox (Thomas Telford, London, 2002) pp.147–8. *Survey of London*, XLVII (2008), p.167.
35. Willan, *Inland trade*, p.32.
36. Manley, *London*, pp.170–1. Manchée, *Westminster*, p.62.
37. Eric Bennett, *The Worshipful Company of Carmen of London* (Carmen's Company, London, 1952), p.44.
38. Stow, *Survey*, p.77.
39. John Dover Wilson, *Life in Shakespeare's England* (Penguin, London, 1944), pp.110, 125.
40. *CSPVen*, 15, 1617–1619, pp.246–7.
41. Bennett, *Carmen*, p.23.
42. Bennett, *Carmen*, p.26. Stow, *Survey*, p.77.
43. Bennett, *Carmen*, pp.26–7.
44. Bennett, *Carmen*, p.32.
45. *Middlesex County Records*, I, ed. John Cordy Jeaffreson (1886), p.266.
46. Bennett, *Carmen*, p.37.
47. Bennett, *Carmen*, pp.37–8.
48. Bennett, *Carmen*, pp.12–13.
49. Bennett, *Carmen*, p.11.
50. Bennett, *Carmen*, p.11.
51. *Commons Journals*, I, 30 April 1604, pp.190–3.
52. Bennett, *Carmen*, pp.131–2.
53. LMA, Corporation of London, Journal of Common Council, xxl, ff.285–6.
54. Thomas Lodge, *A Treatise of the Plague* (1603), Chap.VIII.
55. Rye, p.283.
56. Bennett, *Carmen*, p.14.
57. Manchée, *Westminster*, pp.74–5.
58. *Middlesex County Records*, I, ed. Jeaffreson, p.190.
59. Manchée, *Westminster*, p.76.

60. Mark S.R. Jenner, 'The Great Dog Massacre', in *Fear in early modern society*, ed. William G. Naphy and Penny Roberts (Manchester University Press, 1997) p.48.

61. J. Charles Cox, *Churchwardens' Accounts from the Fourteenth Century to the Close of the Seventeenth Century* (Methuen, London, 1913), p.317.

62. Margaret Wood, *The English Mediaeval House* (Dent, London, 1965), p.292.

63. Stow, *Survey*, p.76.

64. J.M.S. Brooke and A.W.C. Hallen, *The Transcripts of the Registers of the United Parishes of S. Mary Woolnoth and S. Mary Woolchurch Haw... 1538 to 1760* (London, 1886), p.li.

65. John Schofield, *The London Surveys of Ralph Treswell* (London Topographical Soc., 1987), p.94.

66. *CSPD, 1581–90*, p.311.

67. *CSPD, 1595–7*, p.81.

68. *CSPVen*, 10, 1603–1607, p.502.

5. The Whole Trade of Merchandise

1. Stow, *Survey*, p.492.

2. T.S. Willan, *The inland trade* (Manchester University Press, 1976), pp.50–1.

3. *CSPVen*, 10, 1603–1607, p.503.

4. Stephen Inwood, *A History of London* (Macmillan, London, 1998), p.197.

5. Platter, pp.156–7.

6. De Maisse, pp.2–3. *CSPVen*, 10, 1603–1607, p.503.

7. De Maisse, pp.46–7.

8. Manley, *London*, p.90.

9. Manley, *London*, p.92.

10. De Maisse, p.47.

11. *CSPVen*, 10, 1603–1607, p.504.

12. Joan Thirsk and J.P. Cooper, *Seventeenth-Century Economic Documents* (OUP, 1972), p.196.

13. Thirsk and Cooper, *Economic Documents*, p.194.

14. Larkin and Hughes, pp.312–14.

15. Thirsk and Cooper, *Economic Documents*, p.195.

16. Thirsk and Cooper, *Economic Documents*, p.199.

17. *APC*, 1616–17, pp.354–5. Charles Wilson, *England's Apprenticeship, 1603–1763* (Longman, London, 1965), p.73.

18. Thirsk and Cooper, *Economic Documents*, p.471.

19. *Gerard's Herbal*, ed. Marcus Woodward (Studio Editions, London, 1994) p.88.

20. Stephen Porter, *The Plagues of London* (Tempus, Stroud, 2008), pp.68–9.

21. Peter Clark and Paul Slack, *English Towns in Transition 1500–1700* (OUP, 1976), p.77. Cayley Illingworth, *A Topographical Account of the Parish of Scampton* (London, 1810), pp.43–6.

22. Willan, *Inland trade*, p.123.

23. *CSPVen*, 15, 1617–1619, pp.59, 257.

24. Stephen Porter, 'Fires in Stratford-upon-Avon in the Sixteenth and Seventeenth Centuries', *Warwickshire History*, III (1976), 99.
25. *The Winter's Tale*, act IV, sc.III.
26. S. Schoenbaum, *William Shakespeare, A Compact Documentary Life* (OUP, 1987), p.239.
27. R.C. Lang, 'Social origins and social aspirations of Jacobean London merchants', *Economic History Review*, 2nd series, XXVII (1974), 30.
28. Stow, *Survey*, p.492.
29. Lawrence Manley, *Literature and culture in early modern London* (CUP, 1995), p.2.
30. Stow, *Survey*, p.248.
31. Charles M. Clode, *Memorials of the Guild of Merchant Taylors: Of the Fraternity of St. John the Baptist in the City of London* (Harrison, London, 1875), p.352.
32. George Unwin, *Industrial Organization in the Sixteenth and Seventeenth Centuries* (Cass, London, 1965), p.129.
33. Joan Thirsk, *Economic Policy and Projects* (OUP, 1978), pp.93–4. John Strype, *A Survey of the Cities of London and Westminster* (1720), bk 5, pp.236–7.
34. Larkin and Hughes, pp.282–3.
35. Harry J. Powell, *Glass Making in England* (CUP, 1923), pp.29–30.
36. David Hey, 'The origins and early growth of the Hallamshire cutlery and allied trades', in *English Rural Society, 1500–1800*, ed. John Chartres and David Hey (CUP, 2006), p.356.
37. Von Klarwill, pp.396, 422.
38. Von Klarwill, p.376.
39. Henry Crosse, *Vertues Commonwealth: or the high-way to honour* (London, 1603), cited in Jane Schneider, 'Fantastical Colors in Foggy London: The New Fashion Potential of the Late Sixteenth Century', in Lena Cowen Orlin, *Material London, ca 1600* (University of Pennsylvania Press, 2000), p.118.
40. Thomas Dekker, *The Wonderfull Yeare*, 1604.
41. Clare Gittings, *Death, Burial and the Individual in Early Modern England* (Croom Helm, London, 1984), pp.181, 185.
42. Rye, pp.7–8, 73, 90.
43. *Oxford English Dictionary*.
44. Francis Sheppard, *Robert Baker of Piccadilly Hall and His Heirs* (London Topographical Soc., 1982), pp.10–23.
45. James McDermott, 'Farnaby, Thomas (1574/5–1647)', in *ODNB* (2004).
46. Juanita G.L. Burnby, *A Study of the English Apothecary from 1660 to 1760* (Medical History, Supplement No.3, 1983), p.6.
47. *The Worshipful Society of Apothecaries* (2nd edn, London, 2000), p.10.
48. *CSPVen*, 15, 1617–1619, p.257.
49. C.J.S. Thompson, *Quacks of Old London* (London, 1928), pp.34–5.
50. Stow, *Survey*, p.492.
51. David Scott Kastan, *A Companion to Shakespeare* (Blackwell, Oxford, 1999), p.48.
52. Platter, p.154. Marchette Chute, *Shakespeare of London* (Secker & Warburg, London, 1951), p.207.

53. Liza Picard, *Elizabeth's London* (Weidenfeld & Nicolson, London, 2003), p.16.
54. Christopher O'Riordan, *The Thames Watermen in the Century of Revolution* (1992), Chap.3.
55. A.L. Beier, *Masterless men: the vagrancy problem in England 1560–1640* (Methuen, London, 1985), pp.40–1.
56. *CSPVen*, 15, 1617–1619, p.246.
57. Manley, *London*, p.279. Gämini Salgádo, *The Elizabethan Underworld* (Dent, London, 1977), pp.53–4.
58. Germaine Greer, *Shakespeare's Wife* (Bloomsbury, London, 2007), p.152.
59. Platter, p.175.
60. Sir Francis Bacon, 'A Brief Discourse upon the Commission of Bridewell', in *The Works of Francis Bacon*, ed. James Spedding et al., XV (Brown and Taggard, Boston 1861), p.15.
61. *Proceedings in the Parliaments of Elizabeth I, Volume III, 1593–1601*, ed. T.E. Hartley (Leicester University Press, 1995), p.480.
62. Manningham, *Diary*, p.114. De Maisse, p.109.

6. The Time of Life is Short

1. Rye, pp.14, 197.
2. Rye, p.72.
3. Rye, p.7. Von Klarwill, p.326.
4. *CSPVen*, 15, 1617–1619, p.67.
5. Rye, p.73.
6. R.E. Pritchard, *Shakespeare's England: Life in Elizabethan & Jacobean Times* (Sutton, Stroud, 1999), p.24.
7. *The Winter's Tale*, act III, sc.III.
8. Rye, p.7.
9. Chamberlain, *Letters*, p.161.
10. W.H. Manchée, *Westminster City Fathers* (Bodley Head, London, 1924), pp.128–9.
11. J. Charles Cox, *The Parish Registers of England* (Methuen, London, 1910), pp.68–9.
12. Vanessa Harding et al., *People in Place: Families, Households and Housing in Early Modern London* (Institute of Historical Research, London, 2008), p.18.
13. Platter, p.179.
14. Cox, *Parish Registers*, p.64.
15. De Maisse, p.13.
16. James Spedding, *The Letters and the Life of Francis Bacon*, vol.IV (1868), p.252.
17. Charles M. Clode, *The Early History of the Guild of Merchant Taylors of the Fraternity of St. John the Baptist London* (Harrison, London, 1888), p.234.
18. *The Selected Writings and Speeches of Sir Edward Coke*, I, ed. Steve Sheppard (Indianapolis, Liberty Fund, 2003), sect.10.

19. Charterhouse Muniments, G/2/1, pp.3,18. *Charter, Acts of Parliament, and Governors' Statutes for the Foundation and Government of the Charterhouse* (1832), pp.52, 53–4.
20. Stow, *Survey*, p.69.
21. C. Wilfred Scott-Giles and Bernard V. Slater, *The History of Emanuel School, 1594–1964* (The Old Emanuel Association, 1966), p.18.
22. Richard Chartres and David Vermont, *A Brief History of Gresham College 1597–1997* (Gresham College, London, 1998), p.8.
23. Anne Laurence, *Women in England, 1500–1760* (Weidenfeld & Nicolson, London, 1994), p.166.
24. *Epistle to Martin Mar-Sixtus*, 1592, cited in Thomas Deloney, *The Gentle Craft*, ed. Simon Barker (Ashgate, London, 2007), p.xi.
25. Chamberlain, *Letters*, p.12.
26. S. Schoenbaum, *William Shakespeare, A Compact Documentary Life* (OUP, 1987), p.176.
27. 'To the great Variety of Readers', in Shakespeare's *Comedies, Histories, and Tragedies* (1623)[the First Folio].
28. Patrick Collinson, 'Throckmorton, Job (1545–1601)', *ODNB* (2004).
29. *CSPVen*, 10, 1603–1607, p.138.
30. Thomas Helwys, *A Short Declaration of the Mystery of Iniquity*, ed. Richard Groves (Mercer University Press, Macon, Georgia, 1998), pp.vi,xxiv.
31. 2 Chronicles c.15, v.16.
32. Alister McGrath, *In the Beginning: The Story of the King James Bible* (Hodder & Stoughton, London, 2001), p.113.
33. McGrath, *In the Beginning*, pp.163–4.
34. David Norton, *A textual history of the King James Bible* (CUP, 2005), p.18.
35. De Maisse, pp.19, 21–2. Platter, p.176.
36. P.S. Seaver, *The Puritan Lectureships: The Politics of Religious Dissent, 1560–1662* (Stanford University Press, 1970), p.116.
37. Brett Usher, 'Vaughan, Richard (*c.*1553–1607)', *ODNB* (2004).
38. C.S. Knighton, 'Ravis, Thomas (b. in or before 1560, d.1609)', *ODNB* (2004).
39. Thomas Wright, *Queen Elizabeth and her Times*, II (1838), pp.38, 43.
40. *CSPVen*, 12, 1610–1613, pp.136–7.
41. Chamberlain, *Letters*, pp.69, 164.
42. *The Trumbull Papers* (Sotheby's, London, 1989), p.61.
43. *Trumbull Papers*, p.55.
44. *Trumbull Papers*, p.41.
45. Spedding, *Francis Bacon*, IV, p.252.
46. John Howes, *A Famyliar and Frendly Discourse* in, R.H. Tawney and Eileen Power, *Tudor Economic Documents*, III (Longmans, London, 1925), pp.421, 424–5.
47. Roy Porter, *London: A Social History* (Hamish Hamilton, London, 1994), p.58.
48. Philip Stubbes, *The Anatomie of Abuses* (1583), p.59.
49. *CSPVen*, 9, 1592–1603, p.237. De Maisse, p.13.
50. Manley, *London*, p.41.

51. Henry Ellis, *Original Letters Illustrative of English History*, II (London, 1824), pp.283–6.
52. Manningham, *Diary*, p.113.
53. *John Howes' MS., 1582, Being "a brief note of the order and manner of the proceedings in the first erection of" the three Royal Hospitals*, ed. William Lempriere (London, 1904), p.62.
54. A.L. Beier. 'Social Problems in Elizabethan London', in *The Tudor and Stuart Town*, ed. Jonathan Barry (Longman, London, 1990), pp.122–6. LMA, Corporation of London, Remembrancia, III, 159.
55. LMA, Corporation of London, Remembrancia, III, 159.
56. E.M. Leonard, *The Early History of English Poor Relief* (Routledge, London, 1965), p.96.
57. LMA, Corporation of London, Journal of Common Council, xv, f.325v.
58. LMA, Corporation of London, Remembrancia, II, 231.
59. LMA, Corporation of London, Remembrancia, I, 162.
60. *Sutton's Hospital: with the names of sixteen mannors* (1646), (British Library, Thomason Tracts, E344/7), p.3. Andrew Willet, *Synopsis Papismi* (1634 edn), p.1231.
61. *I Henry IV*, act V, sc.II; spoken by Hotspur in the context of the battle of Shrewsbury.
62. Samuel Herne, *Domus Carthusiana: or an Account of the most Noble Foundation of the Charter-House* (London, 1677), p.55.
63. *CSPVen*, 15, 1617–1619, p.321. Ian W. Archer, 'Craven, Sir William (c.1545–1618)', *ODNB* (2004).
64. John Clapham, *Elizabeth of England*, cited in, Leanda de Lisle, *After Elizabeth* (Harper Collins, London, 2005), p.188.
65. Chamberlain, *Letters*, p.122.
66. Ian W. Archer, 'The Charity of Early Modern Londoners', *Trans. Royal Historical Soc.*, 6th series, XII (2002), 223–4.

7. A Quick Eye & a Nimble Hand

1. County of Middlesex, *Calendar to the Sessions Records*, new series, 2, 1614–15 (1936), pp.100, 244, 272, 438, 454.
2. Cited in, Andrew Gurr, *Playgoing in Shakespeare's London* (2nd edn, CUP, 1996), p.269. Chamberlain, *Letters*, p.64.
3. Alexandra Walsham, *Providence in Early Modern England* (OUP, 1999), pp.268–70.
4. Charles Nicholl, 'Marlowe Marley, Christopher (bap. 1564 d. 1593)', *ODNB* (2004).
5. County of Middlesex, *Calendar to the Sessions Records*, new series, 1, 1612–14 (1935), p.416.
6. Henry Ellis, *Original Letters Illustrative of English History*, II (London, 1824), p.291.
7. Chamberlain, *Letters*, p.32.
8. Chamberlain, *Letters*, pp.102, 125–6.

9. Middlesex, *Sessions Records*, 1, 13 April, 10 James I; 16 April, 11 James I.
10. Christopher W. Brooks, 'Fleetwood [Fletewoode], William (*c.*1525–1594)', *ODNB* (2004).
11. Chamberlain, *Letters*, pp.46–7, 76.
12. *The Life of Edward, First Lord Herbert of Cherbury written by himself*, ed. J.M. Shuttleworth (OUP, 1976), pp.63–4.
13. John Dover Wilson, *Life in Shakespeare's England* (Penguin, London, 1944), pp.126–7.
14. Gurr, *Playgoing*, p.176.
15. County of Middlesex, *Calendar to the Sessions Records*, new series, 4, 1616–18 (1941), pp.108–9.
16. Dover Wilson, *Shakespeare's England*, p.129.
17. Stow, *Survey*, p.93n. Platter, p.174. Ellis, *Original Letters*, pp.296–7.
18. Chamberlain, *Letters*, p.25.
19. Von Klarwill, p.340.
20. Paul L. Hughes and James F. Larkin, *Tudor Royal Proclamations*, II (Yale UP, 1969), p.141.
21. Larkin and Hughes, p.284.
22. Chamberlain, *Letters*, p.32.
23. Chamberlain, *Letters*, p.156. *The Court and Times of James the First*, II, ed. Thomas Birch (London, 1848), p.346.
24. Robert Smythe, *Historical Account of Charter-House* (London, 1808), pp.160–1.
25. *Troilus and Cressida*, act V, sc.I.
26. Rye, p.108.
27. *The Winter's Tale,* act IV, sc.IV.
28. R.E. Pritchard, *Shakespeare's England: Life in Elizabethan & Jacobean Times* (Sutton, Stroud, 1999), p.227.
29. *2 Henry IV*, act II, sc.IV.
30. Rye, p.269.
31. Ben Jonson, *Bartholomew Fair*, act III, sc.V.
32. *Court and Times of James I*, p.191.
33. Gämini Salgädo, *The Elizabethan Underworld* (Dent, London, 1977), pp.25, 27.
34. Ellis, *Original Letters*, II, pp.297–8, 303.
35. Middlesex, *Sessions Records*, 2, pp.250, 295–6.
36. Middlesex, *Sessions Records*, I, pp.168, 296, 313, 327, 361, 393, 448.
37. Frank Aydelotte, *Elizabethan Rogues and Vagabonds* (Cass, London, 1967), pp.164–5.
38. LMA, Corporation of London, Remembrancia, III, 159.
39. *Measure for Measure*, act IV, sc.III.
40. Park Honan, *Christopher Marlowe Poet & Spy* (OUP, 2005), p.326.
41. Charles Hughes, *Unpublished Chapters of Fynes Moryson's Itinerary* (Sherratt & Hughes, London, 1903), p.477.
42. Thomas Dekker, *Lanthorn and Candle-light*, in Arthur F. Kinney and John Lawrence, *Rogues, Vagabonds and Sturdy Beggars* (University of Massachusetts Press, 1990), p.228.

43. Middlesex, *Sessions Records*, I, pp.102–3.
44. Aydelotte, *Rogues and Vagabonds*, p.92.
45. Middlesex, *Sessions Records*, 4, pp.64–5.
46. Middlesex, *Sessions Records*, 1, p.268.
47. Dover Wilson, *Shakespeare's England*, p.145.
48. Platter, p.170.
49. LMA, Corporation of London, Remembrancia, II, 54; III, 131–6.
50. LMA, Corporation of London, Remembrancia, II, 126.
51. Ben Jonson, *Bartholomew Fair*, act II, sc.I.
52. *CSPVen*, 15, 1617–1619, p.102.
53. De Maisse, p.66.
54. Aydelotte, *Rogues and Vagabonds*, pp.80–1.
55. *Measure for Measure*, act IV, sc.III.
56. Rye, p.50.
57. Stow, *Survey*, p.491.
58. James Shapiro, *1599 A Year in the Life of William Shakespeare* (Faber, London, 2005), p.72.
59. Gurr, *Playgoing*, p.67.
60. Shapiro, *1599*, p.74.
61. Chamberlain, *Letters*, p.90.

8. A World of People

1. William Smith, *Breffe Description of the Royall Citie of London*, cited in *The London Encyclopaedia*, ed. Ben Weinreb and Christopher Hibbert (Macmillan, London, 1993 edn), p.497.
2. Von Klarwill, pp.325, 326.
3. Von Klarwill, p.327.
4. *CSPVen*, 15, 1617–1619, p.60.
5. *CSPVen*, 15, 1617–1619, pp.61–2.
6. *London Encyclopaedia*, p.498.
7. Von Klarwill, p.316.
8. Rye, p.108.
9. *Calendar of the Manuscripts of the Most Honourable the Marquess of Salisbury*, XXI, 1609–1612, ed. G. Dyfnallt Owen (1970), p.230.
10. Manley, *London*, p.343.
11. A.D. Wraight, *Christopher Marlowe and Edward Alleyn* (Adam Hart, London, 1993), p.436.
12. E.K. Chambers, *The Elizabethan Stage*, IV (OUP, 1923), p.301.
13. Andrew Gurr, *Playgoing in Shakespeare's London* (2nd edn, CUP, 1996), p.217.
14. Michael Hattaway, *A Companion to English Renaissance Literature and Culture* (Wiley, London, 2002), p.141.
15. Stow, *Survey*, p.377n.
16. S. Schoenbaum, *William Shakespeare, A Compact Documentary Life* (OUP, 1987), p.136.

17. Rosalind Miles, *Ben Jonson: His Life and Work* (Routledge, London, 1986), pp.31–2.
18. Chamberlain, *Letters*, p.163.
19. Gwynneth Bowen, 'Oxford's and Worcester's Men And the "Boar's Head",' *Shakespearean Authorship Review*, Summer 1973. R.A. Foakes, *Henslowe's Diary* (2nd edn, CUP, 2002), p.297. Eva Griffith, 'Baskervile, Susan (bap. 1573, d.1649)', *ODNB* (2004).
20. Schoenbaum, *William Shakespeare*, p.131.
21. Platter, p.166.
22. *Hamlet*, act II, sc.II.
23. *Letters, by John Chamberlain*, I, ed. Norman Egbert McClure (Greenwood Press, London, 1979 edn), p.544.
24. Von Klarwill, p.315. Platter, pp.168–70.
25. J.R. Mulryne, Margaret Shewring and Andrew Gurr, *Shakespeare's Globe Rebuilt* (CUP, 1997), p.183.
26. Gurr, *Playgoing*, p.249.
27. Wraight, *Christopher Marlowe and Edward Alleyn*, pp.413–14.
28. Wraight, *Christopher Marlowe and Edward Alleyn*, p.425.
29. Hugh Macrae Richmond, *Shakespeare's Theatre: A Dictionary of His Stage Context* (Continuum, London, 2002), p.505.
30. Andrew Gurr, *The Shakespeare Company, 1594–1642* (CUP, 2004), p.72.
31. Gurr, *Playgoing*, pp.62–4.
32. Gurr, *Playgoing*, p.35.
33. John Taylor, *The True Cause*, pp.5–9.
34. Schoenbaum, *Shakespeare*, p.129.
35. Gurr, *Playgoing*, p.216.
36. Platter, pp.166–7.
37. Gurr, *Playgoing*, p.236.
38. *CSPVen*, 15, 1617–1619, p.110.
39. Schoenbaum, *Shakespeare*, p.129.
40. Charles Hughes, *Unpublished Chapters of Fynes Moryson's Itinerary* (Sherratt & Hughes, London, 1903), p.476.
41. Gurr, *Playgoing*, p.264.
42. *CSPVen*, 15, 1617–1619, pp.110–11.
43. John Dover Wilson, *Life in Shakespeare's England* (Penguin, London, 1944), pp.253–5.
44. Hughes, *Moryson's Itinerary*, p.476.
45. F.E. Halliday, *A Shakespeare Companion, 1564–1964* (Penguin, London, 1964), p.339.
46. Chamberlain, *Letters*, p.135. *The Comedy of Errors*, act I, sc.II.
47. Von Klarwill, pp.316, 340–1.
48. *The Tempest*, act II, sc.II.
49. *CSPVen*, 15, 1617–1619, p.257.
50. Percy M. Young, *A History of British Football* (Arrow, London, 1968), p.54. Middlesex, *Calendar to the Sessions Records*, new series, 2, 1614–15 (1936), p.213.
51. Rye, p.111.

52. Manley, *London*, p.41.
53. *CSPVen*, 15, 1617–1619, p.259.
54. Craig Monson, 'Byrd, William (1539x43–1623)', *ODNB* (2004).
55. Michael W. Foster, 'Morley, Thomas (b.1556/7, d. in or after 1602)', *ODNB* (2004).
56. Marchette Chute, *Shakespeare of London* (Secker & Warburg, London, 1951), pp.140–1, 201–2. Gurr, *Playgoing*, p.25.
57. *Twelfth Night*, act II, sc.III. David Mateer, 'Ravenscroft, Thomas (b.1591/2)', *ODNB* (2004).
58. John Donne, *Selected Letters*, ed. P.M. Oliver (Carcenet, Manchester, 2002), p.4.
59. *CSPVen*, 15, 1617–1619, p.100.

Bibliography

Adamson, John, ed., *The Princely Courts of Europe* (Weidenfeld & Nicolson, London, 1999)

Archer, Ian W., *The pursuit of stability: social relations in Elizabethan London* (CUP, 1991)

Archer, Ian W., 'The Charity of Early Modern Londoners', *Trans. Royal Historical Soc.*, 6th series, XII (2002)

Archer, Ian W., 'Craven, Sir William (*c.*1545–1618)', *ODNB* (2004)

Archer, Ian, Barron, Caroline, and Harding, Vanessa, eds, *Hugh Alley's Caveat: The Markets of London in 1598* (London Topographical Soc., 1988)

Aydelotte, Frank, *Elizabethan Rogues and Vagabonds* (Cass, London, 1967)

Barker, Simon, ed., Thomas Deloney, *The Gentle Craft* (Ashgate, London, 2007)

Barroll, J. Leeds, *Politics, Plague, and Shakespeare's Theater: The Stuart Years* (Cornell University Press, Ithaca, 1991)

Barry, Jonathan, ed., *The Tudor and Stuart Town* (Longman, London, 1990)

Beier, A.L., *Masterless men: the vagrancy problem in England 1560–1640* (Methuen, London, 1985)

Beier, A.L., and Finlay, Roger, *London 1500–1700: The Making of the Metropolis* (Longman, London, 1986)

Bennett, Eric, *The Worshipful Company of Carmen of London* (Carmen's Company, London, 1952)

Birch, Thomas, ed., *The Court and Times of James the First* (London, 1848)

Bowen, Gwynneth, 'Oxford's and Worcester's Men And the "Boar's Head"', *Shakespearean Authorship Review* (Summer 1973)

Brooke, J.M.S., and Hallen, A.W.C., *The Transcripts of the Registers of the United Parishes of S. Mary Woolnoth and S. Mary Woolchurch Haw... 1538 to 1760* (London, 1886)

Brooks, Christopher W., 'Fleetwood [Fletewoode], William (*c.*1525–1594)', *ODNB* (2004)

Brunt, P.A., and Moore, J.M., eds, *Res Gestae Divi Augusti* (OUP, 1967)

Burnby, Juanita G.L., *A Study of the English Apothecary from 1660 to 1760* (Medical History, Supplement No.3, 1983)

Caraman, Philip, ed., William Weston, *The Autobiography of an Elizabethan* (Longmans Green, London, 1955)

Chambers, E.K., *The Elizabethan Stage*, vol.IV (OUP, 1923)

Chartres, John, and Hey, David, eds, *English Rural Society, 1500–1800* (CUP, 2006)

Chartres, Richard, and Vermont, David, *A Brief History of Gresham College 1597–1997* (Gresham College, London, 1998)

Chute, Marchette, *Shakespeare of London* (Secker & Warburg, London, 1951)

Clark, Peter, ed., *The European Crisis of the 1590s* (Allen & Unwin, London, 1985)

Clark, Peter, and Slack, Paul, *English Towns in Transition 1500–1700* (OUP, 1976)

Clifford, D.J.H., ed., *The Diaries of Lady Anne Clifford*, (Sutton, Stroud, 1990)

Clode, Charles M., *Memorials of the Guild of Merchant Taylors: Of the Fraternity of St. John the Baptist in the City of London* (Harrison, London, 1875)

Clode, Charles M., *The Early History of the Guild of Merchant Taylors of the Fraternity of St. John the Baptist London* (Harrison, London, 1888)

Collinson, Patrick, 'Throckmorton, Job (1545–1601)', *ODNB* (2004)

Cox, J. Charles, *The Parish Registers of England* (Methuen, London, 1910)

Cox, J. Charles, *Churchwardens' Accounts from the Fourteenth Century to the Close of the Seventeenth Century* (Methuen, London, 1913)

Cruickshank, C.G., *Elizabeth's Army* (2nd edn, OUP, 1966)

Cruickshanks, Eveline, ed., *The Stuart Courts* (Sutton, Stroud, 2000)

de Lisle, Leanda, *After Elizabeth* (Harper Collins, London, 2005)

Ellis, Henry, *Original Letters Illustrative of English History*, II (London, 1824)

Finlay, Roger, *Population and Metropolis: The Demography of London 1580–1650* (CUP, 1981)

Fisher, F.J., *London and the English Economy, 1500–1700*, ed. P.J. Corfield and H.B. Harte (Hambledon, London, 1990)

Foakes, R.A., *Henslowe's Diary* (2nd edn, CUP, 2002)

Foster, Michael W., 'Morley, Thomas (b.1556/7, d. in or after 1602)', *ODNB* (2004)

George, M.D., *London Life in the Eighteenth Century* (Penguin Books, Harmondsworth, 1965)

Gittings, Clare, *Death, Burial and the Individual in Early Modern England* (Croom Helm, London, 1984)

Goose, Nigel, and Lien Luu, *Immigrants in Tudor and Early Stuart England* (Sussex Academic Press, Brighton, 2005)

Greer, Germaine, *Shakespeare's Wife* (Bloomsbury, London, 2007)

Griffith, Eva, 'Baskervile, Susan (bap. 1573, d.1649)', *ODNB* (2004)

Groos, G.W., *The Diary of Baron Waldstein. A Traveller in Elizabethan England* (Thames & Hudson, London, 1981)

Groves, Richard, ed., Thomas Helwys, *A Short Declaration of the Mystery of Iniquity* (Mercer University Press, Macon, Georgia, 1998)

Gurr, Andrew, *Playgoing in Shakespeare's London* (2nd edn, CUP, 1996)

Gurr, Andrew, *The Shakespeare Company, 1594–1642* (CUP, 2004)

Halliday, F.E., *A Shakespeare Companion, 1564–1964* (Penguin, London, 1964)

Harding, Vanessa, et al., *People in Place: Families, Households and Housing in Early Modern London* (Institute of Historical Research, London, 2008)

Harris, Bernard, 'A Portrait of a Moor', in *Shakespeare Survey Volume 11: The Last Plays*, ed. Allardyce Nicoll, (CUP, 1958)

Harrison, G.B., and Jones, R.A., eds, *A Journal of all that was accomplished by Monsieur De Maisse, Ambassador in England from King Henri IV to Queen Elizabeth Anno Domini 1597* (Nonesuch Press, London, 1931)

Harte, Negley, *The University of London 1836–1986* (Athlone, London, 1986)

Hartley, T.E., ed., *Proceedings in the Parliaments of Elizabeth I, Volume III, 1593–1601* (Leicester University Press, 1995)

Hattaway, Michael, *A Companion to English Renaissance Literature and Culture* (Wiley, London, 2002)

Haynes, Alan, *The Gunpowder Plot* (Sutton, Stroud, 1994)

Healy, Margaret, *William Shakespeare*, Richard II (Northcote House, Plymouth, 1998)

Honan, Park, *Shakespeare: A Life* (OUP, 1998)

Honan, Park, *Christopher Marlowe Poet & Spy* (OUP, 2005)

Hughes, Charles, *Unpublished Chapters of Fynes Moryson's Itinerary* (Sherratt & Hughes, London, 1903)

Hughes, Paul L., and Larkin, James F., eds, *Tudor Royal Proclamations, II: The Later Tudors (1553–1587)* (Yale University Press, London, 1969)

Illingworth, Cayley, *A Topographical Account of the Parish of Scampton* (London, 1810)

Inwood, Stephen, *A History of London* (Macmillan, London, 1998)

Jardine, Lisa, and Stewart, Alan, *Hostage to Fortune: The Troubled Life of Francis Bacon 1561–1626* (Gollancz, London, 1998)

Jeaffreson, John Cordy, ed., *Middlesex County Records*, I, (1886)

Kastan, David Scott, *A Companion to Shakespeare* (Blackwell, Oxford, 1999)

Keay, Anna, *The Elizabethan Tower of London: The Haiward and Gascoyne plan of 1597* (London Topographical Soc. and Historic Royal Palaces, 2001)

Kinney, Arthur F., and Lawrence, John, *Rogues, Vagabonds and Sturdy Beggars* (University of Massachusetts Press, 1990)

Klarwill, Victor von, ed., *The Fugger News-Letters: First Series* (Bodley Head, London, 1924)

Klarwill, Victor Von, *Queen Elizabeth and Some Foreigners* (Bodley Head, London, 1928)

Knighton, C.S., 'Thomas Ravis (b. in or before 1560, d.1609)', *ODNB* (2004)

Knowles, C.C., and Pitt, P.H., *The History of Building Regulation in London 1189-1972* (Architectural Press, London, 1972)

Lamond, Elizabeth, ed., *A Discourse of the Commonweal of this Realm of England*, (CUP, 1893)

Lang, R.C., 'Social origins and social aspirations of Jacobean London merchants', *Economic History Review*, 2nd series, XXVII (1974)

Larkin, James F., and Hughes, Paul L., eds, *Stuart Royal Proclamations, Volume I Royal Proclamations of King James I 1603–1625* (OUP, 1973)

Laurence, Anne, *Women in England, 1500–1760* (Weidenfeld & Nicolson, London, 1994)

Lempriere, William, ed., *John Howes' MS., 1582, Being "a brief note of the order and manner of the proceedings in the first erection of" the three Royal Hospitals* (London, 1904)

Leonard, E.M., *The Early History of English Poor Relief* (Routledge, London, 1965)

Loades, D.M., *The Cecils: Privilege and power behind the throne* (National Archives, London, 2007)

Manchée, W.H., *Westminster City Fathers* (Bodley Head, London, 1924)

Manley, Lawrence, *Literature and culture in early modern London* (CUP, 1995)

Manley, Lawrence, *London in the Age of Shakespeare*, (Croom Helm, Beckenham, 1986)

Mateer, David, 'Ravenscroft, Thomas (b.1591/2)', *ODNB* (2004)

Mattingly, Garrett, *The Defeat of the Spanish Armada* (Cape, London, 1959)

McClure, Norman Egbert, ed., *Letters, by John Chamberlain* (Greenwood Press, London, 1979 edn)

McDermott, James, 'Farnaby, Thomas (1574/5–1647)', *ODNB* (2004)

McGrath, Alister, *In the Beginning: The Story of the King James Bible* (Hodder & Stoughton, London, 2001)

Miles, Rosalind, *Ben Jonson: His Life and Work* (Routledge, London, 1986)

Mitchell, R.J., and Leys, M.D.R., *A History of London Life* (Longmans, London, 1958)

Monson, Craig, 'Byrd, William (1539x43–1623)', *ODNB* (2004)

Mulryne, J.R., Shewring, Margaret, and Gurr, Andrew, *Shakespeare's Globe Rebuilt* (CUP, 1997)

Naphy, William G., and Roberts, Penny, eds, *Fear in early modern society* (Manchester University Press, 1997)

Nicholl, Charles, 'Marlowe [Marley], Christopher (bap. 1564, d.1593)', *ODNB* (2004)

Nicholl, Charles, *The Lodger: Shakespeare on Silver Street* (Allen Lane, London, 2007)

Norton, David, *A textual history of the King James Bible* (CUP, 2005)

Oliver, P.M., ed., John Donne, *Selected Letters* (Carcenet, Manchester, 2002)

Orlin, Lena Cowen, *Material London, ca 1600* (University of Pennsylvania Press, 2000)

Overall, W.H. and H.C., eds, *Analytical index to the series of records known as the Remembrancia* (London, 1878)

Owen, G. Dyfnallt, ed., *Calendar of the Manuscripts of the Most Honourable the Marquess of Salisbury*, XXI, 1609–1612 (1970)

Picard, Liza, *Elizabeth's London* (Weidenfeld & Nicolson, London, 2003)

Pogue, Kate, *Shakespeare's Friends* (Greenwood, London, 2006)

Porter, Roy, *London: A Social History* (Hamish Hamilton, London, 1994)

Porter, Stephen, 'Fires in Stratford-upon-Avon in the Sixteenth and Seventeenth Centuries', *Warwickshire History*, III (1976)

Porter, Stephen, *The Plagues of London* (Tempus, Stroud, 2008)

Powell, Harry J., *Glass Making in England* (CUP, 1923)

Prest, Wilfrid R., *The Inns of Court under Elizabeth I and the Early Stuarts, 1590–1640* (Longman, London, 1972)

Pritchard, R.E., *Shakespeare's England: Life in Elizabethan & Jacobean Times* (Sutton, Stroud, 1999)

Rappaport, Steve, *Worlds within worlds: structures of life in sixteenth-century London* (CUP, 1989)

Rasmussen, Steen Eiler, *London: The Unique City* (MIT Press, Cambridge, Mass., 1982)

Richmond, Hugh Macrae, *Shakespeare's Theatre: A Dictionary of His Stage Context* (Continuum, London, 2002)

Rye, William Brenchley, *England as seen by foreigners in the days of Elizabeth and James the First* (John Russell Smith, London, 1865, new edn 2005)

Salgádo, Gámini, *The Elizabethan Underworld* (Dent, London, 1977)

Schoenbaum, S., *William Shakespeare, A Compact Documentary Life* (OUP, 1987)

Schofield, John, *The London Surveys of Ralph Treswell* (London Topographical Soc., 1987)

Scott-Giles, C. Wilfred, and Slater, Bernard V, *The History of Emanuel School, 1594–1964* (The Old Emanuel Association, 1966)

Scouloudi, Irene, 'The Stranger Community in the Metropolis 1558–1640', in *Huguenots in Britain and their French Background, 1550–1800* (Macmillan, London, 1987)

Seaver, P.S., *The Puritan Lectureships: The Politics of Religious Dissent, 1560–1662* (Stanford University Press, 1970)

Seaver, P.S., *Wallington's World. A Puritan Artisan in Seventeenth-Century London* (Methuen, London, 1985)

Shapiro, James, *1599 A Year in the Life of William Shakespeare* (Faber, London, 2005)

Sheppard, Francis, *Robert Baker of Piccadilly Hall and His Heirs* (London Topographical Soc., 1982)

Sheppard, Francis, *London: A History* (OUP, 1998)

Sheppard, Steve, ed., *The Selected Writings and Speeches of Sir Edward Coke*, I (Indianapolis, Liberty Fund, 2003)

Shrewsbury, J.F.D., *A History of Bubonic Plague in the British Isles* (CUP, 1970)

Shuttleworth, J.M., ed., *The Life of Edward, First Lord Herbert of Cherbury written by himself* (OUP, 1976)

Skempton, Sir Alec W., Rennison, R.W., and Cox, R.C., eds, *A biographical dictionary of civil engineers in Great Britain and Ireland, 1500–1830*, I (Thomas Telford, London, 2002)

Slack, Paul, *From Reformation to Improvement: Public Welfare in Early Modern England* (OUP, 1998)

Smythe, Robert, *Historical Account of Charter-House* (London, 1808)

Sorlein, Robert Parker, ed., *The Diary of John Manningham of the Middle Temple, 1602–1603* (University Press of New England, Hanover, New Hampshire, 1976)

Sotheby's, *The Trumbull Papers* (Sotheby's, London, 1989)

Spedding, James, et al, eds, *The Works of Francis Bacon*, XV (Brown and Taggard, Boston 1861)

Spedding, James, *The Letters and the Life of Francis Bacon*, vol.IV (1868)

Stow, John, *The Survey of London*, ed. H.B. Wheatley (Dent, London, 1987)

Suzuki, Mihoko, 'The London apprentice riots of the 1590s and the fiction of Thomas Delony', *Criticism* (Spring 1996)

Tabor, Margaret E., *The City Churches* (Headley, London, 1917)

Tawney, R.H., and Power, Eileen, *Tudor Economic Documents*, III (Longmans, London, 1925)

Thirsk, Joan, *Economic Policy and Projects* (OUP, 1978)

Thirsk, Joan, ed., *The Agrarian History of England and Wales, V 1640–1750, pt ii, Agrarian Change* (CUP, 1985)

Thirsk, Joan, and Cooper, J.P., *Seventeenth-Century Economic Documents* (OUP, 1972)

Thompson, C.J.S., *Quacks of Old London* (London, 1928)

Thurley, Simon, *The Lost Palace of Whitehall* (London, Royal Institute of British Architects, 1998)

Tudor-Craig, Pamela, *'Old St Paul's': The Society of Antiquaries Diptych, 1616* (London Topographical Soc. and Soc. of Antiquaries, 2004)

Unwin, George, *Industrial Organization in the Sixteenth and Seventeenth Centuries* (Cass, London, 1965)

Usher, Brett, 'Vaughan, Richard (*c.*1553–1607)', *ODNB* (2004)

Walsham, Alexandra, *Providence in Early Modern England* (OUP, 1999)

Ward, A.C., ed., *A Miscellany of Tracts and Pamphlets* (OUP, 1927)

Weinreb, Ben, and Hibbert, Christopher, *The London Encyclopaedia*, ed. (Macmillan, London, 1993 edn)

Weis, Rene, *Shakespeare Revealed: A Biography* (John Murray, London, 2007)

Willan, T.S., *The inland trade* (Manchester University Press, 1976)

Williams, Clare, *Thomas Platter's Travels in England* (Cape, London, 1937)

Williams, Gordon, *A dictionary of sexual language and imagery in Shakespearean and Stuart Literature* (Continuum, London, 1994)

Williams, Sarah, ed., *Letters Written by John Chamberlain during the reign of Queen Elizabeth* (Camden Soc., 1861)

Wilson, Charles, *England's Apprenticeship, 1603–1763* (Longman, London, 1965)

Wilson, F.P., *The Plague Pamphlets of Thomas Dekker*, (OUP, 1925)

Wilson, F.P., *The Plague in Shakespeare's London* (OUP, 1927)

Wilson, John Dover, *Life in Shakespeare's England* (Penguin, London, 1944)

Wilson, Richard, *Secret Shakespeare: Studies in Theatre, Religion and Resistance* (Manchester University Press, 2004)

Wood, Margaret, *The English Mediaeval House* (Dent, London, 1965)

Woodward, Marcus, ed., *Gerard's Herbal*, (Studio Editions, London, 1994)

Wraight, A.D., *Christopher Marlowe and Edward Alleyn* (Adam Hart, London, 1993)

Wright, Thomas, *Queen Elizabeth and her Times*, II (1838)

Young, Percy M., *A History of British Football* (London, Arrow, 1968)

274

List of Illustrations

23. 'This was the parish church of St Olave Silver Street destroyed by the dreadfull fire in the year 1666'. © Stephen Porter.
24. The Swan Theatre on Bankside, built in 1595. © Jonathan Reeve JR1080b3p299 16001650.
25. The Custom House, rebuilt in 1559 after a fire. © Stephen Porter.
26. The church of St Dunstan-in-the-East, shown in Claes Visscher's view of 1616. © Stephen Porter.
27. The coronation procession of Edward VI in 1547. © Jonathan Reeve JR1167b4p710 15501600.
28. The church of St Giles, Cripplegate was close to Shakespeare's lodgings in Silver Street. © Stephen Porter.
29. Elizabeth I at prayer is the frontispiece to *Christian Prayers* (1569). © Jonathan Reeve JR1168b4fp747 15501600.
30. Richard Quiney was a mercer in Stratford-upon-Avon and a friend of Shakespeare's. © Jonathan Reeve JR1065b65fp295 15501600.
31. The Tower of London: Cradle Tower. © Stephen Porter.
32. The Charterhouse: the almsmen's lodgings. Crown copyright, NMR.
33. Temple Church, built *c*.1160–85 for the Knights Templar. © Stephen Porter.
34. Water-wheels for mills on the southern end of London Bridge. © Jonathan Reeve JR1062b10prelims 16001650.
35. Londoners enthusiastically celebrated both civic and national events. © Jonathan Reeve JR258b10p1018 16001650.
36. The Great Hall of the Charterhouse. © Stephen Porter.
37. The former churchyard of St Mary Aldermanbury contains a memorial garden and monument to Shakespeare's friends and fellow-actors. © Stephen Porter.
38. Claes Visscher's Panorama of London of 1616, with St Paul's Cathedral towering above the huddle of buildings leading down to the river. © Jonathan Reeve JR1076b3fp166 16001650.
39. The church of St Mary Overy, Southwark, and London Bridge. © Jonathan Reeve JR1077b3fp174 16001650.
40. A sitting of the Court of Wards and Liveries, shown in a painting of *c*.1585. © Jonathan Reeve JR1068b5fp388 15501600.
41. Inigo Jones's design for Candace, Queen of Ethiopia. © Jonathan Reeve JR1081b3fp326 16001650.
42. Rogues and vagabonds. © Jonathan Reeve JR1085b3fp492 15501600.
43. An ornately carved house front in Hart Street drawn and engraved by J.T. Smith. © Stephen Porter.
44. Costumes of the Elizabethan period. © Jonathan Reeve JR1073b3fp108 15501600.
45. The gatehouse of the Inner Temple. © Stephen Porter.
46. Joris Hoefnagel's illustration of English women's costumes, 1582. © Jonathan Reeve JR1072b3fp98 15501600.
47. Engravings by the Swiss artist Jost Amman, 1539–91. © Stephen Porter.
48. J.T. Smith's etching of 1791 of a house in Sweedon's Passage, Grub Street. © Stephen Porter.
49. Card games were a popular form of recreation during the period. © Jonathan Reeve JR1083b3fp472 15501600.

77. The gunpowder plotters, by an unknown engraver. © Jonathan Reeve JR397b22p1180 16001650.

78. The Gunpowder Plot was foiled when Guy Fawkes was caught, with the cache of gunpowder. He was questioned and tortured and gave this confession. © Jonathan Reeve JR1143b22p1181 16001650.

79. This print shows the execution of the Gunpowder Plot conspirators at the scaffold in St Paul's churchyard in January 1606. © Jonathan Reeve JR1144b42p564 16001650.

80. The area around Smithfield and Newgate, including Christ's Hospital, shown on the 'Agas' plan of mid-sixteenth century London. © Stephen Porter.

81. In 1586 Anthony Babington and his fellow conspirators plotted to execute Elizabeth I and place Mary, Queen of Scots on the throne. © Jonathan Reeve JR204b5p9 15501600.

82. The area around Charing Cross, in the mid-sixteenth century. © Jonathan Reeve JRCD3 893 15501600.

83. The royal barge and its guard of smaller barges are shown passing the riverfront, between the Savoy and Whitefriars. © Jonathan Reeve JR269b10p1073 16001650.

84. Anthonis van den Wyngaerde's drawing of *c.*1544 shows the palaces along the Thames between Charing Cross, in the west, and the Temple. © Jonathan Reeve JR1139b42p7 15501600.

85. The courtyard of Arundel House, in the Strand, drawn by Wenceslaus Hollar. © Jonathan Reeve JR1128b67pxlixM 15501600.

86. Northampton House in the Strand. © Jonathan Reeve JR1138b42p6 15501600.

87. The Savoy. © Jonathan Reeve JR1125b67pxlixT 15501600.

88. London west of the city wall. © Jonathan Reeve JR1101b2p765 15501600.

89. Public executions were carried out at Tyburn and in Smithfield. © Jonathan Reeve JR204b5p9 15501600.

90. This mid-sixteenth century plan-view has the future Oxford Street to the north and the Haymarket along the west, with St Martin's Lane to the east. © Jonathan Reeve JR1140b42p168 15501600.

91. The interior of Middle Temple Hall. © Jonathan Reeve JR1100b2p761 15501600.

92. The nave of St Paul's cathedral, drawn by Wenceslaus Hollar. © Jonathan Reeve JR1123b67pxxxix 15501600.

93. Cornhill, *c.*1630. © Stephen Porter.

94. Cornhill *c.*1599. © Stephen Porter.

95. Outdoor services were held on the site of Paul's Cross, adjoining the cathedral, where the weekly sermons delivered from the pulpit attracted large congregations. © Jonathan Reeve JR209b5p68 15501600.

96. St Mary Overy church, Southwark. © Jonathan Reeve JR1120b67pxxx 16001650.

97. Lambeth Palace. © Jonathan Reeve JR1089b10p1118 16001650.

98. Plan of parts of Bishopsgate Street, Threadneeedle Street and Cornhill, drawn in 1599. © Stephen Porter.

99. The Thames Street and Billingsgate area. © Stephen Porter.

120. Richard Burbage (1568–1619). © Jonathan Reeve JR1130b40p204 15501600.
121. The Swan theatre, redrawn from Visscher's view of 1616. © Jonathan Reeve JR1110b22p1486 15501600.
122. A game of chess between two gentleman. © Jonathan Reeve JR1084b3p477 16001650.
123. Woodcuts showing flutes, pipes and tabor. © Stephen Porter.
124. Ben Jonson (1572–1637). © Jonathan Reeve JR1064b5fp292 15501600.
125. London Wall, Cripplegate and Moorgate in the mid-sixteenth century. © Jonathan Reeve JR1145b41p229 15501600.
126. Westminster Abbey stood at the edge of the metropolis, with Tothill Fields beyond. © Jonathan Reeve JR1129b67plviiB 16001650.
127. The title page of the First Folio edition of Shakespeare's plays. © Stephen Porter.

Index

Also available from Amberley Publishing

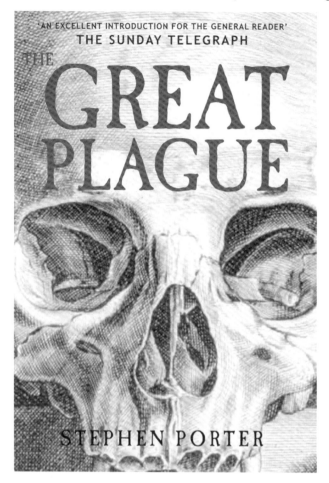

'An excellent introduction for the general reader'
THE SUNDAY TELEGRAPH

The bubonic plague epidemic which struck England in 1665-6 was responsible for the deaths of almost a third of London's population. Its sheer scale was overwhelming and it was well-recorded, featuring in the works of Pepys and Defoe and described in terrible detail in the contemporary Bills of Mortality. Stephen Porter describes the disease and how people at the time thought it was caused. He gives details of the treatments available (such as they were) and evokes its impact on the country. We will probably never know the reasons for the disappearance of the bubonic plague from England after 1665. What is clear is the fascination the subject still holds.

£12.99 Paperback
61 illustrations
192 pages
978-1-84868-087-6

Available from all good bookshops or to order direct
please call **01285-760-030**
www.amberley-books.com

Also available from Amberley Publishing

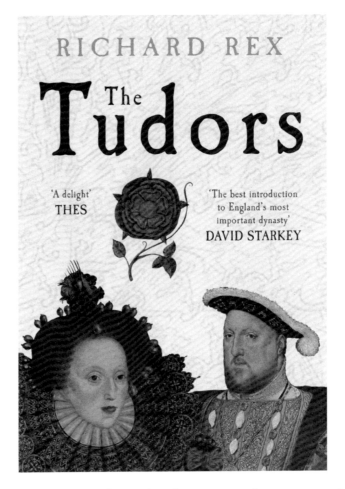

RICHARD REX

The Tudors

'A delight'
THES

'The best introduction
to England's most
important dynasty'
DAVID STARKEY

An intimate history of England's most infamous royal family

'The best introduction to England's most important dynasty' DAVID STARKEY
'A lively overview... Rex is a wry commentator on the game on monarchy' THE GUARDIAN
'Gripping and told with enviable narrative skill. This is a model of popular history... a delight' THES
'Vivid, entertaining and carrying its learning lightly' EAMON DUFFY

The Tudor Age began in August 1485 when Henry Tudor landed with 2000 men at Milford Haven
intent on snatching the English throne from Richard III. For more than a hundred years England was
to be dominated by the personalities of the five Tudor monarchs, ranging from the brilliance and
brutality of Henry VIII to the shrewdness and vanity of the virgin queen, Elizabeth I.

£20.00 Hardback
100 colour illustrations
320 pages
978-1-84868-049-4

Available from all good bookshops or to order direct
please call **01285-760-030**
www.amberley-books.com